A History of Foreign Students in Britain

A History of Foreign Students in Britain

Hilary Perraton

First published 2014 by
PALGRAVE MACMILLAN

Palgrave Macmillan in the UK is an imprint of Macmillan Publishers Limited, registered in England, company number 785998, of Houndmills, Basingstoke, Hampshire RG21 6XS.

Palgrave Macmillan in the US is a division of St Martin's Press LLC, 175 Fifth Avenue, New York, NY10010.

Palgrave Macmillan is the global academic imprint of the above companies and has companies and representatives throughout the world.

Palgrave® and Macmillan® are registered trademarks in the United States, the United Kingdom, Europe and other countries

ISBN: 978–1–137–29494–4

This book is printed on paper suitable for recycling and made from fully managed and sustained forest sources. Logging, pulping and manufacturing processes are expected to conform to the environmental regulations of the country of origin.

A catalogue record for this book is available from the British Library.

A catalog record for this book is available from the Library of Congress.

Contents

List of Figures

List of Tables

Acknowledgements

I have many debts for help, encouragement and information, with the greatest of these being as always to Jean Perraton. I am grateful to Jeff Waage of the London International Development Centre and to the Institute of Education, University of London, for enabling me to base myself there as a visiting fellow while working on the book. This work has benefited from reactions to some of the material in it at seminars organised by Gary McCulloch in the History of Education series at the Institute of Education and by Charlotte Tulinius at the Education across Borders group at St Edmund's College Cambridge. Among many others who have encouraged and helped in various ways, I am indebted to David Bridges, John Kirkland, Bill Lawton, Frances Marshall, Tony Millns, Nick Mulhern and John Stoddart. Laura Broadhurst kindly arranged for me to attend an in-house witness seminar of the Council for Assisting Refugee Academics. John Dawson provided help in using the Venn database of Cambridge alumni. I am particularly grateful also to colleagues who provided help, support and advice and commented on draft chapters: Helen Connell, Charlotte Creed, Christine Humfrey, Jonathan Jenkins, Tamson Pietsch – who also let me have an advance version of her book *Empire of Scholars* – Malcolm Skilbeck, Carew Treffgarne and Peter Williams. Like so many writers, I have debts of gratitude for help from librarians and archivists at the University Library and Faculty of Education Library, Cambridge, the Institute of Education, London, the British Library, the National Archives and the UNESCO Institute for Statistics. Errors, interpretations and misinterpretations are my own.

1
Introduction: Travelling Abroad to Study

Srinivasa Ramanujan was born in a small southern Indian village in 1887, one of six children of whom three died in infancy. His father was a clerk in a silk shop. Ramanujan went to primary and then high school, passing most of his examinations, but with no great distinction except in mathematics where he excelled. At the age of about 16 he was given a copy of the standard English university text Carr's *A synopsis of elementary results in pure and applied mathematics*. Ramanujan devoured the book and began work on a series of his own notebooks in which he extended what was in the text, explored its theorems and suggestions, and went on to discover, infer and go beyond much of what was then advanced pure mathematics. Ramanujan went on to college and entered for an arts degree, but did not complete it as he got poor marks in English, had a vegetarian's objection to the dissection of frogs in physiology and was essentially interested only in mathematics. He got a job as a clerk which gave him an income as well as spare time for mathematics. His capacity here was so remarkable that, despite the lack of a degree, he was soon appointed to a research post at Presidency College Madras. Though he was still isolated from much mainstream mathematical thinking, this put him in touch with local mathematicians; they encouraged him to write to G. H. Hardy at Trinity College, Cambridge, one of the most eminent pure mathematicians of the time. Ramanujan explained in his letter that he was a clerk, with no university training, on a salary of £20 a year, and that he had produced some interesting mathematical results which he enclosed.[1] Hardy's reaction to one group of Ramanujan's theorems was that they 'defeated me completely; I had never seen anything like them before. A single look at them is enough to show that they could only be written down by a mathematician of the highest class.' He went on to explain that 'they must be true because, if they were not true, no one

1

would have the imagination to invent them'.[2] Ramanujan belonged in the Cambridge of Hardy, Bertrand Russell and G. E. Moore, but, leaving aside the complications and cost of travel, a year there would require at least five times his annual salary.

A fellow of Trinity in the heyday of the empire was able to work the levers of power. When the India Office in London rejected the idea of funding such an unorthodox scholar, Hardy found a way of reaching the governor of Madras who duly provided a scholarship for Ramanujan to travel to Cambridge.[3] He cut his hair, abandoned his turban, bought western clothes – all of which he mistakenly thought were necessary – and overcame Hindu objections to travelling over the water before sailing to England in 1913. In Cambridge he began a programme of academic cooperation with Hardy, publishing papers in pure mathematics from 1914 on. Having failed to graduate in India he did so in Cambridge in 1916 and within two years was elected to the Royal Society and to a Trinity fellowship. But his extraordinary academic promise was cut short when he contracted tuberculosis and, having returned to India, died in 1920. He had by then found time to explain that, with his Indian income and his Trinity fellowship, he had more money than he and his family needed and that the surplus should be used as a trust fund for the education of poor boys.[4] And his work in number theory lived on. Within 20 years over 100 papers had been published on his work which continued to inspire further research. In 1974, for example, a paper on the tau conjecture which he had proposed in 1916 confirmed that his conjecture could be established.[5]

British universities have always been a magnet for scholars like Ramanujan, and unlike him, who have overcome improbable obstacles to reach them. University members, like Hardy, and government officials like Lord Pentland, the governor of Madras, have used imagination and administrative flair to support and encourage them. While scholars as able as Ramanujan are exceptionally rare, travel has always been part of student life. In the ancient world, learners from outside the city were welcome in fifth-century Athens and at Taxila in the Indus valley. They were accepted in medieval European universities, and at different times tolerated, embraced and feared in Britain. There was already a handful of foreign students in Oxford at the end of the twelfth century, and monks and friars travelled to England to study until the Reformation. Teachers travelled as well as students so that links between universities helped shape their teaching: the founders of the respected medical school in Edinburgh learnt their skills at Leiden, which in turn owed intellectual debts to Padua. Then for a century and more steamships and imperial expectations brought students from the empire and the

Commonwealth to Britain. As memories of the empire faded, political changes brought increasing numbers from other European countries so that, by the twenty-first century, Britain attracted more students from Europe than from the Commonwealth.

Over the years the number of students from abroad increased so that, for much of the twentieth century, they made up one in every ten of the university total, a figure that had risen to one in five by 2000. By 2010 overseas students made up more than half of all postgraduates. This book sets out to tell the story of foreign students in Britain, concentrating on changes in policy and practice towards them, on the part of schools, colleges and universities, of government, and of society generally.

So far, but not so simple, as the definitions of 'foreign', 'British' and 'student' all turn out to be slippery. Students from Ireland were certainly foreign until 1540 when Henry VIII adopted the title of king of Ireland – or perhaps until the English conquest was completed in 1603 – and again certainly foreign from 1948, or from some other date between the Anglo-Irish treaty of 1922 and Ireland's proclaiming itself a republic and leaving the Commonwealth. But even then the Ireland Act, which has been in force in the United Kingdom since 1949, states that 'Ireland shall not be regarded as a foreign country for the purpose of any law'. Indian students are now regarded as foreign but, in the first half of the twentieth century, were British subjects with a right to travel to Britain and to remain there. Public statistics reflect the changing sense of categories that matter: from the 1920s to the 1980s they distinguished between home, Commonwealth and foreign students, then separated out the European students, and in the twenty-first century dropped the Commonwealth category.

'Overseas' has often been used as a catch-all term but can present difficulties in relation to Scotland and Ireland. Today a distinction is sometimes drawn between international students, who have crossed a border to study, and foreign students, of a different nationality from their hosts.

Just as the sense of foreignness has changed so 'Britain' and 'England' present problems. For simplicity, 'Britain' is generally used in the text as shorthand for the 'United Kingdom of Great Britain and Northern Ireland' (or 'Britain and Ireland' until the 1920s). The earlier story is about the British Isles and begins at a time when students travelling to Oxford and Cambridge from Scotland, Wales and Ireland were as foreign as their contemporaries from France. But even England is not that simple. Queen Elizabeth I's resounding title as 'by the grace of God Queen of England, France and Ireland' reminds us how political realities and claims have shifted. Students from Aquitaine, under her predecessors in the fourteenth century, owed allegiance to the English king and were in that sense less foreign than those from Scotland, though they were clearly more so by the seventeenth century.

The term 'student' is just as tricky. Erasmus came to Britain to teach as well as to learn. Political refugees, from Protestants escaping Catholic Europe in the seventeenth century to central Europeans in the twentieth, travelled to Britain, sent their children to school and themselves went to university. Having arrived as refugees they became students. In another twist, British universities are understandably proud of alumni who went on to fame having enrolled with them, as Jomo Kenyatta did at the London School of Economics, not because they came to Britain primarily to study but because they signed up to study while in Britain for different, individual or political reasons.

Uncertain terminology need not inhibit discussion, as any good pub argument will demonstrate. The terms 'Britain', 'foreign' and 'student' are used with no greater weight or precision than that of their contemporary users, in order to explore and explain student mobility and what it meant. In examining attitudes and even policies there is often a case for treating someone as foreign, or a student, if that is how they were perceived, rather than concentrating on their precise legal status. The uncertainty serves to demonstrate how the typical foreign student has changed over eight centuries. Mendicant friars, encouraged or expected to travel by their orders, formed the largest group in the Middle Ages. The Reformation cut off their flow but students continued to travel from northern, Protestant Europe. By the eighteenth century they were joined by students from the empire, initially from the West Indian plantocracy, and then in small numbers from the west African middle class. In the nineteenth century larger numbers came from India and then Australia. By the twentieth, students from the informal empire – notably Egypt and Iraq – added to the numbers. Children, sent to school from the Caribbean, Africa and India joined their elders. While religion sent the first students, politics and political aspiration now took its place. Kings were made particularly welcome: Harrow had them from Afghanistan, Jordan and Iraq as well as the first prime minister of India, Jawaharlal Nehru. Soldiers went to Sandhurst which educated future generals and military leaders. Some, particularly catechists and civil servants, were sent by their employers, some came on scholarships, but the majority were paid for by their families.

While the students have been various, policy and attitudes towards them have repeatedly been marked by controversy, ambiguity and ambivalence.[6]

Universities have traditionally welcomed foreign students, though the welcome has sometimes been muted. In the Middle Ages Oxford and Cambridge valued the *ius ubique docendi* which encouraged movement to and fro by giving their graduates the right to teach in any European university. The tradition continued: in the 1960s the Robbins Report on higher education confirmed that 'The presence here in institutions of higher education of students from abroad is widely regarded as valuable, and rightly so in our judgment'.[7] Universities' commitment to international values has been a common and consistent feature of university policy, often ranking higher with them than with governments. In the 1930s they, rather than government, made the running in welcoming students and academics escaping from Germany.

For their part governments have usually at least tolerated students from abroad, sometimes wanted to restrain them and at times actively sought to attract them. In the early twentieth century no serious attempt was made to restrict Indian students, even when there were objections to their presence. In the 1930s the Board of Trade wanted to encourage overseas students in the national interest only to be frustrated when industry treated them with suspicion. In the 1960s and 1970s governments tried but failed to hold back overseas student numbers. By the 2000s policy had changed again with the launch of a prime minister's initiative to recruit increased numbers of students from India and China. Over many years international agencies, from the medieval orders of monks and friars to the League of Nations and in its turn the European Union, have encouraged student travel, but without always attracting government support.

Foreign students have mattered to British universities and their presence has influenced university policy. From their beginnings, universities saw themselves as part of an international network of institutions. At different times they were seen as serving the needs of the universal church, of the empire, of the new Europe. Foreigners' needs and interests were likely to have a particularly strong influence on institutions where they were present in large numbers, or as a large proportion of students. These included, among others, the Edinburgh medical school from the eighteenth century, the London School of Economics from its foundation and some London technical colleges favoured by west African migrants in the 1960s. But all universities were affected by the introduction of the PhD at the end of the First World War, designed to attract the kind of students who had previously done doctoral work in Germany. From the mid-1980s, universities themselves created a proliferation of master's courses, mainly targeted at students from abroad. Scholarship and politics alike have been influenced by individual students from abroad, from Erasmus to Wittgenstein or the refugee scientists of the 1930s, some of them first welcomed, then interned, next released and prized for their contribution to military research.

Despite the welcome for talented individuals, there were always sceptical voices. Even where institutions were committed to accepting overseas students, they could not carry all their staff members with them.
Early in the twentieth century schools were ambivalent in expecting to
attract a cosmopolitan elite but reluctant to find places for foreigners.
Oxford academics in the 1900s complained about changes brought by
the first Rhodes scholars; in the 1920s their Cambridge counterparts
complained about the introduction of the PhD in the interest of foreign
students (see Chapter 4). Beyond this general objection to change, the
critical voices have claimed that there were too many foreign students,
that they did not go home, that they were not good enough, that it
was not in the national interest to welcome them and that their loyalty
was questionable. Casual racism affected attitudes. In the late twentieth
century the cost of accepting and teaching them became an issue of
political as well as institutional controversy.

The repeated charge that there were too many foreign students has
sometimes been specific, sometimes general. Before and after the First
World War it was repeatedly argued that there were too many Egyptian and
Indian students, although at this time there was little pressure on university numbers. After the Second World War there was a sharp increase in
the domestic demand for university places, fed by ex-servicemen and by
increasing numbers of school leavers, and reinforced by the availability
of student grants. The resulting apparent shortage of places for overseas
students became a mainspring of government policy in the 1960s and
1970s, with repeated attempts to hold down overseas numbers. Those
attempts led to controversial decisions in the 1960s and 1970s to charge
differential fees to home and overseas students. A Labour government
took the first decision in 1967 while a Conservative one in 1979 took the
policy a step further by requiring them to pay fees that met the full cost
of their education. Each opposition party in turn protested vigorously
and ineffectively but reversed their views when in office. Universities
initially joined the protests, but the protests died away as they came to
enjoy the freedom to generate income by recruiting internationally. The
number question then came back into politics in the 2000s as overseas
students seemed to be swelling the numbers of immigrants. Regardless
of the party in power, the Home Office repeatedly wanted to hold down
their numbers, which became a more consistent policy under the new
government of 2010.

Complaints that students did not return home after they graduated
fed into the arguments that their numbers should be controlled. These
complaints were, at times, reinforced from a quite different direction.
As increasing numbers of students from the colonial empire, and later

from the Commonwealth, travelled to Britain, there were objections that British universities were denuding Australia, New Zealand and later the developing world of their most talented citizens. This complaint was a counterpoint to repeated claims that foreign students were not as good, or as well prepared, as their home-grown contemporaries.

The argument that the presence of foreign students went against national interests took various forms. In the early twentieth century there were commercial objections to their presence, nourished by a fear that they would return home with trade secrets and set up competing enterprises. It was particularly difficult for technical students to get industrial placements for this reason (see Chapter 4). Over a much longer period questions were raised about the loyalty and political or ideological commitment of foreign students. French students were suspect in the fourteenth century, as were students with the wrong religion between the Reformation and the mid-nineteenth century. Many of the future leaders of the Indian National Congress studied in Britain and were, unsurprisingly, seen as being disloyal to the idea of British India. MI5 watched the activities of Forbes Burnham of British Guiana and Kwame Nkrumah of the Gold Coast when they were students and their countries still colonies. In the early twenty-first century academics were encouraged to watch out for potential Muslim activists. University, and national, acceptance of foreign students has been repeatedly tinged with suspicion.

Attitudes towards foreign students have often been marked by the same ambivalence that characterises policy. While many students have been made welcome – and documented the fact – controversies about their presence have also been tinged with racism, demonstrated sometimes by fellow students, sometimes by representatives of the state. This may reflect centuries of xenophobia: a Venetian visitor complained in 1500 that the English 'have an antipathy to foreigners, and imagine that they never come into this island but to make themselves master of it, and to usurp their goods'.[8] In the late nineteenth century, cartoons in Cambridge student magazines consistently derided foreign students while in 1907 a government report quoted with apparent sympathy a student claim that a college lost caste if it had too many Indian students. More than 50 years later a British Council official working in Bombay explained to his superiors that, in recruiting Commonwealth scholars from India, it would not be reasonable 'to expect Rhodes-Scholar standards of conduct from them while allowing that many of them will not be Rhodes material' unlike their mainly white American contemporaries.[9]

Attitudes, like policy, have been influenced by class, race and gender. Class was always important with unflattering comparisons being drawn in the early twentieth century between the middle-class Indian students then coming to Britain and their princely predecessors. Racial distinctions were more subtle and in the early twentieth century reflected the tortuousness of imperial policy: posts in the Indian medical and civil services were in principle open to all, but Indian doctors could not join the west African medical service, and again in principle but not always in practice, British army officers had to be white until the First World War. Only whites could join the Officers Training Corps but if the son of an Arab ruler wanted to do so, then a way would be found round the problem (see Chapter 4).

Gender presented its own difficulties which took different forms at different times. While small numbers of schoolgirls were coming to Britain for their education from the late eighteenth century, women university students remained a tiny minority until well into the twentieth. If problems of gender were perceived, they were seen as following not from the absence of women students but from the presence of the wrong sort of women near the men. A rather puritanical American student, Charles Bristed, was alarmed by prostitutes in Cambridge in the 1840s, and by his contemporaries' casual attitude towards them (see Chapter 7), while by 1901 no less an observer than the viceroy, Lord Curzon, was disturbed that 'some English women of the housemaid class and even higher' were attracted to Indians.[10] Women were seen as such a distraction for male students that in 1953 one Labour MP argued in the House of Commons against making Marshall scholarships available to married men.[11] Issues of nationality, race and gender came together when I was told in 1958 by a representative of the Intervarsity Club in London, set up to bring together young graduates, that it did not accept members from overseas as one of its purposes was acting as an informal marriage broker. Attitudes changed, and by the 1970s sex discrimination was being outlawed and scholarship agencies were beginning to worry about the gender balance among their scholars. Social and cultural changes shifted the ground again so that in the 2000s, while the proportion of female Commonwealth scholars was still below 50 per cent, the Commonwealth Scholarship Commission was also concerned about the shortage of male postgraduate applicants from Canada.

Before exploring the changing student record in more detail we can usefully ask what drives students to travel abroad.

While changing policies and public attitudes, with all their ambiguity and ambivalence, have influenced the lives of foreign students, their decisions to study in Britain were affected by personal choice and personal expectation. Students chose to travel for a variety of reasons and, by following the example of a century-long search for the laws of migration, it is possible to make some generalisations about the drivers of student mobility. Like longer-term migrants, students and potential students have been influenced by their circumstances at home – where these are pushing them towards travel – and conditions in Britain – pulling them towards its institutions – in a process that is influenced by a further set of factors that ease or obstruct student travel.[12] It would be wrong to make this sound deterministic. Individual students also travel for idiosyncratic reasons, to follow an actual or potential partner, or as a response to an unconsidered opportunity: one of the first Commonwealth scholars in Ghana went there in 1967 because he was turning over ideas at the end of his university course and came across a poster about scholarships on the college notice board one day before the closing date.[13] At the same time it is possible to generalise about the factors that have driven large numbers of students, and students in relatively large groups (see Figure 1.1).

Where large groups of students have been pushed to study abroad, they have often come from a population which is already educated to the point where it can benefit from opportunities elsewhere, but where local opportunities at the desired level of education are limited, and there is enough money available to make travel feasible. In the Middle Ages, monks and friars could begin but not complete their education in their own monastery while funds to study in Oxford or Paris were available through their orders or through patronage. Nineteenth-century families in the new and prosperous Bengali middle class, the *bhadralok*, could get a western education by sending their children to school or university in India, but without a British degree or attendance at the Inns of Court could not launch them into the higher levels of the professions. And they could afford to pay. Local opportunities to study may be restricted in terms of the quality and level of what is available, or by religious or political constraints, or by gender. All these can strengthen the push factors. Dire local circumstances repeatedly drove some students abroad, from Huguenots in the seventeenth century to refugees from Hitler and black South Africans in the twentieth.

On the other side, in terms of factors pulling students to Britain, the expectation of financial and social reward, and of an enjoyable experience, has drawn students to British schools, colleges and universities. The *bhadralok* made a shrewd investment when they compared the incomes of local lawyers, the vakils, with those with an English legal qualification who could practise in the higher courts. Future politicians, from Nehru to Clinton, were drawn by the expected benefits of a British education. Study at a British university became a step on the road to

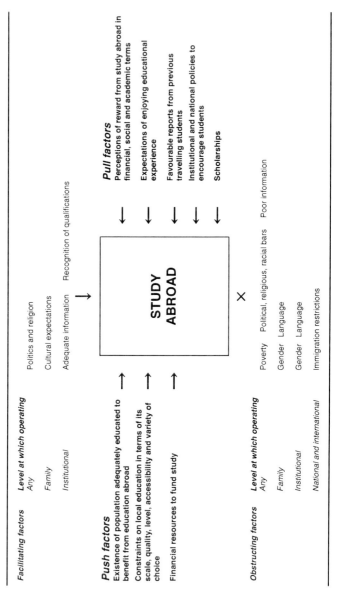

Figure 1.1 Drivers of student mobility

national independence and political power for many leaders of former colonies. Academic expectations bring in international scholars: molecular biologists have been drawn to Cambridge since Watson, an academic migrant, and Crick, announced the double helix in 1953. Anticipation of the quality of the experience has always been important. Rabelais wrote about the *'joyeuse compagnie'* of fellow students in the sixteenth century. These expectations, of long-term reward and short-term enjoyment, are likely to be heightened once the habit of travelling for study has been established so that there is a regular stream from a particular social milieu, in a particular country, with some graduates returning home to encourage others. Deliberate policies, on the part of institutions, governments and international agencies have drawn students that have included Rhodes scholars, East Africans flown in competing airlifts to the United States and the Soviet Union in the 1960s, and Erasmus students funded through the European Union. Institutional policies, including recognition of students' existing qualifications and the introduction of master's and doctoral programmes, have all made institutions more attractive.

Push and pull factors, in terms of a corps of adequately educated students with funds to meet the costs of study abroad, combined with restrictions on local opportunity, and the expectation of reward, sometimes backed by policies to attract students, thus go a long way to explaining student mobility. They have been reinforced, or countered, by a set of second-order factors which encourage or discourage movement and operate either at the level of the individual and family or at an institutional, national or international level. Students have been encouraged to travel where finance is available, where information about opportunities flows freely, and where politics, race or religion are favourable. Scholarships of various kinds have lubricated the process. There have long been handbooks and guidance on studying abroad; Bristed wrote about his five years in Cambridge with the intention of encouraging other Americans while from 1879 the *Journal of the National Indian Association in aid of social progress in India* regularly provided advice for potential students. University marketing departments later picked up that job, using print, academic travel round the small world, and then the internet to inform and attract students.

Many of the obstacles to student mobility are the obverse of these. Poor students have never found it as easy to travel as rich. Political divisions created barriers: student travel across borders was discouraged in mercantilist Europe while, with a handful of exceptions like Pyotr Kapitsa, few came from the Soviet Union in its day to study in Britain. Race meant that for five decades there were no black American Rhodes scholars. Lack of information impedes travel: Ramanujan would not have reached Cambridge unless he had heard of Hardy and his work. On top of this, language has often been a barrier. In the seventeenth century scholars were reported to be reluctant to travel to England because they could not understand the Latin spoken by English academics.[14] In the second half of the twentieth century many British universities decided it was necessary to impose English-language tests on foreign students from some parts of the world. Gender imposed its own barriers. Family expectations, social norms and arrangements to look after children all reinforced the barriers for women even before the shortage of college places and institutional policies could obstruct them. Immigration law has sometimes been a barrier and became a more significant one for many students as the twentieth century wore on and imperial connections fell away. By the end of the twentieth century many students outside the European Union needed a visa, a college place and evidence that they had money to support themselves, in order to enter the country.

A model of the main drivers of student mobility can be no more than that and the personal circumstances of individual students are inevitably more varied than a model would suggest. Many, however, have fallen into one or more of four categories: the rich, the clever, the hopeful and the fearful. Prince Felix Felixovich Yusupov, who went on to assassinate Rasputin, can stand for the rich. He want to Oxford in 1909, armed with letters of introduction from the Bishop of London and Princess Marie Louise of Schleswig Holstein, and accompanied by a chef, a chauffeur, a valet and a housekeeper whose husband looked after his horses.[15] Rutherford will do for the clever. He travelled from New Zealand on a Great Exhibition scholarship in 1895, laid the foundations of nuclear physics in the Cavendish Laboratory in Cambridge, and was awarded the Nobel Prize in chemistry 13 years later.[16] The Indian lawyers, expecting with good reason to make their fortunes as English graduates and barristers, who also dominated the Indian independence movement, can stand for the hopeful. As for the fearful, Gottfried and Ludwig Ehrenberg can stand for many. They escaped from Prague in 1939, went to school with hardly a word of English, rapidly mastered it, got their school certificates, and went on to distinguished careers as Professor Sir Geoffrey and Professor Lewis Elton, with chairs in history, physics and education.[17]

Students, in each of these categories, have left footprints of varying clarity in the sands of history. The earliest university students did not leave memoirs to tell us about their working days but they attended institutions with long memories and good archives. Their records document curriculum, regulations, student behaviour and finance, and analysis of them provides a good picture of student numbers and origins, making it possible to examine the social composition of bodies of students.[18]

From the sixteenth century a growing volume of student reminiscences enriches the literature. College records, and the labour of college and university historians in putting together biographical information, make it possible to trace students and categories of students at least for Oxford and Cambridge.[19] Government documents date back to medieval attempts to influence or control universities; by the nineteenth century they include reports of royal commissions, and by the twentieth accounts by civil servants and politicians as they shaped policy and responded to individual and institutional interests and pressures. By the twentieth century, too, secondary literature on educational history, university development, migration policy, and even the sociology of overseas students and the nature of student mobility, adds to the mix.

The literature makes it possible to explore eight centuries of experience that were influenced both by changing policies and by the changing drivers of student mobility. The exploration casts light on British social, political and intellectual history, and on changing attitudes to foreigners and foreignness. The story is mainly about the experience of foreign university students but not entirely: smaller numbers have travelled to learn techniques, from shipbuilding to surgery, to go to school and to train as soldiers. It is a story about the students themselves, the institutions they attended, the ways in which their presence shaped those institutions and the institutions influenced their lives, as well as about changing practices and policies. Their story has always been part of intellectual and institutional history; for the last two centuries it is part of imperial history and for the last thirty years is woven into the fabric of contentious political debates about immigration, about Europe and about Britain's place in the world.

Following and interpreting the students' footprints demands understanding of four kinds, drawn from narrative, explanation, description and evaluation.[20] Narrative comes first in order to set out an account of what happened as students travelled to Britain and its people and institutions responded to them. Narrative needs, second, to be accompanied by explanation in order to answer questions of 'how?' and 'why?' alongside those of 'what?' and 'what happened?' Narrative and explanation are necessarily interwoven. Then, third, a description of students' experience helps towards a different kind of understanding, found by addressing the question: 'what was it really like?' Fourth, understanding demands some kind of evaluation, exploring outcomes, strengths and weaknesses from the standpoint either of the students or of their host society.

As narrative is the bedrock, the next five chapters provide a sequential account of foreign students in Britain from the end of the twelfth century to the early years of the twenty-first. The narrative is backed by a measure of explanation in looking at the students themselves, at the development of policy towards them and at the forces that encouraged or discouraged their travel. Chapter 2 takes the story from the end of the twelfth to the end of the eighteenth century, from a period when student travel was dominated by the interests of the church to one when universities were beginning to attract students from beyond Europe. The nineteenth century, discussed in Chapter 3, brought new universities and a new perception that they should meet the educational needs of the empire. Imperial needs continued to dominate the story from 1900 to 1945 in Chapter 4, when British universities were seen as the apex of the empire's university system. The years from 1945 to 1979, considered in Chapter 5, saw dramatic increases in student numbers, from home and from overseas, and political changes that were to shape student mobility, from the dismantling of the empire to restrictive immigration policies and Britain's accession to the European Economic Community. Chapter 6 explores the consequences of those changes in the period from 1979 to 2010 as higher education continued to expand internationally, overseas university student numbers went from 10 to 20 per cent of the total, and overseas student policy became both more explicit and more controversial.

The last four chapters move from narrative to explanation, description and evaluation. The extensive literature about students' experience of their time in Britain, which goes back many centuries, so usefully complements the narrative that this is examined next in Chapter 7, with description preceding and providing a context for explanation. The chapter answers the descriptive question of what it was like to be a foreign student, documenting students' responses to repeated accounts of welcome and prejudice. Explanation is then the theme of Chapters 8 and 9. Chapter 8, on poor scholars and endowed scholars, looks at the economics of studying in Britain as a companion to the political explanations within the earlier narrative chapters. It sets out the changing cost of studying in Britain and explores who benefited and who paid when students travelled to Britain with their own or others' money. British experience is then put into an international context in Chapter 9 which looks at the record of international students in other industrialised countries, with revealing contrasts between practice in France, Germany, the United States and in its time the Soviet Union.

Chapter 10, in conclusion, moves on to evaluation, briefly exploring how study in Britain influenced the lives of its former students and going on to see how they have been valued by society. In doing so it looks at the paradox that, while overseas students have travelled to Britain for many centuries, there have seldom been defined, overt, or universally accepted, policies towards them. Insofar as general policies can be discerned, they can be seen as dominated by individual and institutional practice up to the late nineteenth century, by the interests of imperial hegemony from the late nineteenth century into the 1970s, and by a new respect for market forces from the 1980s into the twenty-first century.

Part I
Narrative

2
Internationalism Reshaped, 1185–1800

The University of Bologna celebrated its 900th anniversary in 1988. It was a grand and colourful party with academics travelling from fellow universities to take part: academic dress may be medieval but must now be brighter than the eleventh-century norm. The date was a bit arbitrary, but had a precedent as Bologna held its 800th celebration in 1888 in the first nationalist flush of Italy's existence as a united country. Oxford and Cambridge, founded in the late twelfth and early thirteenth centuries, were both represented and the celebrations had an international touch, with support for a proposed 'Bologna process' of harmonising European higher education (see Chapter 9). The party demonstrated not only the resilience and survival of Europe's universities but also their sense of family. The family was reminded that students and academics, learners and teachers, have always travelled with the pattern of their journeys woven into the university fabric.

The rectors and vice-chancellors of 1988 might not have recognised the medieval university if they had been transported back. Medieval students tended to be younger than their successors, some only in their mid-teens. While the threefold structure of bachelor's, master's and doctoral degrees was already in place, many students stayed for a year or two and never took a degree. Teaching and scholarship were organised within four faculties – arts, law, theology and medicine, sometimes accompanied by music as a fifth – in a pattern that was to survive into the nineteenth century. Oxford and Cambridge were unusual among their European contemporaries in having all four from their earliest days. There were, of course and in principle, no women.

Other characteristics would have been more familiar. The American educator Clark Kerr pointed out that, of 85 institutions surviving with recognisably similar functions since 1520, 70 were universities.[1]

Independence is one defining feature. The medieval university already enjoyed a measure of independence from both church and state, although it served the needs of both and responded to pressure from both. Scholars enjoyed freedoms that followed from privileges granted by one or other of them. Until the Reformation monks and friars ran their own training programmes in such close – though sometimes fraught – symbiosis with Oxford and Cambridge that it is difficult to tell whether a particular activity should be attributed to the university or to one of the orders. Gradually the universities began to meet the needs of the state, as well as the church, in providing the administrators, lawyers and managers needed as state power expanded. As they did so they needed repeatedly to find ways of resolving conflicts that, too, remain recognisably similar, between the freedom and autonomy of the university and the requirements of those who provide its finance.[2]

The universities of Bologna and Paris had emerged from earlier schools at around the same time. Over the course of the next century both attracted students from far beyond their own regions. Their example led to a wave of new foundations, with around a dozen established by 1300, and more following in the next century as European populations grew. Some were created by 'swarms', as university staff moved from one locality to another that looked more congenial, others by deliberate 'planting' when civil or church authorities decided to create a new foundation. A minor swarm from Paris may have helped the establishment of Oxford while Cambridge's founding scholars travelled from Oxford in a deliberate swarm. Organisational patterns were copied. Some universities followed the Bologna model, in which teachers were in effect employed by the students, others the Paris model, later copied at Oxford, in which a guild of masters ran the university. Most of these early universities were in southern Europe with the remoter outliers emerging later in the fourteenth century – Prague in 1347, Krakow in 1364, Vienna in 1365. Oxford and Cambridge were northern exceptions, and were to remain the only universities in England till the nineteenth century. Scotland had to send its university students abroad till the fifteenth century and Ireland till the sixteenth.

Universities shared a common form. The term 'university', or the medieval designation *studium generale*, signal that what they taught was much the same, throughout a western Christendom that could be seen as intellectually united. Scholars and tutors could travel, study and teach with their qualifications universally recognised. For their part, students were attracted not so much by a different curriculum as by their wish to study with a particular master, or to travel for a mix of individual reasons including restlessness, fear and hope. The *studia generalia* had from their beginning the function of 'supranational centres propagating an international culture'.[3] The result was that:

> If one disregards the considerable distances and numerous obstacles and hardships involved in journeys in the Middle Ages, it was in fact relatively easy between the thirteenth and the fifteenth centuries to attend university and become a student. European universities had no national, social, intellectual, or linguistic requirements for admission.[4]

The exchange of ideas, of books and of people was a normal and defining characteristic of the medieval university. The presence of foreign students was a standard feature across Europe. In England, at the end of the twelfth century, 'the presence of foreign students in Oxford is an important consideration in cementing the notion of Oxford as a fully extended university as that was understood within the international academic community'.[5]

The numbers of students travelling seem to have increased up to the early fourteenth century, as universities grew. The English and Scots were among them: there were increasing numbers of English at Bologna and Paris in the late twelfth and early thirteenth centuries.[6] Scots travelled for their education to their national ally, France, where 260 of them have been identified at Paris between 1150 and 1410. From the fourteenth century, however, population changes, politics, religion and the growing number of universities all combined to discourage the travelling student. Plague cut populations and added to the hazards of travel.[7] The Hundred Years' War (1337–1453) intermittently discouraged movement between England and France while religious politics made exchanges between Scotland and France more difficult during the Great Schism (1378–1417), when Scotland recognised the pope in Rome and France his opponent in Avignon.

In England as in continental Europe university numbers gradually increased over their first 150 years, with Oxford always larger than Cambridge. By the late fourteenth century they had between them around 2,000 students and then expanded more rapidly so that, by 1450, there were about 3,000, some 1,700 in Oxford and 1,300 including about 240 friars in Cambridge.[8] This student population was large in relation to the population of 2.5 to 3 million, higher than in France and far higher than in central Europe.[9] The largest numbers were in the general school of arts but one in every three students at Oxford at this time was studying law.[10] This included canon law, an indispensable discipline within a universal church that affected life, death and property, and one highly valued for clerics seeking professional advancement.

A small number of foreign students were among the English. By about 1190 two brothers from Friesland, Emo and Addo, were studying rhetoric and law in Oxford. Thirty years later Henry III gave an open invitation to scholars from the University of Paris who had left the city after a conflict with the civil authorities. But the numbers were small and the records of alumni up to 1500–15,000 from Oxford and 7,000 from Cambridge – show that both universities were predominantly English. Oxford drew about 2 per cent of its students from outside the British Isles and up to a further 6 per cent from Scotland, Wales and Ireland. Figures for Cambridge are lower, amounting to only about 1 per cent in all. Irish students made up nearly half of those at Oxford from Scotland, Wales and Ireland, with the Welsh making up just over 30 per cent of the foreign total. Some of the actual numbers are minuscule, especially at Cambridge: while 315 Irish scholars were recorded at Oxford, there were only 16 at Cambridge, together with 39 Welsh and 19 Scots as against 390 and 129 at Oxford. There were higher proportions of foreign friars, estimated at between 8 and 10 per cent of the total in English convents between 1224 and 1539, mainly from Germany, the Low Countries and Italy.[11] Foreign students may not have been particularly welcome as few of them gained admission to the colleges, which enjoyed greater prestige than halls or lodgings.[12] The Welsh and Irish suffered from a reputation for violence which continued down the years (see Chapter 7) and was reinforced from time to time as when, in 1460, two Welsh students, with little violence but with the help of their tutor, stole a horse to ride home.[13]

It seems that England exported more scholars than it imported. English lawyers were attracted to the law school in Bologna.[14] In the last 20 years of the fifteenth century 137 scholars are known to have left Oxford for another university but at most 16 came from elsewhere.[15] The two-way flow meant that while the English universities had fewer foreign students than some of their continental contemporaries, they were never isolated from the rest of Europe. The small but important flow of scholars from the continent included Peter de Candia from Crete who studied at Oxford and went on to become Pope Alexander V in 1409; later in the same century Lorenzo Gugliemo Trasversagni di Savona was the first humanist to lecture in Cambridge.[16] It was Oxford scholars in Paris who persuaded Erasmus to travel to England. Scholars carried books with them, so that the heretical works of Wyclif could reach Prague and influence Jan Hus and his followers, while fourteenth-century English tracts on logic reached Erfurt and Leipzig where they were used as textbooks.[17]

Students had varying interests: most of the Welsh and Irish read law and the continentals theology. Both universities were unusual in being able to offer a doctorate in theology, a capacity shared only with Paris till the mid-fourteenth century.[18] The major orders of friars encouraged travel and expected their members to go to distant universities and read theology. (Not all did what they were told. Although the Franciscans agreed that a lecturer should regularly be sent to Oxford and Cambridge, John of Barbara successfully argued in 1376 that he should stay in Italy as the English climate would be bad for his health.[19]) Oxford's theologians evidently valued their international links so that when exchanges with Paris were interrupted by the Hundred Years War, contact 'was restored indirectly by German, east European and Italian mendicant scholars who kept Paris and Oxford informed of each other'.[20] The standing of Oxford's theology meant that it attracted students from as far as the University of Prague where in the mid-fourteenth century a scholarship was established to send poor Czech students to Paris or Oxford. Students in Prague who dictated books to their fellows could do so only if they were based on teaching at Prague itself, Paris or Oxford. Franciscan schools, existing alongside the universities, attracted increasing numbers of their friars in the fifteenth century, also to read theology.[21]

Politics and religion affected both the migration of scholars and their treatment once in England. Foreigners were not always welcome. Rioters attacked Italian clergy in 1231, partly out of resentment at papal taxation.[22] Between 1260 and 1261 the chapter in Oxford had to be told 'to receive outsiders and to treat them charitably. They were not, because of preceding disturbances, knowingly to molest the foreign friars'.[23] War with Scotland abruptly cut the flow of students in 1306 and although safe conducts were issued during the Anglo-Scottish wars it seems that few of them were used. War with France led the Oxford chancellor to expel all secular and religious French students in 1369, while four years later the king ushered in a long tradition of concern about espionage when he ordered the Dominican prior to 'remove friars from enemy countries who had come to the priory on pretence of engaging in study but who sought to spy out the king's plans, discover the state of the realm, and pass this information to the king's enemies'.[24] Attempts to control the flow of students fell away, as they repeatedly did in later centuries, and within 30 years foreign students were again coming to Oxford.[25]

For their part the mendicant orders came under suspicion as a brainwashing cult, effectively abducting young men at an impressionable age; they were attacked for doing so in 1357 by the archbishop of Armagh, a former chancellor of Oxford.[26] Suspicions abroad as well as at home could restrict movement. A Franciscan, Peter de Gaeta, was prevented from travelling from Assisi to Oxford by order of the king of Naples in 1340. By the early fifteenth century, and more seriously, suspicions of heresy discouraged students from many parts of the continent from travelling to Oxford as the university embraced Wyclif's teaching.[27] Although his ideas had been welcomed in Prague, the suppression of the Wyclifite Lollard movement then cut the well-established links between Oxford and Prague.[28]

Despite these constraints, movement towards and away from the English universities continued throughout the Middle Ages. The wandering scholars took with them not only their academic knowledge but their familiarity with the arts, living conditions, habits of other societies, opinions, manuscripts and books. While it would be wrong to exaggerate their importance, one assessment is that 'the consequences of academic pilgrimage were, indeed, out of all proportion to the numerically insignificant number of migrant students'.[29] They helped create something like a common European university culture. Domestically they helped both Oxford and Cambridge to grow in numbers and reputation during the fifteenth century, when new colleges were established in both universities. Increased numbers, new foundations, and a growing national and international reputation meant that they were well placed to respond to the new demands of Tudor power and the turbulence of the Reformation.

Before it had its own universities, Scotland was at the periphery of European university culture. Some Scottish students went to Oxford, in particular to Balliol College, others to the continent and especially to Paris where, from the mid-fifteenth to mid-sixteenth centuries, they outnumbered the English by nine to one.[30] In the early fifteenth century, however, some abandoned Paris and settled in St Andrews, seat of the largest monastery in the country. They followed lectures offered by the prior and the archdeacon whose activities were institutionalised in 1412 when the bishop incorporated scholars and teachers as a university. Five papal bulls were then issued to confirm its status. Bishops in Glasgow and Aberdeen, again with papal backing, followed suit in 1451 and 1494 so that by the end of the fifteenth century Scotland had three universities.[31] But at this stage the evidence suggests that Scotland had few if any foreign students.[32]

While it would be an anachronism to talk of a medieval state or university policy towards foreign students, some elements of future policies were already in place by 1500. Universities were benefiting from the presence of foreign students and teachers, and sometimes acknowledged the benefits. They accepted, even welcomed, foreign students though not always treating them as equals. For its part the state had shown its determination to exercise some control over foreign students, as over immigrants generally, and needed to be reassured of their loyalty. Ideology, as represented by the competing mendicant orders, was already promoting and financing student mobility, and arousing opposition as it did so. For their antagonists the mendicant orders were distrusted while French friars, in particular, were repeatedly under suspicion. Scholars were encouraged and funded to travel by the church, especially by the mendicant orders, attracted by the teaching offered in Oxford and Cambridge, intermittently held back by political and religious dispute.

When in the 1640s the English protested that a ban on Christmas celebrations meant the world was turned upside down, they were demonstrating a remarkable patience at a century and more of changes. They had included the Ottoman conquest of Constantinople in 1453, Columbus's journey of 1492, Martin Luther's nailing of his 95 theses on the church door at Wittenberg in 1517 and Henry VIII's Act in Restraint of Appeals in 1533. If it was not an upside-down world, it looked like a new one from an English perspective. The Mediterranean became a half-Christian half-Muslim lake, while Europe discovered a new continent, importing silver and syphilis, exporting measles and missionaries. Silver brought unheard-of inflation in its train. Orthodox Christianity, theologically apart since 1054, became more remote once it was the religion of Moscow but not Constantinople, while Luther's nails soon split Catholic Europe into its separate parts. Henry VIII, with a cheerful disregard for actual documentary evidence, cited 'diverse, sundry, old authentic chronicles and histories' to support the declaration that 'This realm of England is an Empire, and so hath been accepted in the world, governed by one Supreme Head and King': authority began and ended with the Tudor state and with him as its monarch.

The Reformation, and the assertions of Tudor authority, broke up the family of universities to which Oxford, Cambridge and the new Scottish universities had belonged. They had shared a commitment to training for the Catholic priesthood and enjoyed freedom of movement for scholars and tutors. Europe's universities now began to fall into three groups. The English and Scottish universities, to be joined by the University of Edinburgh and Trinity College Dublin, formed part of a group of Protestant universities, mainly in northern Europe. Many, such as Wittenberg, Heidelberg and Geneva, as well as the universities of the British Isles, remained active in training the, now Protestant, clergy. The Counter-Reformation ensured that alongside them there was a group of Catholic universities, including Paris, Louvain, Vienna and those of the Iberian peninsula, committed in the same way to the education of their priesthood. Then a third group, including the Catholic universities of Padua and Orléans and the university of Leiden with the Calvinist Dutch universities, were deliberately tolerant, accepting students regardless of their religion.[33]

Within these three groups religious and political changes transformed universities' constitutional status, relationships and curricula, and 'shattered and remoulded' patterns of student mobility.[34] Change followed swiftly after Henry VIII's break with Rome in 1533 when, a year later, he dissolved the monasteries and appropriated their property. Like the universities they had always enjoyed a certain independence, answering to their own superiors and to Rome, rather than to the local religious authorities. 'It is not too much to say that throughout the middle ages regular orders of various kinds – monks as well as friars – had formed the papal vanguard'.[35] The dissolution of the monasteries demonstrated that such vanguards were no longer acceptable. It also provided much-needed funds to the crown and had three immediate effects on Oxford and Cambridge. First, with their encouragement of travel, within or across frontiers, the mendicant orders had always provided a significant proportion of students at or around the universities. As the mendicants left, the universities became more national and less international institutions. Second, changes to the curriculum inevitably followed. The teaching of canon law, which had formed a major part of the curriculum for clerics, was banned as was lecturing on Peter Lombard's *Sentences*, the standard text of the old theological curriculum. While universities continued to train priests, they now did so for the Church of England, and not the Church of Rome. Third, the dissolution meant that there were spare buildings: Jesus College could take over the nunnery of St Rhadegund in Cambridge while in Oxford Cardinal College, later to become Christ Church, was built on the lands of the priory of St Frideswide.

Tudor policy made it clear that the universities were now state and not church institutions. Their secular nature was important not only as a demonstration of state power over the church but also because they provided a training ground for the government's new and expanded bureaucracies. Queen Elizabeth went on to clarify the universities' status in the Act of Incorporation of 1571 when they were defined as corporations, comparable to boroughs with their burgesses. Authority now came definitively from the crown and not the church so that Cambridge could no longer rely on the papal bull of 1318 with which it had previously justified its authority and privileges. These sixteenth-century changes amounted to what

might be called the 'Englishing' of Oxford and Cambridge. Before the Tudor period they were, like the Church itself, part of a non-English universal community. They owed some of their important privileges and much of their prosperity to the favour and protection of English kings, but the distinctive rights and privileges – the ones that made them universities – they possessed as the result of prescription recognized and confirmed by the Church, the ecumenical authority of the *res publica Christiana*.[36]

In practice the universities retained some of their privileged independence from state control. The extent of that independence and their place in society were to be developed over the next centuries but they gained one new mark of recognition in 1604 when they were each given the right (retained up to the election of 1945) to elect two Members of Parliament.

Along with this status came a responsibility to control university members' religious practice that was to influence the recruitment of students, from Britain or abroad. In principle, alike in England, Scotland and Ireland, they became Protestant institutions. Under Elizabethan legislation university members had to subscribe to the 39 articles of the Church of England. Outward conformity – an Elizabethan principle – eased the strictness of the religious tests. From the seventeenth century, while only Anglicans could matriculate at Oxford, at Cambridge the test was imposed only on graduation. Foreigners had to conform. The conformity acts did not apply to Trinity College Dublin which admitted a number of Catholics until 1641. Unlike Oxford it never required students to sign up to the 39 articles, appropriately enough as an Anglican enclave in a mainly Catholic island. Even so, the Catholics had to avoid noticing that its statutes referred to 'papal and other heretical religions'. Things then became more difficult in the eighteenth century when attendance remained possible but Catholics were faced with an anti-transubstantiation oath if they wanted to graduate.[37] For some, the cachet and contacts that came from attending university were enough and it was not necessary to sign up, register, matriculate and pay the fees these entailed. As the universities had no walls you could reasonably claim that you had been there without getting into the university record books. (For many centuries some continued to do so.)

All this meant that, though universities no longer recruited from Catholic Europe, their gates were in practice more widely open than the religious tests might suggest, to the benefit of both Catholics and Nonconformists. For some students, by the eighteenth century at least, religion was an unimportant barrier. Benjamin Vaughan, who was born in Jamaica, was admitted to Trinity Hall, Cambridge, in 1768 but as a Unitarian did not graduate. This did not stop him from studying law at the Inns of Court, or medicine in Edinburgh before going on to live an active public life into his eighties.[38]

Changes to the role and functions of universities within Tudor society were at least as important as the presence or absence of religious tests. Student numbers at Oxford and Cambridge rose from 1500 and reached a peak in the 1520s before falling dramatically till about 1550 with the removal of monks and friars, the ban on teaching canon law and a reduced demand for law degrees. They then increased between 1550 and 1580 and again in the early seventeenth century when they reached levels not to be seen again till the 1870s. Annual admissions to the two universities rose from about 250 at the beginning of the sixteenth century to about 1,000 in the 1630s before falling to about 330 in the 1750s (see Table 2.1).[39] Changes in class came with changes in numbers. The medieval aristocracy had little use for universities. Even as late as 1514 Henry VIII's principal secretary, Richard Pace, claimed that 'It better becomes the sons of gentlemen to hunt with skill, to teach and manage the falcon. Truly the study of letters is better left to the sons of yokels'.[40] But the demand for lay administrators and professional men created job opportunities which neither the aristocracy nor the gentry were prepared to leave to yokels. Aristocrats now sent their boys to university, and to the Inns of Court, to be joined in the late sixteenth and early seventeenth centuries by considerable numbers of students describing themselves as the sons of plebeians – husbandmen, clothworkers, tailors, drapers and glovers. Oxbridge was not only bigger than it was to be for more than two centuries but was also more diverse in terms of class, although not of nationality.[41]

As universities changed, in England and on the continent, the number of foreign students fell. Even before Henry VIII's split with Rome, Oxford's reputation in theology had declined: by the 1520s only three foreign names appear in the register.[42] At Oxford – and there is no reason to expect a very different pattern in Cambridge – of the 869 matriculants in 1603–5, 91 per cent came from England, less than 9 per cent from Wales and just below 1 per cent from anywhere else – the Channel Islands, France, Ireland, the Isle of Man and the West Indies. By 1683–5 the Welsh had increased their numbers to 10 per cent of the total and the others to 2 per cent.[43] In 1735 only 3 per cent were from outside England and Wales. Ireland sent few students so that only at the end of the eighteenth century did Irish numbers reach between 2 and 5 per cent.[44] Although Protestants fled the Low Countries during the revolt against Spain in the later sixteenth century, they tended to go to the reformed universities of the Dutch Republic, Switzerland and Germany.[45]

The numbers may be an underestimate. Refugees from the Palatinate, Huguenots from France and Protestants fleeing the Thirty Years War all found asylum in England. Total immigration may have been as high as

Table 2.1 University student numbers, 1200–1800

		Measure	Number	Foreign
1400	Total students	Oxford and Cambridge	c. 2,000	
c. 1450	Total students	Cambridge	1,300	1%
		Oxford	1,500–1,700	6%
1570	Total students	Cambridge	1,630	
1600–9	Estimated annual admissions	Cambridge	403	
		Oxford	374	
1603–5	Matriculants	Oxford	857	8.5% Welsh 0.7% other non-English
1650–9	Estimated annual admissions	Cambridge	358	
		Oxford	438	
1651	Total fellows and students	Cambridge	2,522	
1683–5	Matriculants	Oxford	857	10.2% Welsh 2.0% other non-English
1700–9	Estimated annual admissions	Cambridge	249	
		Oxford	316	
1750–9	Estimated annual admissions	Cambridge	149	
		Oxford	182	
1800	Estimated numbers	GB total	1,000–1,500	

Sources: Stone 'Size and composition', 91–2 except for: 1400: P. Moraw 1992 'Careers of graduates', in de Ridder-Symoens *Universities*, 268; 1450: Aston et al. 'Medieval alumni', 13–19; 1570: Curtis 'Oxford and Cambridge in transition', 3; 1603–5 and 1683–5: S. Porter 'University and society', 59; 1651: V. Morgan 2004 *A history of the University of Cambridge 1546–1750*, Cambridge, 464; 1800: estimated from Stone 'Size and composition' and Scottish data.

50,000 with 5,000 Germans in London by 1548.[46] In 1544 2,965 individuals were naturalised by Act of Parliament while the later Protestant Naturalisation Act, passed in 1709 and repealed in 1712, briefly made the process easier.[47] Naturalisation, assimilation and name change, from Schmidt to Smith or Arnauld to Arnold, will have helped immigrants' lot but made their impact difficult to trace. After a generation immigrants may look like any other citizens. And, while there were few students born abroad, the influence of those whose origins lay abroad, like the Huguenots, sometimes counted for more:

> Huguenots set up schools, served as tutors, wrote works that helped to keep England in touch with the march of mind on the Continent. Huguenot names attained distinction in the universities and the Royal Society, or, like Romilly's, in the law. Instead of simply swelling

religious zealotry, as it would have done had it come earlier, the late Huguenot arrival thus promoted England's intellectual as well as economic growth, two processes with many interconnections.[48]

The numbers of registered students also underestimate the total because they omit those attending without registering and those who came for too short a time to register. A survey of Hungarian students visiting Britain between 1526 and 1789 identified 56 who spent at least a fortnight and sometimes several terms at Oxford and 59 who did the same at Cambridge, of whom 12 attended both. A further 21 visitors of higher social rank made brief visits to Oxford and 27 to Cambridge. Only five went to Edinburgh or Glasgow. Their travel brought benefits and they 'translated religious literature from English with great success'. But of the total only half a dozen matriculated – four at Oxford, one at Cambridge and one who wrote a theology thesis at Edinburgh.[49] Hungary cannot be exceptional, at least in this regard, and its figures suggest that once the definition of 'foreign student' is stretched, from 'recognised university member' to 'serious academic tourist', then the total numbers dramatically increase.

The reduction in student mobility did not mean that England or Scotland was cut off from the mainstream of European thinking. The early sixteenth century was a period when both English universities had continuing contact with continental universities and when Cambridge 'went from a provincial status to one of international reputation' in a process that brought it into 'the mainstream of humanist reform'.[50] English logic had an international reputation while, in the early seventeenth century, English scholars were among the first to write on international law.[51] The universities continued to recruit academics and students internationally. Oxford had a handful of students in the 1570s whose fathers were German divines.[52] Cambridge attracted the Frenchman Peter Baro, who had been ordained in Geneva by Calvin himself, and in due course became Master of Peterhouse and in 1574 Lady Margaret Professor of Divinity, a post he retained for more than 20 years.[53] The sixteenth and early seventeenth centuries were a period of academic strength in England as well as of expansion, enhanced status and prosperity for the universities, even though only small numbers of foreign students came to benefit from the strength.

English and even more Scottish students continued to travel abroad. Some went for academic reasons, in search of teaching not available within the British Isles: in medicine they were attracted to universities like Leiden where, in the early eighteenth century, a third of those attending the physician Boerhaave's lectures were from English-speaking countries, or Reims where 60 per cent of the students were at that time from abroad.[54] Some, despite bans that were decreasingly enforced, went as recusants to Catholic universities like Paris. Its intake from England continued unchanged from its pre-Reformation level while Scottish numbers slumped and Irish numbers boomed.[55] They were, however, the exception. By the late seventeenth century the number of foreign students in Europe generally, as in the British Isles, had declined and it was only during the Thirty Years War that English and Scottish universities attracted foreign students in any numbers.[56] Religious tests, the uncertain balance between Catholicism, Anglicanism and Puritanism, and the rival attraction of continental universities, all kept students away. This began to change as English and Scottish universities became more attractive to outsiders, in the late seventeenth and eighteenth centuries. They came in particular from the colonies, from northern Europe and from Ireland.

The sixteenth century had seen universities established outside Europe but on a European model. Imperial powers differ in their educational policies and, unlike his English or Portuguese contemporaries, the Emperor Charles V saw a need to found the first American universities, in the Spanish colonies of Mexico and Peru. Established in 1551, they enjoyed 'all the privileges, exemptions and limitations of the University of Salamanca' and had the job of teaching priests, lawyers and doctors needed for the Spanish colonial empire. A century later the Puritans of New England followed the Spanish example and in 1646 founded Harvard with its statutes modelled on those of Cambridge and its job that of training Puritan ministers.[57] In contrast, neither the colonists and plantocracy of the West Indies nor the British government saw any need to create universities overseas. This was not to be part of the colonising mission for another two centuries. If the plantocracy wanted university education for its sons, it had to be found within the British Isles.

By the end of the seventeenth century the profits made from sugar, grown in slave plantations, meant that plantation owners could easily afford to ship their children home for education. Cambridge records show that two scholars from the West Indies were admitted to the university in the 1690s, Richard Carter, son of James Carter Esquire of Barbados, and John Moore, son of John Moore Gentleman of Jamaica; numbers then built up in succeeding decades so that 43 were admitted in the 1760s. After falling again they then rose to 48 in the 1790s. This meant that students from the West Indies made up some 3.7 per cent of the total of new admissions in the 1760s and were just below 3 per cent in the 1790s (see Table 2.2).[58] According to a contemporary account they included one black Jamaican, Francis Williams, who was sent to school in Jamaica and then on to Cambridge, in an experiment designed to test whether blacks could be educated. Education was assumed to be possible for whites of the right class and, in sending its sons to university, the plantocracy was following the normal pattern of the English gentry.[59] Many of them went on to study law gaining useful skills for managing family estates when 'in a highly litigious society men of means had an obvious need of a modicum of legal skill, which might enable them to deal with the suits of avaricious neighbours and troublesome tenants'.[60] Of the 271 West Indians just over a third (95) went on from Cambridge to the Inns of Court.

The West Indians were joined by new groups of students from northern Europe. As it emerged from the conflicts of the seventeenth century Britain, with its universities, became of new intellectual interest.

> England had at last been fully 'discovered', and had definitely begun to take the place of France as the country most worth visiting for the serious student of human affairs... For the travellers of this time England was above all the land of enlightenment. The influence of English philosophers and scientists, such as Locke, Newton, Shaftesbury and Hume, had opened up the German mind to the significance of England as a cultural factor.[61]

Table 2.2   Students from West Indies admitted to Cambridge, 1690–1799

	West Indies students admitted	Annual admissions of students
1690s	3	238
1700s	7	249
1710s	18	223
1720s	16	225
1730s	12	163
1740s	18	157
1750s	39	149
1760s	43	116
1770s	30	140
1780s	33	171
1790s	48	162
total	267	

Source: Venn database; Stone 'Size and composition', 92.

Students from northern Europe now travelled in increasing numbers to Britain. From the seventeenth century there was a steady flow of students from Scandinavia to Oxford and Cambridge.[62] Continental travellers came to teach as well as to learn. There were industrial and academic links between Germany and Britain where the mining industry in Cornwall, Lancashire and Cumberland was dependent on German expertise. Shared industrial interests brought Peter Stahl from west Prussia to lecture on mining and metallurgy and to teach analytical chemistry in Oxford.[63] English industry and English universities were in their turn attracting students from further afield. At a time when Russia had no universities of its own, Tsar Boris Godunov proposed to send 18 young men to be educated in England, France and Germany. In practice only nine travelled, five to France and four to England.[64] The English four sailed from Archangel with the intention that they should study at Eton, Winchester, Oxford and Cambridge. Their careers illustrate a regular feature of scholarship programmes as, while the tsar intended them to graduate and return home to strengthen the imperial administration, none did so. One went to Ireland and was not heard from again, two went to seek their fortunes in the East India Company, but the fourth, Mikiper Alpheri, successfully went to Cambridge and gained BA and MA degrees, apparently untroubled by the 39 articles. He was summoned to London by the first Russian ambassador to England and instructed to go home but instead renounced Orthodoxy, became an Anglican priest in Huntingdonshire, and managed to survive ejection from his parish under Cromwell and to be reinstated after the Restoration.[65]

A handful of Russian students travelled to England and Scotland in the eighteenth century. Catharine the Great then followed Boris's earlier example and, wanting to establish a theological faculty in Russia, sent four students in 1765. Again they had mixed success: one spent all his money and went to debtors' prison, while the two who got their MAs, Prokhor Suvorov and Vasilii Nikitin, returned home, but rather than starting a theology faculty, together wrote a textbook of *Elements of plane and spherical geometry*, in both languages. As the eighteenth century went on the government nominees were joined by sons of the aristocracy, who were usually sent to Oxford, and probably with different expectations.[66]

The four Scottish universities remained small and predominantly local institutions. Entrants to St Andrews amounted to only 44 a year in the sixteenth century and 60 in the seventeenth while in the early seventeenth century Aberdeen had 17 to 38 a year.[67] Scottish families remained reluctant to educate their sons locally so that until the late seventeenth century more Scots studied abroad than at home.[68] From the outset, however, Scottish universities expected to attract some foreign students. Glasgow, following the practice of continental universities, was organised in four nations: Glottiana for Clydeside, Rothesaiana for south and west Scotland and Ireland, Loudoniana for the rest of Scotland, England and Ireland, and Albania for other foreigners.[69] North-east Scotland had strong connections with the Baltic coast and beyond, but in practice drew few students from there, although the University of Aberdeen did attract small numbers, probably of Nonconformists, from England.[70]

In the late seventeenth century foreign student numbers were declining, in Scotland as in much of Europe. The numbers rose, however, in the next century when Scottish universities benefited in four ways from their particular strengths. First, they were all urban universities, located near to centres of commerce and industry, which helped their curricula respond to new demands for scientific education. Second, Glasgow and Edinburgh established medical faculties in the early eighteenth century which rapidly gained national and international reputations. The American colonists were attracted by the medical faculties as until the mid-1760s their own universities taught theology but not medicine. Aspirant doctors had to cross the Atlantic and often made Edinburgh their first choice.[71] Third, Edinburgh in particular benefited from the achievements of the Scottish enlightenment which made it internationally attractive. And fourth, the religious tests that were still limiting entrance to English universities were more relaxed in Scotland. From the mid-eighteenth century this brought benefits first to Edinburgh and then to Glasgow:

> As these universities did not require any profession of faith in the Church of Scotland and their programmes in the faculty of medicine – the pride of Edinburgh and later of Glasgow – were very flexible, they had an international following of Scandinavian, Portuguese and other students (among them Russians), and were visited by English and Irish dissenters and by Calvinists from the American colonies.[72]

Students came from the east as well as the west. At the time of Catharine the Great the Russians were attracted to work in medicine, political economy and law, with Joseph Black in medicine or with Adam Smith. His student Semyon Desnitskii went home to advise the tsarina on Smith's ideas and to lecture on those of William Blackstone. Others studied with Francis Hutchison in moral philosophy, and James Millar in law. Following his period at Edinburgh Ivan Shishukov made his contribution to Russo-British understanding by publishing a two-volume Russian–English dictionary in 1808–11.[73]

The numbers of registered foreign students are modest but are, once again, potentially misleading as they understate the total number of those attending classes. Very few of the foreign students at Edinburgh in the eighteenth century took a degree there: 'Like Leiden in the seventeenth century, Edinburgh in the eighteenth century is a good example of a study university; thus in the 1780s its faculty of medicine had about 500 students a year, only 20 or 30 of whom took a degree there'.[74]

Ireland waited nearly two centuries longer than Scotland for its first university, Trinity College Dublin, eventually founded in 1592. In its constitution and structure it followed Cambridge precedents and the first heads of the college came from Cambridge. It remained small, as an urban institution meeting the needs of its immediate hinterland, admitting only about 16 students a year in the early 1620s. Numbers then rose gradually so that by the mid-1680s it had 300 to 400 students. By this time it was meeting the needs of the English ascendancy, which increased after the establishment of the plantation of Ulster, though without satisfying all the demands of Catholic Irish. At the extreme edge of Europe, too, Trinity College had limited attraction for foreign students. But with its relaxed attitudes to religious tests and attendance at chapel it drew in some students from Britain and from abroad. In 1792 16 per cent of its students had been born in Britain and 5 per cent overseas, more than half of this group coming from Irish families in India. Many Irish students continued to travel. Alongside the 2 per cent of Oxonians in the early eighteenth century, considerable numbers went to continental Europe. Despite attempts to constrain the flow of Catholic students, about 1,000 studied at the University of Paris between the mid-sixteenth and late eighteenth centuries, many of them aiming for the priesthood either in Ireland or in France itself. Along with students from England and Scotland – but often outnumbering them – they also went to study medicine at the University of Reims which had 558 Irish medical students between 1690 and 1789.[75] Ireland's part in the story of student mobility in early modern Europe is as a sending rather than a receiving country.

Universities in both England and Scotland had survived the Reformation, even as it swept away the monasteries and abbeys, banned the teaching of canon law which had been one of their main functions and rejected the papal authority on which their privileges rested. The English universities' adoption of a new role, serving the needs of the expanded Tudor state and training the clergy of the Church of England, brought them increased numbers, wealth and status. At the same time, the religious and political divisions of the sixteenth and seventeenth centuries forced a redrawing of the map of European student mobility. Medieval student travels spread across Europe but not beyond. They were based on assumptions of university equality with the *ius ubique docendi* ensuring that teachers could travel and an expectation that students might go wherever a teacher was of particular interest to them. For the numbers of mendicants, there was an organisation in the shape of their orders that actively encouraged travel. All that fell away with Europe's religious divisions of the sixteenth century and the wars and civil conflict that continued into the seventeenth. While circuits of Protestant and Catholic universities began to re-establish themselves, mercantilist assumptions then discouraged student travel. Universities in Britain began to attract increasing numbers of students from abroad in the eighteenth century in a new pattern of movement. This was in part a response to new demands in northern Europe, in part a way of meeting the needs of the first British empire and in part, for Scotland, a consequence of the intellectual stimulus of the Scottish Enlightenment. Students were now pushed by the lack of educational opportunities in the West Indies and North America, and its limitations in northern Europe, pulled by the perceived benefits of education in Britain, from law in the Inns of Court to medicine in Scotland.

3
Revival and Reform, 1800–1900

The English universities entered the nineteenth century in a state of torpor. While student numbers rose in the first two decades they then remained stagnant from the 1830s to the 1850s with annual admissions to Oxford and Cambridge at between 800 and 870. In the country as a whole the proportion of young men going to university fell from 732 per million in 1821 to 541 in 1861.[1] Universities had little to do with England's burgeoning industry.[2] Oxford, for example,

> seemed to many to be tied to an earlier age, affluent, idle, Anglican, aristocratic, having, in the minds of its radical critics…all the defects of moribund privilege. Fellows were still elected because of their regional qualifications and family connections and with too little regard to scholarship. Once elected the majority had no obligation to pursue either a course of study or research, retaining their positions until a college living offered an opening for preferment and the opportunity for marriage. At most colleges many fellows were non-resident and one or two sufficed for the instruction of undergraduates.[3]

Oxford had no faculties of science, modern languages, English or history. Cambridge was little different. Both retained religious tests for entry, resisting changes that brought Catholic emancipation to the country generally and removed bars on the admission of Jews and dissenters to public office. Both universities resisted proposals for reform made by royal commissions in the 1850s. Both still required Latin and Greek for entry and still refused to let their dons marry. There were fewer of the middle- and even working-class students who had been so visible in the seventeenth century and at least some of their more aristocratic successors were happy with torpor.[4] All this limited the universities' appeal for international students. In Scotland, Edinburgh University was suffering from infighting among its professors and a ferocious conflict with the city authorities, and had lost its earlier Enlightenment vigour.[5] Only its medical school retained its strength and even here, with respect for a dying tradition and a dead language, the faculty continued to conduct its written and oral examinations in Latin until 1832.[6]

Innovation was to be found away from the ancient universities. Although London had traditionally trained lawyers at the Inns of Court, and doctors through the royal colleges and its hospitals, it had no university till the nineteenth century when, in quick succession, University College and King's College were founded in the 1820s to be followed by the University of London in 1836. It was a deliberately different kind of institution. With no religious tests, it followed Scottish precedents in making no residential requirements. As a degree-giving body it provided accreditation for both King's and University College but went so far beyond them that by 1859 it was examining students in Manchester and Liverpool as well as London, and by 1865 was doing so outside the British Isles, initially in Mauritius. London was followed by Durham, which gained its charter in 1836. It, too, sought an international role and established links with Codrington College in Barbados and Fourah Bay College in Sierra Leone. Industrial cities followed Durham's example and, building on the experience of their mechanics' institutes, created new university colleges, which were to gain university status in the late nineteenth and early twentieth century. They were joined by polytechnics, technical colleges and municipal colleges in London and the larger provincial towns. Unlike Oxford and Cambridge these were inner-city institutions, with finance from industry, which wanted from the outset to teach in disciplines new to English higher education; only after their foundation could students graduate in chemistry without travelling to Germany.[7] They grew rapidly so that, while there were only some 600 students in the provincial university colleges in 1861, within 20 years their 5,000 exceeded the total at Oxford and Cambridge.

Having resisted calls for reform in the 1850s, Oxford and Cambridge finally began to change within 20 years. New subjects came into the curriculum. Cambridge introduced courses in natural sciences and moral sciences in the 1850s and these were followed by the construction of the Cavendish Laboratory. Oxford's Clarendon Laboratory had been built in 1869. Gradually both universities gained in academic strength, in the sciences as well as the humanities. In response to imperial interests both introduced teaching in oriental languages, initially for British rather than Indian students. Oxford opened its doors to non-Anglican students in 1854 and Cambridge in 1856, and religious tests for university teachers were abolished in 1871.They were retained for degrees in divinity until after the First World War and colleges might still expect regular attendance at chapel. Students of any religion or none could now, however, enter without religious conversion or perjury.

They still had to pass examinations in Greek and Latin. That linguistic door was prised open, mainly for the benefit of Indian students. Cambridge moved first, and for some years attracted more Indian students than Oxford, but from 1884 Oxford allowed Sanskrit as a substitute for Latin or Greek and from 1907 allowed one oriental language and English as a substitute for both Latin and Greek. Life changed for college fellows who were now allowed to marry – from 1840 at Trinity College Dublin and 1878 at Oxford and Cambridge. Admitting women students was, however, a step too far. Although London introduced a special examination for women in 1868 and awarded its first degrees to them in 1880, the Oxford and Cambridge women's colleges, which go back to 1869, only enabled women to attend and to sit examinations; they could not formally become members of either university till the next century. Trinity College Dublin was slower than Oxford or Cambridge in admitting women to the fringes of the university but then, in 1904, leapt ahead and admitted them as full members. Reform encouraged expansion and university numbers increased from the 1850s.

Despite the changes, which increased the universities' international appeal, Britain enrolled few from the continent. Though figures are sparse Britain was now apparently sending more students to continental Europe than receiving them, with Germany to the fore: an estimated 9,000 British students enrolled in German universities between 1844 and 1914.[8] Universities slowly made life easier for those who came to Britain. In 1871 Oxford introduced a category of special students and began awarding BLitt and BSc degrees, and diplomas in economics and forestry in a move away from the constrictions of the centuries-old BA. More than half of the special students came from the continent, with others coming from America, Asia and the colonies.[9] From 1895 advanced or research students could be admitted to Cambridge without passing a language examination and this too brought in students from overseas. The professor of mathematics, J. A. Ewing, reported that granting advanced status to these students brought 'not only from the home university colleges and universities, but more especially from the colonies, a band of most admirable young men, young men full of enthusiasm for their work, of much more than average ability'. London and Edinburgh followed the Cambridge example in easing entry for research students.[10]

Expansion and reform together equipped Britain with a network of university institutions capable of meeting changing national or international demands. By the end of the century, it was possible to study engineering, physics at the highest levels, brewing, Indian languages and mining technology, as well as classics, regarded as a vocational qualification for future rulers of the empire. Race was never a formal barrier to entry within Britain, religion fell away as one, and there were new ways round the linguistic barriers of Greek and Latin. One consequence was that university numbers increased, most dramatically in the last 30 years of the century, almost doubling in the 1870s and doing so again between 1880 and 1900. Another was that the proportion of overseas students rose for the first time for centuries, doing so most rapidly in the last decades of the century (see Table 3.1).

Figures from Oxford and Cambridge illustrate the changes. In 1810, 95 per cent of entrants to Oxford were from the British Isles with 2 per cent from Europe and 3 per cent from North America and the empire. The proportion from outside the British Isles then rose to 7 per cent in 1835/37, 8 per cent in 1860 and 10 per cent in 1885 to reach 24 per cent in 1910.[11] Figures from Trinity College, Cambridge for 1898 suggest a similar pattern at the end of the century with 19 of 199 new undergraduates coming from abroad.[12] In Oxford by 1810,

> there had appeared a sprinkling from Scotland, India and Western Europe to join the swelling Irish contingent, which now amounted to 6 per cent of the whole. In 1885 the proportion of outsiders was still only 16 per cent, although Australia and New Zealand were now sending a trickle of students, and the Indian contingent was increasing. But the big change came between 1885 and 1910, when there was a truly massive influx from the United States and the Empire, and also from western Europe.[13]

London and the provincial universities are less well documented but the figures from Scotland follow the same trend. Among the Scottish universities Edinburgh always had the largest proportion from overseas which increased from 9 per cent of the total in 1870 to 16 per cent in 1900. By that time Glasgow and Aberdeen each had 6 per cent and St Andrews 4 per cent.[14] It seems safe to conclude that, across the whole country, there was a marked increase in absolute numbers of students from abroad during the century and that the proportion increased from around 5 to around 10 per cent of the total, suggesting that there were some 2,000 of them by 1900. There was then to be a further marked increase in the early twentieth century (see Chapter 4).

Table 3.1   University student numbers, 1800–1900

	Measure		Total student number	Foreign number
1800	University students		1,000–1,500	
1810	Oxford matriculants		324	2% Europe 3% North America and empire
1835–7	Oxford matriculants		1,175	2% Europe 5% North America and empire
1860	University numbers	Britain	3,385	
1860	Oxford matriculants		394	2% Europe 6% North America and empire
1870	University numbers	Britain	5,560	
1880	University numbers	Britain	10,560	c. 100 Indians
1885	Oxford matriculants		749	2% Europe 8% North America and empire
1890	University numbers	Britain	16,013	c. 200 Indians
1892/3	University numbers	Scotland	6,488	c. 640 (10%) overseas
1900	University numbers	Britain	20,249	c. 340 Indians

Sources: 1800 estimated from Stone 'Size and composition' and Scottish data; Oxford matriculants: Stone 'Size and composition', 101; British numbers 1860–90: K. H. Jarausch 1983 'Higher education and social change', in K. H. Jarausch (ed.) *The transformation of higher learning 1860–1930*, Chicago, 13; Scottish numbers 1892/3 in J. Kerr 1913 *Scottish education school and opportunity*, Cambridge, 378ff. with overseas proportion estimated from R. D. Anderson 1983 *Education and opportunity in Victorian Scotland*, Oxford, 296–8;1900: British numbers, UGC *Report 1929/30–1934/5*, 52, Indian numbers, Lahiri 'Indians', 5.

It was easy to travel to Britain in the nineteenth century, whether to study or as a response to its expanding economy. Passports were rare before 1915 and there were no legal barriers to migration into Britain. The country's standing as an imperial and industrial power drew travellers, immigrants and students. The costs of travel fell as railways crisscrossed Europe and steamships shortened journeys. From 1869 the Suez

Canal brought India closer. As the century went on it became easier and cheaper for students of all kinds to reach Britain.

Although the categories sometimes overlap, the overseas students who were drawn to Britain in the nineteenth century fell into four groups. First were the children of empire, including those from the colonies of settlement, together with the North Americans. Then there were the children of the affluent and internationally minded middle class, which had developed in countries like Egypt or Russia, and looked to Britain particularly for higher education. Members of a third group were sent to acquire professional qualifications needed by their societies and not available at home. Indian students made up the fourth group. Their numbers grew so dramatically in the second half of the century that they demand separate treatment though some might be included in each of the other three categories.

Some of the children of the empire were literally that. The more prosperous members of the West Indian plantocracy continued to send their children to school as well as to university in Britain, as they had in the previous century. They were now joined by children of the developing middle class as 'anyone with the means sent his children to England for all but the most elementary education'. In Jamaica where class tended to match colour, a black Jamaican commented in 1824 that 'the Browns were far above most of us in fortune, and some of them had been educated in a very respectable manner in Britain'.[15] They included girls as well as boys. In Jane Austen's *Sanditon*, 'Mrs Griffiths was a very well-behaved, genteel kind of woman who supported herself by receiving such great girls and young ladies, as wanted either masters for finishing their education, or a home for beginning their displays'. Among her three charges, the richest and therefore most important, who had a maid of her own, was a 17-year-old described as 'half mulatto'.[16] Similarly, in the 1820s and 1830s, the Sierra Leone middle class, whether European or African, continued to send their children to England. Kenneth Macaulay, who had travelled to Sierra Leone as a government writer, sent his children there apparently 'hoping that on return they would show the Settlers a better example of moral family life than their fathers had provided' while Thomas Carew, a property developer of Afro-Caribbean origin, sent two of his children for all the benefits that English education might bring.[17]

The Sierra Leoneans were joined by children of the aristocracy from the Gold Coast, the Gambia and southern Nigeria. Under a British Asante treaty in 1831 two sons of the royal family travelled to Britain to be educated at the British government's expense. Both duly returned home where one of them worked at various times for the Asante state, for Methodist missionaries and for the colonial government. Things were not always so benign; the son of the Asantahene spent six years at Surrey County School, Cranleigh, but was expelled in 1884 for immoral conduct with a servant girl. While the numbers are small, they confirm that 'throughout the century, English educational institutions, from pioneering elementary schools to the most advanced vocational departments of the universities, received a trickle of West Indian and black African students'.[18]

It is safe to assume that larger numbers of the children of empire went to university in Britain than to school. If they wanted a university education most of them had to travel as, until the 1850s, and with the limited exception of the Ionian Academy from 1824 to 1864, the only imperial universities outside the British Isles were in Canada and Malta. For the rest, subjects of the empire could graduate without travelling only with the establishment of universities in Australia and India from the 1850s, in New Zealand from the 1860s and in South Africa from the 1870s. Hong Kong, west Africa, the West Indies and the rest had to wait till the next century.

Despite the decline of the sugar industry, which ruined many fortunes, university students from the West Indian plantocracy continued to travel to Britain. Like the school children they were now joined by Afro-Caribbeans: by the 1820s there was a barrister in St Lucia who had been educated in England and a doctor in Trinidad who had graduated at Edinburgh.[19] Similarly the west African middle class sent its sons to British universities as well as schools, providing the region with doctors, lawyers and pastors. By the 1850s five students had travelled from Sierra Leone to study medicine though only two qualified – William Davies in London and James Africanus Horton in Edinburgh. Edinburgh continued to recruit black students from the West Indies and occasionally the United States with increasing numbers towards the end of the century. Others followed the medical students to study law, the humanities and theology. The Sierra Leoneans included Christian Cole, who graduated in greats at Oxford in 1876 where he is reported to have been the first African BA and another doctor, D. P. H. Taylor, who got his MRCS in London in 1874 and returned to Africa, leaving behind his son, the composer Samuel Coleridge Taylor, who never visited his father's country.[20] Throughout the nineteenth century British universities, along with the schools of medicine and Inns of Court, were meeting professional needs within the colonies and the family interests of their middle class.

Small numbers were also coming to England from the colonies of settlement and from North America, despite the existence of established universities in both Canada and the United States. The first Cambridge student recorded as born in Australia, John Mcarthur 'of a well-known Australian family' arrived in 1811 and by 1840 had been followed by ten more, typically the children of senior civil servants, lawyers and doctors.[21] Students from the United States were sufficiently rare for Charles Bristed to return from graduating in Cambridge in 1845 and write his book of guidance, *Five years in an English university* (see Chapter 1). He was followed by William Everett who published his guide *On the Cam* as a series of lectures in 1865. Bristed had already graduated at Yale, spent a year wondering what to do next and whether to become a clergyman, before sailing to England where he signed up as a fellow commoner, a status that cost more but got him privileges including a better seat at dinner and in chapel and a velvet cap with a metallic tassel. As his grandfather, John Jacob Astor, was the richest man in the United States, he could afford to do so. Bristed read classics and argued for their strength as an educational tool for his home country. Everett, too, came from a privileged background and was at Cambridge because his father was a minister in the embassy in London. Though both came from unusually wealthy backgrounds, their example suggests that a proportion of the colonial and American students who made their way to England in the early nineteenth century were drawn by the status of its universities rather than the utilitarian value of an English education.

As the colonies of settlement developed their own universities, this, paradoxically, increased the flow of students to Britain rather than reducing it. The early colonial universities were planted, as in the middle ages, by groups of scholars who went from Britain, bearing assumptions about university quality and the superiority of British models. Within Australia, British assumptions were reinforced by local expectations that the best was to be found in Oxford or Cambridge. A letter from the senate in Sydney to a selection committee in England explained that:

> We consider it most important that the Classical and Mathematical Professors should bring with them the prestige of high Academical distinction at one of the Universities of Oxford and Cambridge. And we hope we shall not inconveniently fetter your choice by confining it to first class men at either University in Classics, and the first ten Wranglers in Mathematics at the University of Cambridge.[22]

The expatriate professors, and their peers in the other new colonial universities, then had to resolve the tension between nostalgia for the education that they had left behind, and the colonial community's expectation that a university supported by public funds should be demonstrably useful. Donnish memories and assumptions could easily suggest to students that 'a classical education was the ideal and the colonial interest in practical things a difficulty to be surmounted', tempting them to travel to Britain in search of the metropolitan ideal.[23] Even if they avoided that temptation, early colonial graduates generally had to look abroad if they wanted to pursue research or work for a higher degree. The metropole was a magnet for this group.

Ernest Rutherford was one of them. He got double first degrees in mathematics and physics in New Zealand, published two papers on electromagnetism while still studying, and moved to Cambridge in 1895 to work with J. J. Thomson as the Cavendish Laboratory's first research student. He was one of a growing number of invigorating migrants to English universities like the Australians in the 1890s who, in Ernest Barker's eyes, 'blew into the antiquity of Oxford with the challenge of their own and their country's youth'.[24] They also blew into Cambridge where Australian numbers almost doubled from the 1860s to the 1870s (increasing from 82 to 161) though falling to 118 in the 1890s. While some, like their predecessors, went to school in England before entering university, an increasing number now moved to Britain after studying at Australian universities.[25]

The paths of these colonial students were eased by constitutional changes within Oxford and Cambridge. Reformers succeeded in persuading both universities to interest themselves in students outside their walls, promoting the extension movement within Britain and strengthening links with universities in the empire overseas. Both universities introduced procedures to allow institutions in the empire to become affiliated so that their graduates would get advanced standing once they had travelled to Britain. Cambridge introduced its affiliation procedures in 1879 and went on to approve the affiliation of, among others, the University of New Zealand in 1886 and Calcutta University in 1887.[26] Oxford's scheme followed in 1887 and by 1900 it had affiliated universities in Australia, South Africa, New Zealand, Canada and India. Students who came with the right qualifications from their home university were exempted from responsions, an examination taken in the first year.[27] Overseas alumni could now graduate at Oxford or Cambridge in a shorter period than was possible for ordinary – even English – school leavers.

The second category of students, alongside those from the empire and America, came from an international and increasingly affluent middle and upper class that was sending its children to western Europe. Many of these students were from outside the formal empire, with Egypt as one important source. It had a cosmopolitan middle class and a large expatriate population, which was to number 286,000 by 1907. But even by 1902 there were only three state secondary schools and, under what amounted to British rule in the late nineteenth century, the British Consul-General,

Lord Cromer, carefully cut expenditure on education.[28] Higher education had to be sought elsewhere and both the prestige and the practical
usefulness of British degrees drew Egyptian students. Among the first in
Cambridge were Abdul Aziz Izzet Bey who arrived in 1886, went on to
the Royal Military College at Woolwich, and went home to marry the
king's niece and follow a career as a politician and diplomat, serving as
foreign minister in the 1930s. He was followed in the 1890s by Gaston
Raphael De Menasce, of a family of bankers in Alexandria, who went to
school in England before going on to Cambridge.[29] Outside the informal
empire, prosperous families in Russia, like those in Egypt, sent their children abroad. Although it had its universities, which expanded rapidly in
the nineteenth century, they imposed quotas which meant that, as it was
'difficult for those from the petty bourgeoisie, the middle class and the
Jewish communities to study, their sons and daughters went abroad in
droves to obtain their university degrees' (see Chapter 9).[30] While many
went to Paris, Berlin and Zurich, smaller numbers reached England. They
were joined by the children of Russian exiles, attracted to England for
its tolerance and lack of immigration policies, and seen from a Russian
standpoint as an early example of brain drain.[31]

Students in the first two categories were generally sent and paid for by
their families or, less often, travelled with scholarships. The third category comprises those who were sent, often with public funds, because
their societies wanted to benefit from education and training abroad.
In Egypt, again, from 1809 Muhammad Ali began to send students to
western Europe to acquire the skills needed for his programme of national
modernisation. 'It was typical of him to send men of his own kind to
Europe to see for themselves what was lacking in the country and what
the Westerners had to give and teach…rather than to depend solely on
the advice of foreigners who happened to be in the country.' He sent
students to England to learn ship-building, the management of ships and
mechanics.[32] These missions continued through the century until Cromer
put a stop to them.

Students were sent from the formal empire in the same way though
Britain, unlike Egypt, saw little need to train local engineers or mechanics
for its overseas territories. Religion and medicine were a different matter.
Missionary agencies sent students to Britain, and also set up training
programmes abroad: both Codrington College in Barbados and Fourah
Bay in Sierra Leone had the training of catechists among their functions.
The empire also needed doctors and did so at a time when English and,
even more, Scottish medical faculties, were attracting an international
corps of medical students.

Almost from its beginnings, the East India Company saw the need for a medical service to care for its own staff; it assigned surgeons to its ships travelling to India and then employed them at its factories within India. After 1857 the Indian Medical Service operated in parallel with the Indian Civil Service, drawing many of its doctors from Scottish medical schools. Local paramedical staff were needed, alongside the Scottish doctors, and from 1824 training institutions were set up to train sub-assistant surgeons, apothecaries and dressers. The Native Medical Institution of Bengal, which was one of these, became Calcutta Medical College and in the 1850s moved on from producing licentiates, and 'native doctors', to providing full medical qualifications.[33] Indian medical education then followed two parallel paths with some doctors travelling to Britain to train and others doing so within the subcontinent. The first three to be sent to Britain went there in 1845, to be followed by many more. The University of Aberdeen, among others, went on to support both approaches to the training of doctors. It had longstanding links with Ceylon and between 1860 and 1900 produced 40 medical graduates who had been born in Ceylon. At the same time it worked with the Ceylon Medical College and from 1884 gave students of its courses advanced standing if they travelled to Aberdeen to complete a degree.[34]

Students from India, including future doctors and many others, form the fourth category. They were virtually unknown before the middle of the nineteenth century, but by 1900 dominated discussion about overseas students. The expansion of British rule and commerce in India meant that the Indian empire now interpenetrated upper-class and upper-middle-class society in the way that the West Indian sugar interest had in the eighteenth century. British rule in India could rank with diplomacy as, in John Bright's phrase, outdoor relief for the aristocracy. More soberly Cain and Hopkins have pointed out that 'from the 1850s, military and civil appointments in India became a large, vested interest of the educated middle class' to the extent that by 1913 65 per cent of the government of India budget was spent on the army and civil administration.[35] British universities played their part: Oxford and Cambridge trained India's future civil servants while, alongside their new examinations in Indian languages, Oxford created an Indian Institute in 1877 for the academic study of the subcontinent.

From the early nineteenth century Britain interested itself in education within India. The East India Company began funding education with a grant of Rs 100,000 (£10,000) in 1813. Educational policy then flowed from Macaulay's much-quoted minute of 1835 with its claim 'that a single shelf of a good European library was worth the whole native literature of India and Arabia'. In accordance with that principle he urged that funds should be used to support a system of English schools in the main towns whose beneficiaries would be '"Indian in blood and colour, but English in tastes, in opinions, in morals and in intellect": a class who would serve as interpreters between the government and the masses'.[36] The expansion of English-style schooling led inexorably to demands for higher education and by 1845 plans were being sketched for a university that might be modelled on the recently established University of London. Ten years were to pass but in 1858 India's first universities, in Calcutta, Bombay and Madras, were established by Act of Parliament. All three followed the London university model in which the university was an accrediting body with teaching left to separate colleges.

British rule, as Macaulay's minute suggests, demanded an educated local population: British administrators and soldiers were always so vastly outnumbered by local citizens that control of India rested on the labours of Indian, and normally subordinate, staff. The East India Company came to recognise this dependence in its recruitment policies: in 1833 it abandoned earlier restrictions that had been based on race. Once the government took over political responsibility from the company a clear principle of equality, without discrimination, was reasserted, with regal authority. In 1858 the queen's proclamation laid down that 'it is our...will that, so far as may be Our Subjects, of whatever Race or Creed; be freely and impartially admitted to Offices in Our Service, the Duties of which they may be qualified, by their education, ability, and integrity duly to observe'.[37] The dependence, and the principle if not always the practice of equality, had profound effects on the development of education in India, on the Indian class structure and on students' passages to Britain.

Under the queen's proclamation, the Indian Civil Service, with all its power, prestige and expatriate domination, was now in principle open to all comers, provided they were qualified. By 1864 it had its first Indian member in Satyendranath Tagore, elder brother of the poet Rabindranath Tagore. British rule also created new opportunities outside the civil service that were just as dependent on higher education. The introduction of English property law in 1793 led to the growth of litigation about land rights, creating work for lawyers. They became the most highly paid profession in the British raj where successful Indian lawyers could earn more than their British counterparts. The profession expanded so rapidly that, by 1911, alongside smaller numbers of British lawyers, the Bombay High Court had 150 Indian solicitors and 234 advocates.[38] Professional opportunities were seized, not by the old Indian aristocracy, but by a new middle class, who enjoyed new levels of prosperity.

Opportunities for advancement were in practice less widely open than the queen's proclamation might have suggested. While the Indian Civil Service could not operate a colour bar, Indian candidates had to overcome formidable obstacles that might almost be mistaken for one. Examinations for entry were held in London, not in India, and in practice candidates with a British or Irish degree, were at a great advantage over those with an Indian one. There were age limits on entry, which fluctuated – with changes in 1859, 1866 and 1877 – that were partly an attempt to control the activities of crammers in England but also operated against Indian candidates.[39] While Indian medical qualifications were recognised by the royal colleges, strict controls on engineers remained. (Suspicion lingered for many years: the education officer of the Institution of Mechanical Engineers told me in the 1960s that, in order to avoid any risk of corruption, its examinations in India were conducted only by members of the Institution, whose professional integrity was apparently taken for granted.) Both locally trained vakils and lawyers from the Inns of Court in London could practise in India, but only the latter had access to the higher courts. All this meant that, within ten years of the Indian universities' foundation, there were students with the educational background required by British universities, families who could afford to send them and potential rich rewards for the 'England returned'. The Suez Canal was open. Even the timing of religious change was right as religious tests had been abandoned in England while Hindu culture was beginning to relax religious bans on travel over the sea. By the 1890s Bengal had an 'Indian Sea Voyage Movement' to establish that sea voyages were compatible with Hinduism.[40]

There were, too, English voices, arguing a case which one of them, that of Hodgson Pratt of the Bengal civil service, set out in his title: *University education in England for natives of India considered with a view to qualify them for the learned professions or the public service and to create a class who shall mediate between the Indian people and their English rulers.* Echoing Macaulay's intentions he paid tribute to the achievements of the Indian schools and colleges but wanted to encourage a small number of their graduates every year who were ready to begin the specialist study needed for the bar, medicine, engineering, divinity, manufacturing or commerce. He combined high hopes for them with an exalted view of English university life:

In England natives of India would have not only a higher kind of competition than in their own country, where their class-fellows are men of their own race and standing, not only the higher teaching of an English University as compared with that of a Colony; not only the higher standard of attainment so requisite; but, – what I would chiefly lay stress upon, – the free association with professors and fellow students, with the first minds in the world. Besides, many may like to associate themselves for a time with mercantile houses and commercial undertakings, and in other ways to obtain experience and knowledge altogether beyond the sphere of a University.[41]

Indian students began to travel to Britain and did so in increasing numbers in the last third of the century. Hodgson Pratt reinforced his argument by quoting the example of 'four native gentlemen' who, despite the danger of loss of caste, had in the 1860s 'come from Calcutta to this country, and at their own expense, for the purposes of completing their education'.[42] They went to the universities and to the Inns of Court where Manmohan Ghose was the first Indian to be called to the bar in 1866.[43] In Britain as a whole there were 40 to 50 Indian students by 1873, 100 by 1880, 200 by 1890 and over 330 by 1900. The first at Oxford matriculated in 1871 and by 1893 49 had done so, with half of them going on to become barristers. Those at Oxford were mainly from Bengal and from Bombay including a number of Parsees; 20 per cent were Muslims. Most were paid for by their families but the Gilchrist trust offered two scholarships a year for 'deserving natives' from 1868 and the government of India established two in 1886.[44]

The students had a mixed reception. In Oxford, they were welcomed by Benjamin Jowett, the reforming master of Balliol from 1870 to 1893. He had sat on the government committee in 1854 that developed selection procedures for the Indian Civil Service and persuaded his own college to accept ten ICS probationers from 1875 in an understandable belief that Oxford was the right place to train them. 'Logically enough, Indian students were encouraged as well' with the result that 22 of the 49 Indian students entering Oxford in his mastership went to Balliol.[45] Others were less fortunate: some 16, while admitted to the university, did not get college places and remained as non-collegiate students.[46]

Beyond Oxford the National Indian Association in Aid of Social Progress in India, set up in 1870, was there to welcome students, to promote 'friendly intercourse with Indians who come to England', and to support the education of women. Its journal carried advice on the practicalities of entering university and the Inns of Court, including detailed information on the likely costs, where and how to apply, and on the documents needed. One of its writers, S. Satthianadhan of Corpus Christi College, Cambridge, was clear and forthright in his advice: Cambridge was the place to go for maths, Oxford for languages, London for medicine and the Inns of Court for law. Cambridge had the edge over Oxford as it had more maths, and Sanskrit or Arabic were already an alternative to Greek. But, over and above these distinctions, 'To put it in plain words – An English Education pays best in India'.[47] Some families began almost as a matter of course to send their children to England: the names of Dutt, Banerjee and Nehru recur among these and continued to do so into the next century.[48] Michael Madhusudhan Dutt, for example, went to London in 1862 to study law and was followed eight years later by his family who established themselves in Cambridge.[49] At the same time, there were tensions for the middle-class intelligentsia, to be played out until 1947, as its members both studied in Britain and came to lead the home-rule movement in India (see Chapters 4 and 7).

Despite barriers at home and abroad, women as well as men travelled to Britain. Cornelia Sorabji found her way to Oxford, where she originally intended to study medicine, but switched to law and found herself under Jowett's wing. He arranged for her to attend lectures in All Souls and like Satthianadhan she went on to write a book about her experience in order to encourage others.[50] She qualified and practised as a lawyer and remained a supporter of British rule. In contrast Pandita Ramabai, who also travelled to England in the 1880s, both studied and taught at Cheltenham Ladies College, converted to Christianity, objected to the male leadership of the Church of England, and went on to support both home rule and feminism. Both returned to India and worked to improve the lives of Indian women while remaining ideologically far apart.[51] Women, however, remained a small minority of Indian students. By 1900 only four had entered Girton or Newnham at Cambridge. Three were sisters and had been sent to school in Croydon before going to university. They were a remarkable four of whom two went on to qualify as doctors, one married a Scottish colonel as well, and one became the first woman president of the Indian National Congress. It was easier for men. Downing College, which with St Johns was the most welcoming Cambridge college, accepted 16 male Indian students between 1850 and 1900. (They studied alongside ten from British families with an Indian raj background and a further 12 British who later went to India to serve the raj.)[52]

British authorities and universities were edging towards clear policies on Indian students in the late nineteenth century although these were to be articulated only in the 1900s. With the exception of Jowett's Balliol, the students were generally neither shunned nor particularly welcomed. As British subjects, they could travel freely to and from Britain (unless they were princes when protocol and the viceroy could get in the way). They, and other overseas students, benefited from the affiliation schemes introduced by Oxford and Cambridge. For the most part, however, apart from the acceptance of Sanskrit in place of Greek, changes to university practice were made mainly in the interest of domestic students: scrapping religious tests benefited dissenters as well as Hindus or Muslims. The academic study of Indian languages was stimulated by British scholars and seen as of value for British scholarship and British interests. Manchester University was to introduce the study of Asian languages in the new century in the interests of locally based trade. Both students and universities had to resolve the paradoxical and unintended consequences of Macaulay's minute that now brought students in their hundreds to Britain.

By 1900 the children of the empire and of the world's affluent middle class, the intending professionals and the rapidly growing number of Indians were drawing another map of student mobility. They had been pushed towards Britain by the growth of that class, within and beyond the empire, and by limited local opportunities for higher education. They had been pulled partly by the standing of British universities, partly by their expectation of eventual benefits – intellectual for Rutherford and his like, social and financial for the Indian lawyers. Responding to those pressures, the overseas students had grown in numbers, and in academic strength, to the point where they could shape and influence university policy. By 1900 they made up a larger proportion of the total than they had for centuries. Meanwhile the new map looked different from the old as student mobility was less a matter of exchanges between European universities on a basis of equality, and more one of attracting students from the overseas empire and from universities of subordinate status. If the mendicant wandering scholar was the symbol of the Middle Ages, and a student of English humanism or the Scottish Enlightenment one for the following three centuries, the Indian student watching the 1897 Diamond Jubilee parade of all the empire's peoples could stand at that imperial apogee as one for the nineteenth century.

4
Universities for the Empire, 1900–45

Jawaharlal Nehru's memories of Edwardian Cambridge could have been written by any nostalgic graduate:

> life was pleasant, both physically and intellectually, fresh horizons were ever coming into sight, there was so much to be done, so much to be seen, so many fresh avenues to explore. And we would sit by the fireside in the long winter evenings and discuss unhurriedly deep into the night till the dying fire drove us shivering to our beds…It was the pre-war world of the early twentieth century. Soon this world was to die, yielding place to another, full of death and destruction and anguish and heart-sickness for the world's youth.[1]

Nehru was one of some 750 students from India whose life of privilege was shared by only 20,000 university students in a country where less than 1 per cent of the age group got to university. The number of overseas and of home students then grew over the next 30 years. Over that time public attitudes and policies for overseas students developed and changed, influenced by the students themselves and their interests, by national and international politics, and by educational change within Britain and its colleges and universities.

In 1900 the British Isles had 13 universities with six in England, four in Scotland, two in Ireland and one in Wales. They had limited government funding and, proudly autonomous, took little account of government policy. For the most part it intervened when granting, or refusing, university charters or when the national interest seemed to demand a commission of enquiry, as for Oxford and Cambridge in 1922. Four university colleges were poised to get their charters within the next ten years, to be joined in the same decade by the London School of Economics. 'To be sure, the end of the nineteenth century was what Germans called a *Gründerzeit*, a time of founders'.[2] University numbers more than doubled in the next 20 years, rising to almost 28,000 in 1910 and exceeding 48,000 in 1920. The growth was in part a response to the expansion of secondary education, in part a reaction to the country's emergence from the great depression of the late nineteenth century, in part a product of the civic pride that stimulated the rise of civic universities and helped London University grow. Expansion was also spurred by the need to strengthen industry, agriculture and medical research, and to meet new demands for secondary school teachers.[3] It was affected, too, by the continuing overseas demand for university education, especially from the empire.

After the rapid increase in student numbers between 1900 and 1920, they rose much more slowly in the next two decades. As ex-servicemen left university, the total fell to 46,000 in 1921 and rose only by 4,000 to reach 50,000 in 1938. Only one university – Reading – gained its charter between the wars with the other university colleges having to wait till after 1945. 'The dilemma of the 1960s – too many candidates competing for too few places – would have seemed fantastic in the 1930s. The dilemma of the 1930s for some of the smaller institutions was how to attract enough students to justify their survival'.[4] Growth was uneven. Oxbridge and London expanded by 17 and 41 per cent between 1921 and 1938, while numbers fell slightly in the civic universities, in Wales and in Scotland.

The national system of higher education now had institutions of five kinds. First, Oxford and Cambridge dwarfed the others in scale and prestige; for much of this period they attracted one student in every five. Second, the large federal University of London took another one in five: it had 9,400 students in 1921, roughly the same as Oxford and Cambridge combined. Third, in the same year some 16,000 students were enrolled at the burgeoning civic universities and university colleges along with the federal university of Wales. Fourth, Scotland had 10,000 to 11,000 students between the wars. Alongside these four was a fifth group of civic institutions often providing London external degree programmes. Detailed figures for this group are lacking until many of them emerged as polytechnics in the 1960s. Ireland had universities or university colleges in Dublin, Belfast, Cork and Galway but with only small numbers of overseas students.

The universities, with Oxford, Cambridge and London in the lead, saw themselves as at the apex of an imperial university structure. Imperial interest in British universities was demonstrated at a colonial universities conference in 1903 and by the first ever Congress of Universities of the Empire held in London in 1912. This was attended by vice-chancellors, professors and university board members from round the empire, and by local grandees who were present in such force that the only people below the rank of viscount listed on the front page of the congress report were the prime minister and the archbishop of Canterbury. The congress led to the establishment of the Universities' Bureau of the British Empire – later the Association of Commonwealth Universities.[5]

The available figures suggest that overseas numbers rose rapidly in the first decade of the century. At Oxford, overseas student matriculations rose from 10 per cent in 1885 to 24 per cent in 1910 with overseas numbers growing more rapidly than those for home students.[6] Their ranks were swollen by the Rhodes scholars of whom the first 12 arrived in 1903 with a further 72 the next year.[7] Figures from Scotland tell a similar story of expansion. In 1900 overseas students made up between 4 and 16 per cent of the total at three of the four Scottish universities (with fewer at St Andrews); numbers then rose so that by 1910 Edinburgh, which always had the strongest international connections, drew 20 per cent of its students from outside the United Kingdom.[8] By that time the universities and university colleges funded by the board of education in England had overseas totals amounting to 9 per cent.[9] All in all, though the figures are incomplete, the evidence suggests that overseas numbers amounted to at least 10 per cent of the total by 1910. University numbers shrank and the flow of overseas students dwindled during the First World War. Rhodes scholarships were suspended, not because of the danger of crossing the Atlantic but because the Oxford experience would itself be diminished.[10]

The estimate that overseas students already made up 10 per cent of the total in 1910 fits with the pattern that emerged after the First World War. From the early 1920s to the mid-1980s the proportion of overseas students was remarkably consistent, steadily remaining at around 10 per cent, rarely dropping below 8 or rising above 12 per cent. Actual numbers of overseas students changed little between 1921 and 1931 but then rose from some 4,400 to 5,200 in the next seven years (see Figure 4.1). Figures for all students then dropped during the Second World War, as they had in the first so that at the lowest point, in 1943, total university enrolment was only 35,600.

There were few women among foreign as among British students but, as data often took no account of gender, figures are uncertain. Oxford and Cambridge had quotas for women, and few women's colleges, which kept down their number. For the rest, in 1920 just over a quarter of students in universities and university colleges receiving a government grant were women while by 1937 they made up only 22 per cent of full-time university students in England and Wales.

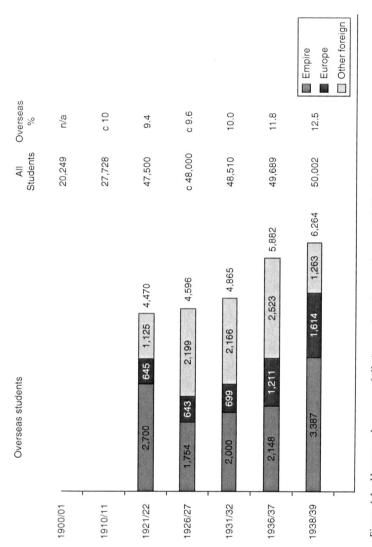

Figure 4.1 Home and overseas full-time university enrolments, 1900–45

Note: There are minor differences between UGC and AUBC figures. Totals for the student body are for Great Britain (1921–39) but overseas numbers also include students in Ireland.

Source: 1900 and 1910: *UGC Report 1929–35*; 1921–38: *Yearbook of universities of empire*; 1938/9: *University returns*

Institutions varied widely in their recruitment of overseas students. Between the wars the university of Wales was never popular with overseas students, with less than 2 per cent of its enrolments from outside Britain, while some institutions steadily built up an international reputation: Manchester's Institute of Science and Technology (as it was to be renamed) increased its overseas enrolment from 12 per cent to 31 per cent between 1921 and 1938. Consistently in this period, four institutions dominate the story of overseas enrolments: Oxford, Cambridge, London and Edinburgh. Between the wars they took about half of all full-time enrolments but often over three-quarters of those from overseas (see Table 4.1).

Students from India formed the largest single group, making up between a quarter and a third of the total from overseas before and between the two world wars. Their numbers rose from about 340 in 1900 to between 700 and 800 in 1907 and about 1,750 in 1913. While most of them went to university, a large number were potential lawyers studying at the Inns of Court; just before the First World War one in every three Indian students was reading for the bar. Some, like Nehru, went for both qualifications. He took things the easy way, first doing his Cambridge degree and then qualifying as a barrister, but many students signed up with the Inns of Court, and ate their requisite dinners, while reading for a university degree. In 1921 1,200 Indians were at British universities, with about another 800 at the bar. Numbers increased to 1,500 in 1931 before dropping to 1,350 in 1938.

Beyond India, British education drew students from the dominions and colonies to provide a further 30 to 35 per cent of the overseas total – 1,400 students in 1921 and 1,500 in 1938 – with the largest contingent

Table 4.1 Most popular universities for full-time overseas students, 1921–38

	1921/22	1926/27	1931/32	1936/37	1938/39
London	1,165	2,114	2,322	2,994	3,208
of which					
Medical schools	n/a	543	595	649	713
Imperial	91	215	230	227	301
LSE	192	393	354	526	533
UCL	194	366	418	662	620
Oxford	684	468	429	534	523
Cambridge	600	500	371	640	632
Edinburgh	550	528	532	445	412
Percentage of total overseas	74	79	76	78	76

Source: Yearbook of universities of empire; University returns for 1921/2.

coming from South Africa. Between the two world wars the United States often followed India in the statistics with its figures rising from 400 in 1921 to 700 in 1931, falling again to 520 in 1938 in reaction to the depression. Outside the formal empire, though inside the informal one, Egypt was always an important source of students with numbers rising from 300 in 1921 and running consistently at 6 to 7 per cent of the overseas total. (Indian students complained in 1913 that London hospitals were accepting Egyptian medical students in preference to them.[11]) Students from countries under British influence in the near east added to a loosely defined imperial total. A report on numbers, prepared by the board of education in 1926 for a forthcoming imperial confer- ence included 54 students from Mesopotamia and Palestine under the heading 'Dominions'.[12] By 1938 there were over 220 students from Iraq and Palestine. (See Figure 4.2 and Table 4.2.)

While the great majority of students came from the English-speaking world, Europe came next. In 1910 almost a quarter of the overseas matricu- lants at Oxford were from Europe. After the war, and in the country as a whole, Europe provided 14 per cent of overseas students in 1921, a figure which rose to 26 per cent in 1938. In the years before both world wars Germany was the most important source of European students. It provided half of Oxford's 60 new European students in 1910, numbers that had increased from single figures in the previous decade. Their presence marked a new kind of international bond with German scholarship; despite the *entente cordiale* there were only three French matriculants in 1911 alongside

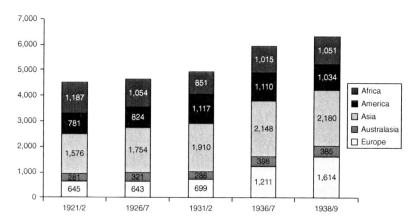

Figure 4.2 Numbers and proportions of overseas university students from each continent, 1921–38

Source: Yearbook of universities of empire.

Table 4.2 Countries sending over 100 full-time overseas students, 1921–38

1921/22		1926/27		1931/32		1936/37		1938/39	
Country	No.	Country	No.	Country	No.	Country	No.	Country	No.
India	1,240	India	1,518	India	1,361	India	1,313	India	1,350
South Africa	832	South Africa	624	USA	694	USA	592	South Africa	532
USA	400	USA	449	South Africa	465	South Africa	568	Germany	532
Egypt	294	Egypt	338	Egypt	292	Germany	416	USA	517
Canada	200	Australia	196	Canada	200	Egypt	348	Egypt	383
Australia	178	Canada	156	Australia	166	China	295	Canada	278
China	143	West Indies	129	West Indies	141	Canada	280	Australia	253
New Zealand	102	New Zealand	123	Germany	141	Australia	248	China	233
West Indies	101			China	136	Palestine	157	Poland	195
				New Zealand	122	West Indies	150	West Indies	160
						New Zealand	148	New Zealand	131

Note: Canadian figures include Newfoundland.

Source: Yearbook of universities of empire.

the 43 from Germany.[13] Oxford demonstrated its, and Britain's, European connections in the summer of 1914 when the majority of those receiving honorary doctorates were from Germany. 'The First World War severed this Anglo-German cultural tie. Despite attempts after the war, both on a personal and an institutional level, to revive the mood of Anglo-German friendship in Oxford, the old bonds were never fully restored.'[14] German numbers fell after 1918 but rose again in the 1930s, increasing from 140 in the country as a whole in 1931 to 530 in 1938, as German refugees added to student numbers. By 1938 there more students from Germany than from any other country apart from India and South Africa. The refugees had created new and different bonds to replace the old.

Overseas students could be classified in various ways. Solomon Bandaranaike, later prime minister of Ceylon, went to Oxford in 1919 and identified two groups among his contemporaries:

> There are those who come here to take up some qualifying exam-ination such as the I.C.S., or to go through a course such as that of Forestry, at Oxford or Cambridge, which make their sojourn in this country imperative. About these there can be no question of the desirability or otherwise of their coming here.
> But there are a great many – certainly the majority of those who do come to this country – who are under no such constraint. They come to the English universities, as the average English public schoolboy does, for the advantage of a University training, to put a final finish and polish, as it were, to their education.[15]

Many of those in Bandaranaike's first category came at the expense of their family, following the path staked out by their nineteenth-century pred-ecessors. They included the potential lawyers who came for solid reasons of professional advantage. Alongside them governments and scholarship agencies sent a smaller group who sought qualifications rather than pres-tige in the expectation that their higher education would bring public as well as private benefits. Students from India could compete for scholar-ships provided by the government of India, by provincial governments and by the princely states.

In the first half of the twentieth century an increasing number of scholarships became available. By 1900 the empire was already at a point where colonial governments looked to British universities to meet

their educational needs. In that year some 40 students held scholarships from colonial governments, mainly at Edinburgh, Oxford and
Cambridge but with others at technical institutions.[16] The government
of India introduced technical scholarships in 1904 which took some 66
scholars to Britain in the next eight years to study practical subjects that
included textiles, engineering, metallurgy and pottery.[17] Meanwhile the
number of Indian probationers joining the Indian Civil Service gradually rose, and they too travelled to Britain to learn how to govern their
own country (see also Chapter 8).

Bandaranaike's second group, seeking their final polish, followed the
example of the wealthy English who, from the sixteenth century, had
attended Oxford or Cambridge as a rite of passage. Some eased their
progress to Oxbridge by going to school in England: before he went to
Oxford, Nehru was at Harrow with the sons of the Gaekwad of Baroda
and the Maharaja of Kapurthala.[18] Abdul Rahman, the twentieth child
of Sultan Abdul Hamid of the Kedah royal family, and later prime
minister of Malaya, went to Cambridge where his fast cars and lifestyle
troubled the authorities.[19] Wealthy Russian families, like the Yusupovs,
continued their two-century-old tradition in sending their sons to
Oxford or Cambridge. The Russians continued to come even as their
families went into exile: Vladimir Nabokov reached Cambridge in 1919
where he interested himself in girls and butterflies but even more in
football and tennis.[20] This group tended to study law or the humanities
and, in the early years of the century, contented themselves with pass
degrees – an award later effectively dropped by Oxford and Cambridge.

A third category might be added to Bandaranaike's two to include
those attracted to Britain because of the academic strength of its universities. Just as Rutherford had been drawn from New Zealand by the
strengths of the Cavendish Laboratory so in his turn he drew students
from abroad. Pyotr Kapitsa, one of an intellectual family which had
sent previous generations to Cambridge, joined him in 1921, sent by
the Soviet Union as a talented scientist. Rutherford told him he had
no room for another researcher, prompting Kapitsa to ask about the
level of accuracy he expected in his results and to argue that his addi-
tion to the number of research students would be within the margin of
error.[21] Kapitsa went on to a career of such distinction that a laboratory
was built for his work, and duly shipped back to Moscow when he was
recalled there.[22] From the creation of the PhD (see below) as a research
qualification British universities had an increased international appeal
for scholars pursuing an academic career. Just as some of the empire's
wealthier families saw attendance at Oxbridge as a normal part of family

life, so a British PhD became a passport for an academic career within the universities of the empire.

Alongside the students who came for social, professional and academic reasons there were others who were driven or encouraged by political hopes or threats. By the beginning of the twentieth century the prestige of British universities was attracting some of the world's rulers. Authority tended to regard them benignly: ruling Indian princes were seen as 'practically English gentlemen' in contrast with the disloyal Indian National Congress.[23] But, while the princes were rulers of the last generation, the rulers of the next were likely to be drawn from the disloyal. Aspirant politicians, and leaders of independence movements, valued their time at British universities both for what they learned and because their degree certificates helped in meeting the British on their own terms. With hindsight it is not surprising that the able, articulate, 'England returned' should go home and form the leadership of both the Indian National Congress and the Muslim League. Within Britain,

> Indian students had the opportunities to meet with not only other students but various political activists as well. They could meet with British Communists, Egyptian nationalists and Irish Home Rulers. They met with Indians from other regions and social backgrounds. They also crucially met with a wider spectrum of British society, noticing differences in the ways the British acted away from India.[24]

Their activities provoked reactions that had a bearing on the development of policy. Both before and after the First World War students from throughout the empire were expected to demonstrate loyalty and respect for British institutions. In practice, their political activities led to suspicion about their imperial loyalty which extended to the highest levels of government and society. In 1921 Lord Curzon, then both foreign secretary and chancellor of Oxford University, wrote to the vice-chancellor with disquiet about student loyalty. Five years later Lord Birkenhead, as secretary of state for India, wrote to heads of colleges to encourage action against communists who were thought to be influencing students.[25] Scotland Yard seized documents from the Communist Party which showed – not surprisingly – that S. Saklatvala, a communist MP, had been asked by the party to meet selected Indian students.[26] A decade later overseas students at Oxford, Cambridge and London claimed, with some reason, that they were under regular surveillance (see Chapter 7).[27]

It is possible that the authorities were looking in the wrong direction. Many of the future leaders of the south led exemplary and ordinary student lives. Bandaranaike made his mark in the Oxford Union and looked as if he was to return home to the life of privilege and comfort from which he had come: he was welcomed home with garlands, bands, elephants and a parade by the boy scouts that do not sound like acclaim for a revolutionary.[28] Norman Manley, who was to become the first prime minister of Jamaica, arrived in Oxford as a Rhodes Scholar in 1914, enlisted like his British fellow undergraduates, but unlike them did so in the ranks, returning to complete his degree after the war. Grantley Adams, later premier of Barbados and prime minister of the short-lived West Indian Federation, involved himself in liberal politics in Oxford but also spent a lot of time playing cricket.[29] Eric Williams had a distinguished academic career at Oxford although this was held back when he failed to win a fellowship at All Souls in 1935.[30] His assumption that prejudice played a part in this is understandable: it was not many years since a contemporary noticed that 'the election of a Polish Jew from Balliol [the historian Lewis Namier], much the strongest candidate really, was prevented'.[31] Namier and Williams both went on to greatness elsewhere.

While political aspirations carried some students to Britain, others were driven by the turbulent politics of Europe. Belgian and Serbian refugees, including students, arrived in the First World War when Oxford relaxed its entry requirements to admit them. Threats from the left and then the right drove White Russians after 1917 and Germans and central Europeans after 1933 to become student refugees. Those who reached Britain did so despite the increasingly restrictive legislation of the twentieth century in which the Aliens Act of 1905, the introduction of passports in 1915 and the Aliens Order of 1920 made entry increasingly difficult for those outside the empire. The consequence was that, after Hitler came to power in 1933, Britain was a place of restricted refuge for those fleeing Nazism with only some 10,000 refugees admitted between 1933 and 1938. Some relaxation of the rules in 1938 meant that a further 40,000 arrived that year while, in 1938 and 1939, some 10,000 children arrived on the *Kindertransport*.[32] British universities showed their concern and their compassion by establishing the Academic Assistance Council (later the Council for Assisting Refugee Academics) to help threatened academics escaping from central Europe.

Along with the established academics were junior researchers and students whose contribution to British academic life was rich and varied. A single academic strand can demonstrate its strength. The British nuclear programme existed in part because of Rutherford's early theoretical work after he arrived on a Great Exhibition scholarship. It was then boosted in the 1930s by the refugee nuclear physicist Rudolf Peierls who joined the Tube Alloys project. He in turn encouraged Klaus Fuchs to come from Germany and work with him so that it is not too far-fetched to see nuclear weapons in both Britain and the Soviet Union as flowing from student mobility of the 1930s. There are more benign examples. Eric Hobsbawm moved to Britain from Berlin in 1933 and to school in Marylebone and university at Cambridge. As a British subject, born in Alexandria of an English father and an Austrian mother, he was not technically a refugee but he explained 'in every other respect we were immigrants from central Europe ... in a country unknown to all of us'.[33] Max Perutz, like Hobsbawm, came to Britain before the *Anschluss*, leaving Vienna to work with J. D. Bernal in Cambridge.[34] Their examples could be multiplied.

As before the First World War students were pulled towards British universities by the opportunities they offered, with increasing numbers pushed by political aspirations and by the political pressures and disasters of their home countries.

University students attract more attention than those at other levels of education, or at less prestigious institutions. But alongside the overseas university students there were also children, soldiers and young people seeking practical qualifications. Some travelled to Britain to study, some studied because they were already there.

The children were, at first, of the rich. In the early twentieth century upper-middle-class families in India continued to send their children to school in Britain.[35] Prosperous Egyptian families, faced by restricted opportunities within Egypt, did the same, as did middle-class families in west Africa and the West Indies.[36] Even where they could afford to do so, it was not always a simple process. Bryanston School in Dorset was launched in 1926 with a letter to *The Times* commenting on the 'difficulty experienced by boys from the Dominions in gaining admission to the public schools'.[37] Though school histories are remarkably quiet on the issue, prejudice against foreigners and against Jews meant that quotas and restrictions were placed on both groups. One Harrow headmaster in the early part of the century tried, apparently without success, to require all his housemasters to admit some 'Jewish and foreign boys': 'As an Imperial school, Harrow could not afford to deny admission to sons of wealthy or aristocratic subjects of the Empire ... Yet the ambivalence remained, pride in educating a cosmopolitan elite vying with the reluctance ... to accept foreigners.' The school reached a compromise by arranging for Indian and Siamese boys to be housed separately from the British.[38] Access to British schooling was sufficiently important in India for the committee on establishing a military academy there to argue against anything that would restrict access to Sandhurst for Indian boys at school in Britain.[39]

From 1933 the children of the wealthy were joined by the children of refugees. They had to go to school, and often to learn a new language, which they did with mixed fortunes. Some, in the more conventional schools, were bullied. Some were more fortunate. Among these were the pupils of Frensham Heights School in Surrey which accepted children who could speak no English; refugees approached 10 per cent of their numbers between 1935 and 1939 and they found the school a 'haven of rationality and kindness'. One of them, Wolf Rilla, recalled arriving there:

> It was one of those golden September days when the school and its grounds look their best. Everything was deceptively quiet and peaceful and beautiful. But I wasn't deceived…I braced myself for what I knew was to come. The musty smell of school corridors which stuck with loathing in my nose. The cold and hostile stare of many eyes. The quiet sarcasm of the masters. The many small but sharp cruelties which I knew to be the lot of a new boy for weeks. And this was going to be even worse. I had never been to a boarding school. Moreover my command of the language reduced my fourteen years for all practical purposes to four.
>
> It was with a considerable shock that I realised that none of this was forthcoming. There was no musty smell, no stone passages. Nobody thought I was odd – or if they thought it they didn't show it. I was accepted with a naturalness that was unbelievable.[40]

While fortunate children found rationality and kindness, this is not what military cadets expect. In the first half of the twentieth century, they were trained at the Royal Military College at Sandhurst and the Royal Military Academy at Woolwich, both of which had spare capacity after 1918. Just as the universities had a role in educating the elite of the empire so Sandhurst and Woolwich now began to train its future military leaders. Racial restrictions on becoming an army officer had been relaxed and from that time ten places a year were reserved for Indians at Sandhurst. They were joined by others from the empire and beyond so that between the wars, 254 overseas cadets were trained at Sandhurst and 70 at Woolwich. Like the schoolboys sent by wealthy families, many came from a privileged background, and from the informal empire and friendly countries as well as from the empire itself. There was 'a sprinkling at any one time from Egypt, Iraq, Siam, China and Persia'. In stories that may be apocryphal the Chinese were taught bicycle riding by a tall guardsman while the Egyptians insisted on being addressed by their correct name and not as 'gyppy number four in the front rank'. The most distinguished foreign cadet was reported to be the King of Afghanistan; King Farouk of Egypt was charming, lazy and obedient, while the best horseman was the Maharaja of Jaipur who offered a job as master of horse to his Sandhurst riding instructor.[41] The Indians at least were only moderately successful. Whereas British cadets had a failure rate of only 3 per cent, the Indian rate was 30 per cent.[42]

The handful of royal cadets at Sandhurst were looking forward to a political career of one kind or another, in a presumed expectation that this was their right. Sandhurst, however, taught military leadership not only to kings and princes but also to ambitious officers. Iskandar Mirza was one of the first Indian officers trained there and was to become president of Pakistan in 1956; two years later he declared martial law, only to be overthrown within less than a month by Ayub Khan, himself a Sandhurst graduate. Sandhurst as well as Oxford and LSE had its impact on the leaders of the world.

One other group of soldiers edge themselves into the definition of overseas students. From 1917 'khaki colleges and universities' were set up for Canadian and Australian servicemen based in Britain and awaiting deployment on the continent or, later, their return home. The aim was both to occupy the troops and to enable them to get credit they could use at home or in Britain. By May 1918 there were 11 khaki colleges and more than 50,000 Canadians were estimated to have attended them.[43] American students were to follow in their wake after the Second World War (see Chapter 5).

Education and training of the less privileged, and for less prestigious qualifications, fell neither to universities nor to military academies but to local education authorities. In 1933, when some 2,400 foreign students were attending London University, London County Council had about 1,400 students in special classes for foreign students. These included courses in English for foreigners, particularly for the catering trades, with students mainly from Cyprus and Italy. Most of the council's students were from Europe with the largest number from Germany, followed by France. Russians and Poles tended to study at the Robert Montefiore Institute in Whitechapel where a 'very considerable proportion of them' were seen as 'very ill educated people' while Regent Street Polytechnic attracted a 'very good type of student indeed' and had some 500 to 600 of them. Three polytechnics had from 16 to 45 per cent overseas enrolments on their engineering courses. Most of these students were lower middle class or 'artisan class'. There were few Indians as 'Indian students come rather from the upper class families in India' and were not be found in Whitechapel or the polytechnics. While, at this time, some institutions charged differential fees to home and overseas students, the council drew no such distinction and the level of fee depended solely on whether a student lived within or outside the county of London.[44] These students, and those in similar institutions in the other major cities, attracted less attention than those in universities but their numbers, just in London alone, were significant and the students were forerunners of much larger numbers after 1945.

During the first decade of the twentieth century, as overseas student numbers increased, Britain inched towards the development of a policy addressed to them. Discussions were dominated by the needs of the empire and by what *The Times* called 'the problem of Indian students'. At the same time, there was no formal statement of policy, nor was there any one institution with the capacity or the responsibility to develop one. Rather, policy emerged from the activities of interested parties that initially included the universities, the students themselves, and those concerned with imperial education and above all the interests of India. Insofar as policy can be discerned, or inferred, it was for many years ambivalent and uncertain as the needs of overseas students came up against other and weightier interests.

The empire was all-important and imperial voices were heard from far and near. In 1902 the South African politician Henry Fremantle pressed Oxford to call a conference on colonial education, arguing 'that the Universities of Oxford and Cambridge ought to be without question the two points of convergence for the intellectual and social aristocracy of the whole Empire'.[45] The Colonial Office held such a conference in the same year. The colonial universities conference that followed a year later was opened by James Bryce, the Liberal politician and former professor of law at Oxford, who brought race, empire and education together as he explained that:

> We have two aims, and those two aims are closely bound together. One aim is to develop the intellectual and moral forces of all the branches of our race wherever they dwell, and therewith also to promote learning, science and the arts by and through which science is applied to the purposes of life. The other aim is to strengthen the unity of the British people dispersed throughout the world.[46]

His view, and Fremantle's, were to be echoed and re-echoed in the next few years. In 1912 William Temple, the quintessential establishment man – son of an archbishop of Canterbury, former Oxford don, at that time headmaster of Repton and later himself archbishop – claimed that, 'It is the supreme function of the Universities to guide the thought of those who mould the destiny of the nation and the empire'.[47] Imperialism shaped the thinking of new universities as well as old. Dahrendorf, writing with authority as its director as well as historian, characterised the Edwardian London School of Economics in terms of education, economics, efficiency, equality and empire, and argued that 'if one were to single out one intellectual current which provided much of the tension, creative or otherwise of LSE in its first fifteen years, it would not be Equality, or even Efficiency, by itself, but Empire'.[48]

The same intellectual current flowed in Canada and Australia. At the congress of universities of the empire in 1912 the professor of physics from the University of Manitoba explained that:

> we are British and we are at present dominated by British ideals, and, seeing the great opportunities of culture that are presented in this country, we desire our students to profit by them so that they may obtain the manifold advantages that a country so rich in history, so wonderful in its literature, possesses.[49]

A council member from Melbourne University asked:

> Why can we not come to a common understanding by which students can proceed from a University in any part of the Empire to a University in any other part, subject to reasonable conditions, and get credit in these places for exactly that which they have done? [50]

Universities within Britain were moved both by a sense of imperial destiny and by their wish to recruit good students, and so to recruit internationally. As early as 1894 there was concern in Oxford that, while it wanted to attract foreign students, the period of residence was likely to be double that needed in Germany for a PhD. In 1902 Sidney Webb wanted London University 'to become the foremost postgraduate centre of the intellectual world' while the principal of Birmingham University wanted to expand postgraduate study in order to 'attract workers from many parts of the world, and certainly from the colonies'.[51] A year later the colonial universities conference identified postgraduate teaching, and questions of advanced standing, as issues that were holding back the exchange of students. While the concessions by Oxford and Cambridge to affiliated institutions eased the problem, they went only some way towards resolving it.

Moves to meet the specific needs of overseas students repeatedly came up against the barrier of established university practice, although there were some exceptions. Oxford was persuaded to introduce a one-year diploma in anthropology partly for future administrators in India, Sudan and the colonies, but partly in the interest of overseas students such as Rhodes scholars. It also agreed to open a forestry school in 1905 on the closing of Cooper's Hill college on the Thames, set up to train engineers for India. Oxford had the edge over Cambridge as the country nearby was better wooded.[52] Applicants still, however, required an ancient language to be admitted and would need a foreign language to complete the practical part of the course, usually in Germany. For another ten years and more after the 1903 conference universities were unwilling to change residence or entry requirements and rules about advanced standing.

The complacent view that British universities were properly and benignly at the apex of the imperial structure of education did not mean that overseas students were universally welcomed. Even the Rhodes scholars, with their trails of imperial and American glory, led Henry James to protest 'vehemently against the desecration of Oxford by an eruption of young barbarians…there was genuine apprehension that the Rhodes Scholars might be uncouth, difficult to assimilate and, worst of all, out to change things'. Even 30 years later three Oxford colleges still regarded Rhodes scholars as 'if not undesirable aliens at least as quaint exotica'.[53] While nearly all the Rhodes scholars were white Americans, students from the empire, and particularly from India, were likely to face greater difficulties.

There were issues of class as well as of race here as the Indian 'sojourners' were no longer 'invariably the sons of well-to-do citizens [who] came with introductions and recommendations which frequently gave them access to English society'.[54] In 1907 the secretary of state for India responded to the perceived problems of Indian students by commissioning an enquiry led by Sir William Lee-Warner, a former Indian civil servant and at that time a member of the Council of India. He was to report 'upon the position in this country of young Indians who come to England, otherwise than as Government scholars, to study for University degrees, or for the Bar or other professions, and to make recommendations'.[55]

The Lee-Warner report identified four types of problem beyond general difficulties of the lack of information on the practicalities of studying in Britain. First, some Indian students were intellectually ill-prepared for British university courses. Some arrived with neither university entrance nor, in some cases, the educational background it demanded. Second,

they encountered prejudice. From Cambridge 'Witness after witness testi-
fied to the prejudice which at present exists against them', an unpopularity which was 'of comparatively recent origin'.[56] Third, Indian students
were seen as facing moral hazards. This applied with particular force to
those reading for the bar where benchers had no desire to control the
private lives of their students. Lee-Warner and his colleagues felt strongly
that 'for the young Asiatic, a stranger from a distant land, and for the
most part unattuned to his new surroundings, the entire absence of guidance and control in a large European city may be fraught with serious
consequences'. The committee was warned that for ten out of 74 recent
law students 'their sojourn in London and the companions they had
made had so degraded them that they were not likely ever to become
respectable men'.[57] The fourth problem was the political one that many
students demonstrated 'antipathy to British rule in India' which was
reportedly 'aggravated by residence in England'. Some had even been
'imbued before leaving India with the political opinions of the advanced
section of the Indian Opposition'. To compound the problem it emerged
that 'Extremists of Indian politics...spare no pains to win adherents to
their cause among the Indian students as soon as they arrive'.[58]

   The report was stronger in identifying problems than suggesting solutions. It argued for a standing advisory committee and for an information
bureau. Students with Indian government scholarships were expected to
set an example to their countrymen and the government should announce
that it would exercise its 'power of rejection in case of candidates whose
declared political opinions are inconsistent with the continued existence
of British rule in India'.[59] But the report rejected any suggestion that 'steps
should be taken to diminish the flow of young Indians' on the grounds
that the British government could not 'interfere with the discretion of
Indian parents' and that 'for many years to come the educated classes of
India will find it necessary and beneficial to visit Europe and America'.[60]
In that spirit the government continued with a half-hearted attempt at
regulation by issuing identity cards to Indian students, a policy introduced
in 1903 and abandoned as impractical in 1913.[61] Meanwhile prejudice
against them was reinforced when Sir Curzon Wyllie, adviser to students
at the India office, was assassinated by one of his charges in 1909; some
Oxbridge colleges closed their doors to Indians in response.[62]

   The sensitivity of the issues in the report meant that government
decided against its publication. Following Lee-Warner's recommendations,
the secretary of state set up an advisory committee, an information bureau
and an Indian students' department at the India office.[63] The department
was able to provide practical information to students on accommodation

and on university entrance and to press their interests with universities and government. In doing so its work was inevitably tinged with ambivalence and paradox. One paradox was that imperial expectations were in conflict with everyday practice where discrimination and prejudice were lawful and widespread. The department reported in 1914 that it had 'occasioned great regret that Magdalen, the [Oxford] College selected for the residence of the Prince of Wales should be one of the very few Colleges in either [sic] University to refuse to share in its imperial obligation and to open its doors to British subjects from the East'.[64] Students' freedom to travel to Britain as subjects of the empire did not guarantee a welcome.

Another paradox was that, while the department was set up to ease the difficulties faced by Indian students, they regarded it with almost universal suspicion as existing 'to exercise surveillance over their political opinions'. Ironically, the limits on imperial power frustrated some policies that the raj would have favoured: the Indian students' department could only rail impotently on the preference given to lawyers trained in England over vakils trained in India.[65] (Government's inability to interfere with the practice of the bar echoes Lord Curzon's annoyance that he had no power as viceroy to change the curriculum of Indian universities: plural institutions, encouraged by the British, kept getting in the way of imperial intent.[66]). Nor did public policy fit with commercial interests. The Indian technical scholarships reflected a government policy of encouraging technical education – engineering and technology rather than law and the humanities. But the policy ran into difficulties, duly reported by the students' department, when students had difficulty in getting practical experience in Britain or jobs on their return home.[67]

Indian students' moral and physical welfare were not forgotten in the aftermath of the Lee-Warner enquiry: in 1916 the Indian Gymkhana Club was established to provide 'opportunities for healthy exercise and social intercourse with Public Schools and other English athletic clubs of good standing'. (Some students will have got more from the establishment of Indian majlis in Oxford and Cambridge and Indian associations at Edinburgh, Glasgow and Manchester.)[68] Beyond the creation of the Indian Students' Department and these limited measures, however, the report did not result in any clear or overt student policy on the part of the British government or the universities.

Despite the inconsistencies and ambiguities, it is nevertheless possible to discern the elements of consistent practice in early twentieth-century Britain, if not of articulated policy. There was a consensus that universities needed to serve the educational needs of the empire and not just of the kingdom. Students from India and Egypt were seen as presenting problems to which there were no easy solutions within universities that were autonomous and an empire that allowed freedom of movement to its subjects and had few restrictions on aliens. Various arms of government were beginning to show an interest in overseas students with the India Office and the Colonial Office to the fore. With some reluctance, universities were beginning to adjust their practices and their curricula in response to overseas needs.

The First World War unexpectedly took the Foreign Office on a rare excursion into university policy.

From the late nineteenth century universities had to reconcile the dilemma that, while they preferred overseas students to have gained a first degree at home, their own degree structures did not suit those who had done so. Students were often reluctant to spend time acquiring a second bachelor's degree but British universities offered few research degrees that would meet their needs. There was no British equivalent to the German PhD. The war brought a new sense of urgency and a solution. Canadian universities pressed their British counterparts to 'modify and enlarge their graduate facilities to meet the needs of students from the Universities of the Dominions'.[69] The Foreign Office wanted to attract to Britain some of those, particularly from North America, who had previously sought doctorates in Germany, and wanted to see something that would compete with offers from France and Italy. In 1917 Arthur Balfour, then foreign secretary, called a meeting of universities to facilitate arrangements for research. He had the backing and the company of H. A. L. Fisher, president of the Board of Education and an ex vice-chancellor, and future delegate to the League of Nations. The universities responded with uncharacteristic speed: Oxford agreed to introduce a DPhil degree in 1917, Cambridge and London their PhD in 1919. The degree was to meet the needs of home as well as overseas students but, in the next 25 years just over half of all Oxford's doctoral students, and a third of Cambridge's, were from overseas.[70] Within seven research universities, of the 2,500 doctoral students between the wars, overseas students made up 40 per cent of the total, with the figure rising to 58 per cent in the social sciences.[71]

The post-war establishment of the University Grants Committee in 1919 brought into existence a new potential player on university and overseas student policy. But the committee was hardly a policy-making body. It reported to the Treasury, not the Board of Education, and saw its role as one of funding universities while keeping itself and them at arm's length from government. Only after the Second World War did its quinquennial grant come with a *Memorandum of general guidance*. After Fisher's involvement in the 1917 meeting, the Board of Education kept an occasional watching brief but little more though civil servants from the board were in the 1930s to provide staff to the Ramsden and Tyrrell enquiries, discussed below, which had a bearing on university policy.

Neither the Board of Education, nor the University Grants Committee, nor the government's overseas departments developed formal statements of policy on overseas students between the wars. But it is possible to discern how thinking developed from changes in university practice and from a series of government enquiries on foreign students. The secretary of state for India moved first, setting up a committee on Indian students in 1922 with Lord Lytton in the chair, an old India hand at that time under-secretary for India.

The Lytton committee did not find it easy going: figures for the number of students were not available from government sources; the original idea that the committee should take evidence in India was scotched when the legislative council refused to vote funds for the visit; Indian students and the London Indian Association declined to give evidence.[72]

As in 1907, the committee's main recommendations were to strengthen the flow of information and to improve the welfare of Indian students at British universities. It sought closer cooperation between British and Indian universities as one means to that end. But there were two significant changes from the earlier report. First it noted how India had 'now been set on the road to self-government and autonomy'. While it accepted that British universities had a responsibility to the whole empire, it looked forward to the time when India could itself 'provide an adequate education even for the ablest of her sons'.[73] It supported proposals to reform the system of courts in India and so remove the need for English legal qualifications. Second, in a discussion of the needs of 'industrial students' which took up nearly a third of its chapter of conclusions, it recognised what would later be called education for development. Self-rule, decentralisation in education, and development were all now on the agenda.

The committee concluded with evident concern at the scale of the empire's educational needs:

> While [British Universities and Colleges] are fully aware that as educational institutions at the heart of a great Empire they have responsibilities towards those of its members who wish to come to the United

Kingdom in order to obtain an education which they cannot get in their own country, the demands made by the various parts of the Empire – Canada, Australia, New Zealand and South Africa, as well as India – are large when taken together.[74]

Like the Lytton committee, a royal commission on Oxford and Cambridge, which also reported in 1922, raised an imperial flag. The commission noted that since the end of the war both universities were attracting growing numbers of research students and argued that they had 'the chance of becoming to a much greater extent than formerly centres of research, and of graduate study for the whole Empire and for foreign guests'.[75] Overseas universities continued to sound a note of imperial dependence. The Pro-Chancellor of the University of New Zealand told the congress of universities of the empire in 1936 that

> our little country is the most remote and isolated of the Dominions. In consequence it becomes all the more necessary that the cream of our intellectual youth should have the opportunity of absorbing some of the culture and learning of the Old World, of sitting at the feet of the great teachers of the old Universities whose traditions are part of their heritage and of making contacts with those who are destined to be the leaders of the thought and action of the British Empire.[76]

Universities within Britain continued to value overseas students for academic as well as imperial reasons. At the London School of Economics, William Beveridge as its director 'emphasised the value to the general body of students of being brought into contact with, and having special opportunities of learning the views and ideas of, students from other lands and peoples'.[77] Universities also continued to respond to proposals for courses that were needed in the imperial and international interest. Oxford and Cambridge provided specialist courses for Indian and colonial administrators. A colonial service course at Oxford, originally set up for tropical Africa, was widened in 1934 to embrace the whole of the colonial empire. The Oxford forestry course continued to serve the needs of the empire. The Institute of Education in London, which built up a close relationship with the Colonial Office, introduced a course on colonial education in 1927; while initially for teachers and missionaries going abroad it attracted immediate attention from the government of Bengal and recruited a steadily increasing number of overseas students.[78]

At the same time academic conservatism, a concern for resources, and nationalist views that merged into racism meant that university responses to overseas students remained at times muted. The PhD was a disappointment for some and still attracted academic suspicion. In 1929 the Cambridge faculty of English claimed that:

> It tends to attract to Cambridge a number of candidates, particularly from America, with testimonials too good to refuse, but with little real qualification for research in English. It encourages men to attempt to research who would be better employed in gaining a general mastery of a subject already vast than in trying to extend its boundaries. Under such conditions 'research' becomes an enemy both of learning and of education; it wastes the time not only of the candidates themselves but of supervisors who are sometimes none too well provided with leisure for research of their own.[79]

As late as 1944 the economist I. G. Patel, later to head the London School of Economics, found that 'at Cambridge a PhD degree was still regarded as a weakness of foreigners, particularly Americans and the Indians'.[80] The University Grants Committee had a more measured reaction but was at once disappointed and relieved about the number, rather than the quality, of PhD candidates:

> It is true that the introduction of the PhD degree has had less effect than was originally expected in the way of attracting to our Universities students from other countries, but it is perhaps not wholly to be regretted that our Universities have not had among other serious preoccupations to improvise arrangements for dealing with a large and sudden influx of foreign students in search of some particular academic label.[81]

Ambivalence towards overseas students meant that they were often welcome only in small numbers. Balliol College in Oxford explained to the India Office in 1915 that, before the war they had 'quietly operated an informal restrictive quota system for Indian students without attracting adverse comments'. They would treat Americans, French and probably working-class applicants in much the same way. This provoked the slightly acid response from the under-secretary for India that the 'suggestion of a proper "proportion" of Indian Students in a College is at least capable of being presented in the form that the Indian Students are an undesirable and indigestible element in a College, to be tolerated in a strictly limited dose'.[82] Reluctance to admit overseas students sat awkwardly with the consensus that they would gain the greatest benefits if they lived cheek by jowl with their British contemporaries. While the Lytton committee thought prejudice had declined since 1907, it recognised that it remained and that Rhodes scholars and public-school men should take some of the blame.[83] Prejudice also created particular difficulties for the Colonial Office where the junior minister asked the Cambridge vice-chancellor in 1926 if he could 'in the interests of the Empire' find a way of reserving places for eight to 16 students a year who were 'usually young men specially picked in their respective colonies for their ability, and...likely on their return to their homes, to develop into men of influence'. The college replies were unpromising: two did not reply, five would not commit themselves and the others offered reluctant small numbers.[84] Casual racism was a fact of life.

Ambivalence about imperial priorities, race and the overseas student were played out in the Officers Training Corps (OTC). The corps had two divisions, the junior operating in schools and the senior in universities, and was designed to do just that – train officers – providing a route for university graduates to join the army. While public-school boys of any race could, with the headmaster's permission, join the junior division, only university students of 'pure European descent' could join the senior division, with a colour bar matching that of the pre-war army. When large numbers of British students enlisted or joined the OTC in 1914, Indian students were barred from doing so which 'caused inevitable disappointment'.[85] The bar was briefly lifted towards the end of the First World War, but then reimposed. Subhas Chandra Bose, who went to Cambridge in 1919, 'was vocal in his discontent at this exclusion'.[86] Ten years after the war Lawrence Kentwell, an Oxford-educated barrister and journalist later tried for collaboration with the Japanese in the Second World War, claimed that his enmity to Britain followed from his being rejected by the OTC because he was half-British and half-Chinese.[87]

Resentment at the exclusion rumbled on. Between 1927 and 1935 the Indian Sandhurst committee, charged with planning an Indian equivalent of Sandhurst, the governor of Ceylon and the National Union of Students – a trio who might have agreed on little else – all argued for lifting the ban.[88] The army was not sympathetic. The presence of Indians within the OTC might hinder recruitment of British undergraduates and the war department deployed a series of supporting arguments: most Indian undergraduates belonged to 'the non-martial races' whose desire to join the OTC was 'purely political'. As Scottish regiments wore the kilt, 'if Indians were allowed to appear in the Scottish national dress considerable resentment might arise'.[89] Neither Whitehall nor New Delhi wanted to change but they did set out their policies. The commander in chief in India saw difficulties with the proposal and the secretary of state for India preferred that it should not be taken any further 'unless the Universities themselves express themselves in favour of such a course'.[90] The Colonial Office understood that the rule 'causes disproportionate mischief in India and embitters Indians both in that country and at the English Universities' and saw that if it were relaxed for India it might also be relaxed for the colonies.[91] This would not do as it could not 'be seriously contended that any negro or person with a good deal of negro blood would be regarded as suitable to hold a commission in a British regiment of white troops' or even in charge of the black soldiers in the King's African Rifles or West African Frontier Force.[92]

Pragmatism found a way with a recommendation that went to the secretary of state:

> It seems to me that we can lay down two definite propositions in regard to this matter:-
>
> (1) As a matter of principle, no British subject should be barred from the Senior Division, Officers Training Corps, on grounds of colour.
>
> (2) As a matter of practice, applications from British subjects who are coloured, for admission to the Senior Division, Officers Training Corps, should be refused if there is no reasonable opportunity for the applicant to make use of the training thus gained when he returns to his own home in the Colonies.[93]

Pragmatism meant, too, that class could be used to overrule race in an extreme and unlikely case 'if the son of the Sultan of Zanzibar was at College here and wished to join the O.T.C. (But he would be an Arab and the son of an allied, though independent, potentate and rules are stretched in such cases)'.[94]

Prejudice about race was always in conflict with rhetoric about empire.

The next government enquiry was to put trade into the policy mix. In 1933 the Department of Overseas Trade was anxious to promote British exports to Europe, China and Latin America. Trade missions had 'been unanimous in saying that the export trade would receive considerable benefit if a greater number of students from overseas countries were to come to the United Kingdom...instead of going to other countries, for instance Germany and the United States'.[95] The department set up an enquiry to explore 'what further steps could usefully be taken to encourage suitable students to come to the United Kingdom for education and training'. Eugene Ramsden, a Yorkshire MP, chaired the enquiry and soon found his fears confirmed. On a tour of Scandinavia with the committee secretary 'there was no doubt in the minds of our informants that the policy pursued by Germany, France and other countries had...the effect of influencing business in their direction'.[96]

At home, however, the committee's ideas got a mixed reception with a muted welcome from universities. The secretary of the Bureau of Universities of the British Empire gave his personal view that they were 'prepared to take more overseas students, provided that they are suitable', a view which university evidence was to support. The Chinese and Siamese were probably the most, and the Egyptians the least welcome.[97] (The Lee-Warner report had welcomed the Siamese government policy, which continued long after, of dispersing its students round the country in twos and threes.) The National Union of Students would have liked to restrict Indian students: 'We should not encourage more to come, because there are more than can be comfortably looked after in this country. And the same applies to Egyptian students'.[98] While the Board of Trade wanted to welcome students in the interest of the economy, industry was against the idea. The Silk Association of Great Britain and Ireland registered 'a formal protest against the idea that United Kingdom resources should, in these trying times, be expended on the education and training of foreign nationals'. Their doubts even extended to the empire where industries might be set up 'in direct competition with our own'.[99] They were joined by the Pottery Manufacturers' Federation which considered that 'the training of Asiatics is particularly dangerous in this respect'.[100] Even the Board of Education was sceptical about the committee's idea of offering scholarships arguing that there was 'no case for this which would be in the least likely to impress the Treasury'.[101] It is not surprising that his civil servants noticed that a mood of despondency had overtaken the chairman half-way through.[102]

Hitler came to the rescue as Germany followed Italy's lead in aggressively recruiting foreign students. The Ramsden committee produced an interim report in May 1934 recording its 'firm conviction that the...student question was only part of the much wider problem of ignorance overseas of British achievements in the fields of education, culture and science, and technology'.[103] It went on to make the cautious recommendation that government 'should encourage the flow of carefully selected students from overseas' but it was then sidelined by a Foreign Office initiative.[104] By the summer of 1934, and in a politically changed world, the Foreign Office was arguing that 'cultural propaganda has been recognised as an effective and necessary instrument of national policy' and set up a quite separate cultural relations committee. It had broader terms of reference than the Ramsden committee and, benefiting from the political backing of the Foreign Office rather than the Department of Overseas Trade, effectively took over Ramsden's remit. Its work led directly to the establishment of the British Council for Relations with other Countries – soon to drop the last five words of its title – and to a recognition that the encouragement of overseas students formed part of foreign policy. (The British Council's interests were broader than countering the fascist countries; in March 1935, for example, it was concerned at the risk of French 'cultural ascendancy' in Egypt.[105]) By 1938 the new council was providing scholarships for foreign students; a year later it was able to offer 236 of them. It was to become a vigorous player on student policy, claiming a place in discussions not just about the welfare of its own scholarship holders but about all overseas students.

International politics, along with the needs of the empire, of development and of trade were beginning to influence overseas student policy.

With few if any formal statements of policy between 1900 and 1945 British universities, government and society slowly developed a set of attitudes and practices towards overseas students, although these were marked by inconsistency and ambivalence. The educational needs of the empire were recognised as a priority, alike by government, the universities and universities in other parts of the empire. Student numbers stayed at around 10 per cent with higher proportions in the universities of the highest status. While these numbers were enough to demand some attention and recognition, universities were hesitant in adapting to overseas students' interests. A thin red line of military cadets, and a longer line of privileged children, had limited influence on institutional policy and even less on its national development. The refugee children of the late 1930s were to have a much greater effect on society.

Within government, the early explorations of policy were stimulated by the India Office, holding a brief for the large number of Indian students. Individual government departments edged towards a policy that would meet their interests: the Foreign Office did so in pressing for the establishment of the PhD and again in the 1930s with the beginnings of cultural diplomacy. Political and economic development got a nod from the India Office and brought in the Colonial Office. The Board of

Education showed occasional interest. And the Board of Trade tried with little success to bring British economic interests to bear. There was no mechanism for bringing all these interests together, nor any expectation that this might happen: inconsistencies were inevitable. Inconsistencies followed, too, from the fact that overseas students came into a society in which open xenophobia and deeply embedded racism sat awkwardly beside a national open-door policy for subjects of the empire. Doors were no longer open in the same way for those categorised as aliens.

More rapid change was to come with the rethinking of social and imperial policy during the Second World War when the Education Act of 1944 was to reshape secondary education at home while the first Colonial Development and Welfare Act was passed, the Devonshire committee proposed a reform of Colonial Office training, and the Asquith commission provided a blueprint for university development overseas. All these were to have major implications for educational, colonial and Commonwealth policy after 1945.

5
Recovery and Expansion, 1945–79

Education can thrive on war. The French educational system was reformed at the time of the Napoleonic wars, the Morrill Act was passed during the Civil War to create America's land grant colleges, while the Humboldtian university 'was forged in the aftermath of the battle of Jena'.[1] In Britain, not only did the 1944 Education Act promise secondary education for all but government welcomed proposals to double the university grant, double university numbers, and triple the production of scientists and technologists. The post-war government went on to accept recommendations from a quartet of committees, Goodenough, Barlow, Clapham and Scarbrough, to expand teaching in medicine, science and technology, social science, and oriental and Slavonic studies. University enrolments grew four-fold in the 35 years from the end of the Second World War. It was noted at the time that 'Apart from electronics and natural gas, higher education has grown faster than any major national enterprise in the 1960s'.[2] Nor was this just a British phenomenon:

> Never before in history had the expectations placed on the universities been greater than in the fifty years following the Second World War. Never had Europe seen so many universities and other institutions of higher learning being founded in such a short time. Never before had they hosted such crowds of teachers, students and administrative personnel. Never, to such an extent, had they been at the centre of public discussion. Never had governments had such an influence on the universities' development; at the same time universities were cooperating on an unprecedented scale at the national and international level.[3]

In Britain successive governments committed themselves to expand education, even at a time when the country had to recover from the war, American lend-lease funds had been abruptly cut off, new houses were needed by the hundred-thousand and the Beveridge plan had to be implemented. In the mood of post-war optimism the Labour Party manifesto of 1945 set out plans for 'Jobs for all'. The jobs were created and full employment ensured there were tax revenues to fund recovery. The Ministry of Labour had to worry not about unemployment but about labour shortages. Within the plans for recovery, education at all levels was a priority. In January 1946, almost with her dying breath – which came three weeks later – Ellen Wilkinson as minister of education persuaded the cabinet to raise the school-leaving age.[4]

In higher education, universities grew in number, variety and size, in three waves of expansion. Between 1948 and 1955 five university colleges gained their charters and one was established. Some 12 technical colleges became colleges of advanced technology (CATs) in 1956 and gained university status within ten years; they were joined by a new round of green-field foundations. By 1979 Britain had 46 universities, up from 11 in 1945, while student numbers rose from their pre-war level of 50,000 to 300,000. In 1965 the next group of technical colleges followed the CATs on their upward path and gained a new status, emerging as 30 polytechnics in a binary system of higher education. Other sectors of education continued to grow: full-time numbers in further education – much of it for qualifications below degree level – increased seven-fold between 1938 and 1962 to reach 43,000.[5]

Expansion was stimulated by demand, repeatedly underestimated. In 1953, when one in 31 of the age group were getting to university, the University Grants Committee anticipated that, after an increase in the 1960s, numbers were then likely to remain stable.[6] Within five years, when university numbers had risen again, the committee conceded it had got that wrong as more children were staying on at school to the age of 17 or more.[7] An acute sociological observer, Michael Young, argued in 1962 that universities would not be able to expand to accommodate the students from the post-war bulge in the birth rate and that an open university was needed to meet the anticipated demand.[8] His forecast was wrong as, with unprecedented resilience, universities increased their numbers almost two-thirds in five years, between 1961 and 1966. Yet more surprisingly the country got its Open University, but for a different purpose and different audience. By 1972 the education minister in a Conservative government, Margaret Thatcher, accepted that 22 per cent of the age group would be entering higher education.[9] In the 35 years after the war all governments consistently wanted to ensure that higher education had enough places to meet national demand.

Expansion was driven by policy as well as by demand and by a new recognition of links between education, prosperity and development. Using data from intelligence tests on conscripts, the Crowther report on education for 15- to 19-year-olds found in 1959 that able children were leaving school too young, so that 'the available resources of men (and presumably also of women) of high "ability" are not fully used by the present system'.[10] It was in the national interest to strengthen education for this age group. The Robbins committee then took the argument further, arguing that places in higher education should be made available for all qualified school leavers who wanted to take them up, even as this group grew in size. Robbins and his colleagues stressed the economic case for educational expansion:

> Meanwhile we wish to state unequivocally that – always provided that the training is suitable – there is a broad connection between the size of the stock of trained manpower in a community and its level of productivity per head. ... if productivity is to advance at anything like the rate now deemed desirable there is a strong presumption that a substantial increase in the proportion of the population that is skilled and versatile will be necessary. And in modern societies the skills and the versatilities required are increasingly those conferred by higher education.[11]

That conviction, reinforced by public demand from school leavers and their parents, continued to fuel the expansion of higher education for the next two decades.

Similar arguments applied abroad as at home with the result that the number of overseas students in British institutions rose as rapidly as the domestic numbers. As between the wars, the proportion of overseas full-time university students remained between about 8 and 12 per cent of the total (see Figure 5.1). In 1946 when ex-service students, some of them from the colonial empire, were swelling student numbers, there were nearly 7,000 overseas students in universities. In the next 30 years overseas numbers rose five-fold to exceed 34,000.

The numbers were driven in part by rising prosperity as the world recovered from war. In 20 years from 1946 students from the United States increased eight-fold. Two devaluations helped reduce their costs while the fall in the cost of transport, as planes replaced ships, and jets replaced propellers, made international travel easier and cheaper. New sources of wealth became available; oil revenues lubricated student mobility and brought increasing numbers from Nigeria and the middle east.

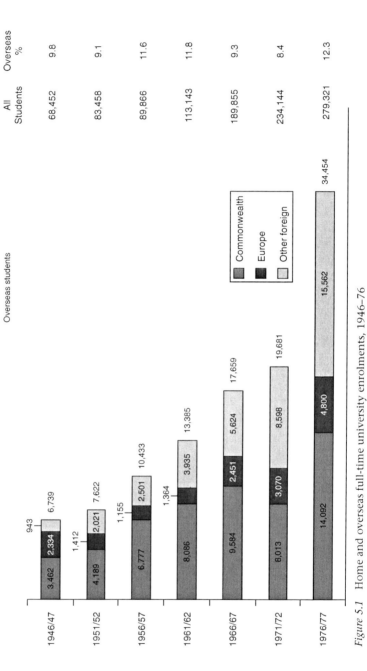

Figure 5.1 Home and overseas full-time university enrolments, 1946–76
Note: GB universities.
Source: ACU Yearbook.

The politics of decolonisation also drove student numbers. Indian independence was in sight at the end of the war and self-government was a visible target rather than a distant intention for the African colonies, even though these were seen as good for another 40 years. At least as important, assumptions about higher education shifted with a new recognition that the colonies would need large numbers of professionals in medicine, law, technology and agriculture, and not just a small cadre of administrators. The numbers needed were of a different order from those that had been achieved in the mid-1930s when Makerere had 17 degree students in east Africa and Fourah Bay in west Africa had 17, mainly in theology.[12] War-time planning brought simultaneous reports in 1945 of the Asquith commission on higher education in the colonies, the Elliot committee on west Africa and the Irvine committee on the West Indies, which set out a British 'blueprint for the export of universities to her people overseas' with a role for British universities in their development.[13] One immediate effect of the policy was to increase the demand for university education in Britain in order to produce future university teachers alongside the other professionals. Increased funds became available to bring students to Britain in the interests of colonial development (see Chapter 8). British universities were seen as a necessary destination for students from the colonies and ex-colonies.

With changes in the politics and finance of international student mobility came changes in its geography. The proportion of overseas university students from the developing world rose from 49 per cent in 1938, with students from India very much to the fore, to 63 per cent in 1954 and 70 per cent in 1962. It remained at about that level into the 1970s.

There were continuities as well as changes among students, many of whom continued to come from the Commonwealth, the informal empire and the United States (see Table 5.1). Into the 1960s, more than half of all overseas students continued to come from the Commonwealth; their numbers reached 65 per cent of the overseas total in 1951, before falling back to just over 40 per cent by the 1970s. The Commonwealth itself changed so that, while Australia, Canada and New Zealand continued to send students to Britain, the modal Commonwealth student by the end of the period was black, not white. The countries of the informal empire, Egypt, Iran and Iraq, continued to send large numbers of students, often appearing among the top ten sending countries. Egyptian numbers continued to rise despite a change of regime with the fall of Farouk (an ex-Sandhurst king). An Egyptian student got one of the longest ovations during the Cambridge Union Society debate on the Suez war in 1956 when he pointed out that the Anglo-French ultimatum required

Table 5.1 Top eight sending countries – universities, 1946–76

Universities

1946/7 Country	No.	1951/2 Country	No.	1956/7 Country	No.	1961/2 Country	No.	1966/7 Country	No.	1971/2 Country	No.	1976/7 Country	No.
India	966	India	831	India	1,532	India	1,660	USA	1,991	USA	2,095	Malaysia	4,081
Poland	690	USA	710	USA	910	USA	1,146	India	1,711	Canada	973	USA	2,871
South Africa	417	West Africa	557	Nigeria	896	Nigeria	1,124	Pakistan	952	Malaysia	792	Iran	2,055
West Africa	363	Egypt	458	Pakistan	459	Canada	559	Nigeria	904	Pakistan	783	Greece	1,770
Germany	328	South Africa	405	South Africa	407	Pakistan	526	Canada	742	India	720	Iraq	1,307
West Indies	276	Australia	401	Canada	392	WI	476	Norway	681	Nigeria	608	Hong Kong	1,299
Egypt	261	Canada	380	Australia	344	Kenya	400	Iraq	596	Greece	561	Nigeria	1,172
Canada	244	West Indies	314	Ghana	337	South Africa	397	Malaysia	561	Iraq	514	Canada	879

Sources: 1946–61: ACU Yearbook; 1966–76: British Council statistics.

the Egyptian forces to retreat well within their own national frontiers.[14] With increased oil revenues and governments sympathetic to Britain, university numbers from Iran and Iraq rose sharply in the early 1970s, as they did in technical colleges and polytechnics (see Table 5.2). The student numbers from the United States recovered from a low point immediately after the war, when they made up less than 4 per cent of the overseas total, to make up a steady 10 per cent.

Students from Europe were at a high point in 1946 when they made up 35 per cent of the overseas total, partly because of refugees who were still at university; students from Poland and Germany formed the second and fourth largest overseas contingent that year. European numbers then fell so that they were below 20 per cent in 1951 and then remained at between 10 and 15 per cent. Within Europe, Greece, which had a restricted university system, continued to send the children of its educated middle class often making it the largest European sending country. Norway, with historic links with Scotland, regularly came high in the European list even before oil and gas revenues boosted its economy from the 1970s.

Change came from Asia and Africa. India continued to dominate the list of countries sending students for two decades after the war. While Indian and Pakistani students were still numbered in their hundreds, and Pakistan even sent its probationary civil servants to Oxbridge until 1959, the number of Indian students then fell from over 1,700 in 1966 to less than 500 in 1981.[15] By this time university opportunities within India had themselves increased as numbers rose from 198,000 to nearly 3 million between 1961 and 1981. Devaluation of the rupee increased the cost of studying abroad. The fall in the numbers travelling was also associated with a declining sense of the prestige and value of an English degree. By the 1950s it was reported that:

> Formerly the holder of a first-class degree from an English university was assured of a glowing public welcome on return. He was regarded as a good match for the daughters of the best families in his subcaste, who were prepared to offer a sizable dowry and their influential backing in getting a position; he could choose from among several high-ranking job offers and he would look forward to a bright future. Today the man who is foreign-educated has his picture in the paper on his return, is congratulated by his relatives and friends, and thereafter is on his own to make his way in life. In short, foreign education gives a person less bargaining power than it did in the old days.[16]

As numbers from India declined, those from Hong Kong, Malaysia and Singapore increased. Between them they sent 65 students in 1946;

Table 5.2 Top eight sending countries – technical colleges, polytechnics and nurse training, 1962–76

1962/3		1966/7		1971/2		1976/7	
Country	No.	Country	No.	Country	No.	Country	No.
Technical colleges all courses		**Polytechnics and technical college advanced courses**					
Nigeria	2,827	Nigeria	1,468	Malaysia	750	Malaysia	3,987
Iraq	1,408	India	498	Sri Lanka	488	Iran	1,800
India	915	Ghana	414	Nigeria	352	Nigeria	2,522
Ghana	844	Malaysia	345	India	330	Sri Lanka	1,225
Iran	768	Iraq	332	Norway	312	Greece	790
Kenya	512	Norway	289	Greece	310	Hong Kong	780
Pakistan	478	Ceylon	260	Kenya	298	Singapore	637
Norway	441	Pakistan/ Kenya	202	Pakistan	268	India	559
		Technical colleges non-advanced courses					
		Nigeria	1,827	Malaysia	975	Iran	5,344
		Kenya	650	Iran	964	Malaysia	3,860
		Cyprus	565	Cyprus	882	Hong Kong	2,075
		Hong Kong	538	Kenya	745	Nigeria	1,806
		Malaysia	501	Uganda	739	Sri Lanka	965
		Ghana	486	Hong Kong	619	Greece	716
		Tanzania	444	Nigeria	569	Jordan	683
		India	436	Pakistan	482	Kenya	654

Nurse training

Jamaica	3,543	Jamaica	3,129	Malaysia	3,726	Malaysia	3,087
Nigeria	1,401	Trinidad	1,831	Mauritius	2,167	Ireland	2,764
Trinidad	1,133	Barbados	1,459	Jamaica	2,079	Philippines	913
Barbados	1,043	Guyana	1,081	Ireland[a]	2,010	Jamaica	844
British Guiana	844	Mauritius	1,019	Trinidad	1,828	Trinidad	577
Malaysia	601	Nigeria	1,011	Ghana	724	Sri Lanka	467
Ghana	399	Malaysia	845	Barbados	653	Ghana	391
Hong Kong	333	Ghana	543	Philippines	603	S. Rhodesia	386

Note: a. Ireland not regarded as a foreign country in earlier British Council statistics

Source: British Council statistics.

within 20 years this had grown to almost 1,900 and within 30 to exceed 6,000 of whom over 4,000 came from Malaysia. (At this time China kept its academic isolation so that the 48 students shown as Chinese in 1976 are more likely to have been refugees than government nominees.) This rapid growth was driven by expanding economies, expanding education systems and by the demands of those systems themselves. A Malaysian student who did his doctorate (on termites, which had to be imported from France) at Aston University in the early 1970s explained what led him to come to Britain as a Commonwealth scholar from the newly established University of Penang (later the Universiti Sains Malaysia):

> I was among the first staff to be appointed to biology and we had a very forward looking vice-chancellor...I had then only a master's degree and during the interview he said 'Look, I want the university to be populated by PhDs, especially in the science schools'. Would I have any problems if I was encouraged to complete my PhD as quickly as possible? I had always had in the back of my mind a desire to complete my doctorate. So I said I wouldn't have problems and I was invited to join as an assistant lecturer. And the university then began thinking about their task and policy which I think was fairly innovative for that period. South Africans would now call it 'growing your own trees'...I took the chance and applied to the university for a scholarship and I got the award.[17]

The profile of African students was also changing. As apartheid tightened its grip, numbers from South Africa fell and it no longer appeared among the top ten sending countries after 1956. Meanwhile the expansion of education in west Africa, and oil revenues in Nigeria, drove up their numbers: there were 360 students from 'British West Africa' in 1946, almost 1,500 from Ghana and Nigeria in 1961. Nigerian numbers then varied with the vicissitudes of the country's politics and economics and changes in British immigration law; they exceeded 1,100 in 1961, had fallen to 400 ten years later, but then recovered to more than 1,100 in 1976 and 2,000 in 1981.

While there were changes as well as continuities in their geography, overseas university students remained predominantly male as they had been before the war. In 1961 only 14 per cent were female, with no difference between graduates and undergraduates.[18] Some 28 per cent of home students were women. Until the late 1970s figures were seldom disaggregated but by 1981 the British Council, which had long distinguished between foreign and Commonwealth students but not between men and women, at last noticed gender, reporting that 26 per cent of overseas students were women. The home figure had by this time risen to 40 per cent.

Just as there were differences in the nationality of pre-war and post-war cohorts of students, so there were changes in the subjects they studied. In 1961 almost half of the overseas undergraduates studied humanities and social sciences and less than a third science and technology, while by 1976 the first group had fallen to 34 per cent and the scientists and technologists risen to 59 per cent. Over the same period the proportions studying medicine and health, and agriculture, forestry and veterinary science all fell significantly, as overseas universities expanded in these areas. At postgraduate level there were similar but less marked changes; here students in the humanities fell from 18 to 7 per cent of the total while social scientists increased from 16 to 23 per cent. While postgraduates in the sciences remained at about 20 per cent, those in engineering and other technologies rose from 18 to 25 per cent of the total (see Table 5.3).

Table 5.3   Overseas full-time university students' choice of degree subjects, 1961–76

	Percentages			
	1961/2	1966/7	1971/2	1976/7
	Undergraduates			
Humanities	27	15	19	14
Education	–	3	1	1
Social studies	20	20	18	19
Science	11	11	14	16
Technologies	18	38	34	43
Agriculture, forestry, veterinary	4	2	1	1
Medicine and health	21	11	12	7
Total	100	100	100	100
	Postgraduates			
Humanities	18	18	17	12
Education	12	6	6	7
Social studies	16	21	22	21
Science	21	20	21	23
Technologies	18	22	23	25
Agriculture, forestry, veterinary	2	3	4	3
Medicine and health	12	11	8	8
Total	100	100	100	100

Sources: 1961: *Robbins report Annex 2A*, 260; 1966–76: *British Council statistics*.

Individual groups of students went against these trends. Rhodes scholars from the United States had always favoured the humanities – 88 per cent before the war and 84 per cent after – but the proportion of Rhodes scholars from the Commonwealth in the humanities more than doubled from 30 per cent to 65 per cent by 1954.[19] (This may reflect no more than the preferences of the Rhodes selectors.) The profile of law students also changed. With independence, reading for the English bar no longer offered the same advantages to Indian lawyers. Although they had made up 25 per cent of admissions to the Middle Temple in 1936, by 1950 their numbers had fallen to 3 per cent. The bar, however, continued to attract overseas students: by 1959, two-thirds of those beginning to read for the bar were from overseas with the largest contingent coming from Nigeria, followed by Ghana and the West Indies.[20] Lord Denning, who chaired an enquiry into legal education for African students, saw a continuing role for the English bar in the post-colonial world when 'On the transfer of power the territories will not only need legislators and administrators. They will also need judges and lawyers'.[21]

For much of the twentieth century universities expressed a preference for postgraduates rather than undergraduates. The proportion of overseas postgraduates steadily rose from 47 per cent in 1961 to 61 per cent in 1971 only to fall back to 54 per cent in 1976 and 52 per cent in 1981, in response to a continuing demand for undergraduate study, despite the growth of universities outside Britain. Some voices always made the undergraduate case. In a memorandum to the Robbins committee the British Council noted the expansion of universities in the developing world but added that:

> In practice, the basic training provided overseas is likely to be of a low level of proficiency.... In the light of our experience with India, Pakistan, Ghana and Nigeria it may be regarded as axiomatic that the number of overseas students of undergraduate status seeking admission to courses of higher education will continue to increase, unless it is prevented by artificial means e.g. currency restrictions.[22]

Lord Robbins thought this argued against 'a fairly commonly accepted principle, namely, that it is better for foreign students to take their first degrees at home and to come here for their graduate training' but without convincing the council's director general. The council also regretted that there were more Greek students in Germany than in Britain, suggesting that it retained political as well as developmental concerns.[23] In practice, in three of the four countries cited – India, Pakistan and Ghana – undergraduate numbers declined in the next two decades while postgraduate numbers grew. Nigeria was the one exception where undergraduate numbers fell in the 1960s only to rise again in the oil-rich 1970s, though still far exceeded by the growth in the number of postgraduates.

To sum up, in 35 years of university expansion the growing number of overseas students kept pace with the increasing numbers from within Britain, and continued to include both undergraduates and postgraduates. The Commonwealth and informal empire remained a prime source for students, but a changing one. Numbers from South Africa fell away as those from west Africa increased. The proportion of students from Europe decreased while that from southeast Asia began to rise. In terms of discipline, there were moves away from the humanities and towards science and technology. Men continued to dominate the numbers.

While the largest single group of overseas students were at university, others came to do degrees and other advanced courses in the state sector of technical colleges and polytechnics, to obtain lower-level qualifications and to qualify as nurses. As with university students, the numbers for these three groups rose, with marked increases in the 1970s and a complicated history of rise and decline for the nurses (see Figure 5.2). Alongside these there were, as earlier in the century, smaller numbers

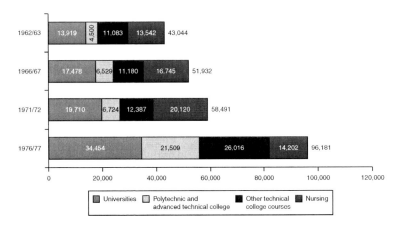

Figure 5.2 Categories of overseas students, 1962–76

Note: There are minor discrepancies between British Council figures and the ACU figures used in Figure 5.1.

Source: *British Council statistics.*

of school children, who were then joined by English language students, the first of what were to become large numbers. And, as before the war, Britain continued to train overseas soldiers.

From earlier in the century some overseas students had followed advanced courses at the larger technical colleges, either for London external degrees or for professional qualifications. Although they had fewer overseas students than the universities, by 1976 there were over 21,000 at these colleges, the larger of which were now polytechnics. Their geography was different. Australia, Canada and the United States all appeared among the top eight sending countries for universities but not for the state sector: these students wanted university prestige. From the time when statistics were centrally collected in the 1960s, Malaysia and Nigeria were consistently prominent here. Increased numbers also enrolled for technical college courses at a lower level, designated as further rather than higher education. Here, too, Malaysia and Nigeria were prominent in sending the hopeful and ambitious who might be classified as students or as migrants.

Changes in immigration policy affected many of these students more directly than those at universities who were for many years treated as temporary visitors of little interest to the Home Office. Citizens of the colonies had a right to move to Britain which was reconfirmed in the 1948 British Nationality Act. Despite hesitations within government on the arrival in the same year of the *Empire Windrush* with its 500 Caribbean immigrants, Commonwealth citizens retained the right to travel and stay in Britain until the Commonwealth Immigrants Act of 1962. Over the next 20 years a second Commonwealth Immigrants Act in 1968, the Immigration Act in 1971 and the British Nationality Act in 1981 steadily restricted the right of entry. The migration laws had a pronounced effect on those who came with the intention of combining work and study.

Restrictive legislation had its effect even before coming into force. In the late 1950s the hesitant were encouraged to move quickly as new controls on immigration looked increasingly likely. There was then a further stimulus in a period of grace between the announcement of the Commonwealth Immigrants Bill in October 1961 and its coming into effect in July 1962. Nigeria's oil and Malaysia's strengthening economy helped its young men – mainly men – to travel. Others came from Hong Kong, Cyprus and Greece. Many stayed in London, some with the expectation that they would stay, some planning to return home with a qualification. Many in both groups intended to study full or part-time which brought a concentration of overseas students in some London colleges that created a sense of alarm. The Robbins committee was told in 1962 that some drew 79 per cent of their students from overseas and that 'in many cases the students of these colleges are there to study for their G.C.E. and in fact the colleges are secondary schools'.[24] Others were studying privately. The Associated Examining Board ran an open centre in London for candidates who were not registered with any school or college: in the early 1960s its centre regularly had several hundred candidates for its GCE ordinary level English language examination with the alphabetical roll dominated by Nigerian names beginning with As and Os.[25]

While most of these students travelled hopefully and individually, Britain went out to recruit trainee nurses. The country was always cautious about the professions for which it would recruit overseas. At no time in the century did it recruit large numbers of overseas teachers; early in the century prospective teachers were warned that they would pay a larger fee than the locals, and might not be able to teach even when qualified.[26] At the time of the Robbins report only 2 per cent of students in teacher-training institutions were from overseas.[27] But while Britain was wary of letting foreigners care for its children, it had a different attitude to health, life and death so that, from its founda-tion, the National Health Service relied on large numbers of staff from overseas. In the 1950s, with full employment, British schools were not producing enough potential nurses. While governments had previously been more willing to recruit labour from European displaced persons and prisoner of war camps, the service responded with recruitment drives for nurses in the Caribbean.[28]

The number of overseas nurses in training exceeded 20,000 in 1971, with the majority coming from the Caribbean, Mauritius and Malaysia, only to fall to 4,300 ten years later. Unlike most overseas university students, they were expecting to stay rather than return home. This large programme was run with no national planning or coordination: even in 1979 the Royal College of Nursing reported that 'there is still no meaningful national policy regarding the recruitment of nurse learners from overseas'. Most were women, and men were sometimes discouraged: the director of Nigerian students in London was told in 1956 that it was 'impossible to place male candidates for training and no more should be sent'.[29] The nurses attracted less public attention than the predominantly male migrants on the *Empire Windrush* and its following ships, and often quietly put up with their lot. One in four of them were not met on arrival; four out of five felt lonely; they were expected to find their own way around so that one nurse from Grenada reported that on her first day 'the one thing I found hard was that no one showed me the canteen. I just stayed in my room and cried.' When they completed their course and became employees not students, the new immigration laws meant they were plunged into a legally grey area, unable to work till a work permit arrived.[30]

The changes in immigration policy made for dramatic reductions in the numbers of scholar-migrants who left west Africa for south London. And, while Britain continued to import health workers from abroad, the large programmes of nurse recruitment and training were a temporary phenomenon rather than a permanent part of health service policy, cut back during the 1970s.

Just as some of the internationally affluent continued to seek university places for their children, so there was a continuing demand for school places. A review of public schools in the mid-1960s found that they drew about 4 per cent of their boarder and 2 per cent of their day boy entrants from overseas, making up a total of some 3,400 from abroad.[31] Numbers increased in the late 1970s when schools began to recruit more vigorously overseas in a response to their own rising costs and a fall in demand at home that followed a decline in the British birth rate in the late 1960s.[32] As with universities, the schools drew large numbers of students from Asia, more than a third of the overseas total in the 1970s, with middle east countries to the fore, but also drew one in five from Europe and evidently had a surge of popularity in America in the 1970s.[33] These students presented schools with their own institutional strains. At Harrow a 10 per cent quota for overseas pupils was imposed in the 1970s but, regardless of the quota, quality mattered as well as quantity: 'As long as the majority of foreign Harrovians possessed impeccable pedigrees, such as the kings of Jordan and Iraq, prejudice could be constrained.' By the mid-1990s the actual quota was to rise to 16 per cent.[34] The hope of university entrance in turn increased the demand from families seeking the specialised sixth-form education that English universities expected. In response to that demand another private-sector school, Sevenoaks, in 1962 opened an international house for pupils planning to spend one or two years preparing for university entry.[35]

Another group of privileged students – but perhaps less privileged than the Harrovians – began to flow into England from the 1960s as English-language schools grew in size, status and reputability. Frank Bell, for example, who had worked for the Cambridge extramural board where he was responsible for re-establishing academic links with Germany, set up his Bell school of languages in Cambridge in 1955. He had failed to persuade the extramural board to do more than run an annual short course in English, but had the mayor and both the outgoing and incoming vice-chancellors in attendance and was criticised for 'such a flourish of academic trumpets'. He saw this not principally as a way of creating a viable business (which it was but one that he turned into a charity) but as a contribution to international understanding. His was apparently the second in Cambridge and he initially had 55 students.[36] Their numbers grew steadily. By 1972 Cambridge had 16 language schools with almost 7,000 students, figures that rose to 46 and 14,000 within ten years.[37] One national estimate suggests there were 180 schools with some 86,000 annual enrolments by the mid-1970s. Some 50 new schools had opened in ten years in response to the demand for English teaching and 'increasing affluence in Europe, the Arab countries and Japan'.[38] While language students slip under the net of international statistics, as they generally stay for less than a year, their image is often the one conjured up by the term 'foreign student' in attractive towns from Bournemouth to Cambridge where Bell and his successors built their schools.

Military students continued to come to Britain after the war. (The first, and least military, were the American servicemen who attended new versions of the 1918 khaki colleges. In Cambridge they enjoyed their gap months between the war and repatriation at Bull Hostel, later incorporated into St Catharine's College.) With independence, it was no longer necessary to keep places at Sandhurst for the Indian army, leaving it with spare capacity: by 1955 the British army needed only 960 officer cadets in residence at any one time, releasing 140 places. Political, colonial and military priorities then determined who should get them. Malta and the Gurkhas came first as they provided officers for the British army. The RAF regiment, treated not quite as a foreign power, came next, after which it was 'obviously important and desirable to give sympathetic consideration to bids for vacancies from the Colonies and new Commonwealth countries'. These were in turn followed by countries with which there were close treaties and to which British officers were seconded such as Iraq, Jordan and Libya. Neither India, nor Pakistan, nor Egypt now fitted the bill, although both Egypt and Pakistan later sent small numbers.[39]

They were not universally welcomed, even within Sandhurst. It was claimed that 'Afro-Asian students contribute very little to the courses they attend. I am sure, however, that we must continue to have them because if we do not, the chances are they will go to Russia'.[40] There were repeated suggestions that the policy might be reviewed amid concerns both about the cadets' behaviour in England and at their potential activities abroad. In 1958 one internal minute to the director of military training argued that it was time to consider whether the policy was in the national interest:

> Throughout Africa and Asia the 'students' are now exerting an improper political influence, and they are filled with an aggressive nationalism. Those who come to Sandhurst are probably typical of these 'students', and their heads are filled with restless, muddled, and intransigent ideas. This makes them prickly customers and the British Sandhurst Cadet is not renowned for tolerance towards those who do not conform to the normal British patterns of behaviour. ...
>
> I cannot but be impressed by the fact that two of the Iraqi Army Officers now in the revolutionary Government of that country were Cadets in England and that their anti-British sentiments are said to stem from their treatment when they were at Woolwich and Sandhurst.[41]

Further enquiries suggested that the military academies were not to blame as one of the Iraqi students had failed and one had been withdrawn. The policy remained in place and was seen by the Foreign Office as 'sustaining British influence in some countries', though a cabinet committee argued for a review in 1973.[42]

In terms of a model of student mobility, international students were pushed towards Britain in the post-war years by the expansion of secondary and tertiary education overseas that still left university opportunities restricted, especially in the developing world. Public and private finance continued to lubricate the flow of students. They were pulled towards Britain partly by the strengths of its university system and the value of British qualifications and partly by deliberate policies, including an expanded commitment to education for colonial and post-colonial development. Almost in opposition to that commitment, the policy of recruiting and training overseas nurses to work in Britain took them away from the same colonies and ex-colonies. The gates of Sandhurst were kept open in the interest of foreign policy. Immigration law acted to facilitate student mobility until the early 1960s and then increasingly to constrain it.

As between the wars there were no formal statements of public policy towards overseas students. Practice evolved in response to the competing interests of students, government departments and institutions. Tensions were inevitable and were at their most strained between the desire to welcome students from abroad, the shortage of funds to pay for them and the demand for places from home students.

Education expanded within financial constraints that constantly preoccupied governments. The devaluation of sterling in 1947, and a further reluctant devaluation in 1967 followed by expenditure cuts, all demonstrated the weakness of the national economy. The strain on finances was compounded by the rapid inflation of the mid-1970s and demonstrated again by the need for support from the International Monetary Fund in 1976. At the same time any attempt to hold back the demand for university places for home students would have had an insurmountably high political cost.

One theme of policy was a wish to hold down the number of overseas students because of the scale of home demand. It was reported in 1946 that the Ministry of Labour had advised the committee of vice-chancellors and principals 'to accept the entry of students from abroad only for special reasons', apparently in happy ignorance that there were nearly 7,000 already there; the committee, like the ministry, could in any case only advise.[43] Two years later the secretary of state for the colonies claimed that universities were required to reserve 90 per cent of their places for ex-servicemen (which seems improbable at this point) and, despite the advice of his own staff, argued a touch plaintively that

> it would be, most unwise that there should be any great increase in the number of students coming to this country, and while I do not wish to suggest that any steps can, or should, be taken by administrative means to prevent the movement of persons to the United Kingdom for study, I earnestly hope that parents and guardians and students are made aware of the great difficulties which exist at present.[44]

But, along with the claims for home students and the calls for economy there were voices to sound a welcome for those from overseas. They came with particular strength from the three overseas departments – the Foreign Office, the Colonial Office and its Overseas Development successor, and the Dominions or Commonwealth Office – and from the universities themselves.

For its part the Foreign Office was consistently warm towards overseas students, having realised their importance within soft diplomacy in the 1930s (see Chapter 4). In a minute written on Boxing Day 1946, as the German control commission was trying to negotiate a university place for a German student, it explained that:

> we were not aware that we had agreed with the Ministry of Labour and the Committee of Vice-Chancellors that at present aliens were

only to be admitted in special circumstances. The fact is that we were not consulted before the Ministry sent a circular to the Committee advising them, inter alia, to accept the entry of students from abroad only for special reasons, and on receiving a copy we informed them that in fact we 'attached great importance to foreign students and were most anxious that their numbers should not be unduly restricted'.[45]

The Foreign Office went on to demonstrate its confidence in the value of overseas students by initiating Marshall scholarships in 1953 to bring American scholars to Britain. These were described in the House of Commons as an 'expression and a token of our gratitude' to the United States as a wartime ally which would 'make its own contribution to the cause of Anglo-American understanding'. It was expected that 'scholars will be enriched by their experience, and that our universities will benefit from the new ideas and outlooks' they would bring. Herbert Morrison gave bipartisan support to the proposal, explaining that it had been his idea in the first place when he was foreign secretary in the previous government.[46] Almost the only critical comment came from Emrys Hughes, the left-wing labour MP for South Ayrshire, who 'had no hope at all of the Foreign Office being able to educate Americans' and wanted the Ministry of Education and the Scottish Office to be involved.[47]

The Foreign Office wanted friends for Britain but also to compete with its rivals abroad. Throughout the cold war, a welcome for overseas students was part of the armoury of foreign policy with scholarship programmes seen as being in competition with those from the Soviet bloc. (Their numbers tended to be exaggerated and it was some years before African students' criticisms of their time in the Soviet Union began to get publicity (see Chapter 9).) A Fabian pamphlet published in 1962 suggested that 'The generosity of the Soviet government and the efficiency of the Friendship University's methods, especially in the teaching of Russian are both a model and a warning to our Government and institutions'.[48] One analysis of policy summed up that alongside the need 'to attract the best students and to secure influence abroad, there are also common responsibilities towards Third World nations and a shared interest in winning "the battle for the minds of men" against totalitarian regimes and military dictatorships'.[49]

In the climate of the cold war government wanted to counter Soviet initiatives at home as well as abroad and expressed the same anxieties about communist influence on students as it had about the loyalty of students before and after the First World War. In 1949 it suggested to colonial governors that students offered scholarships in the Soviet bloc might be discouraged from taking them up; if that failed their activities should be watched on their return home.[50] The parliamentary secretary in the Colonial Office claimed that when he addressed groups of students 'the Communists gather round after my speech in order to try and counter it among the coloured students. I hear too that the Communists are working through prostitutes in London and other big cities to get their policy across.'[51] For its part MI5 was more cautious and, out of a total of '3,200 coloured students in the United Kingdom and Eire', it knew of 'less than a dozen who might be labelled as Communists'.[52] (In neither case do the files explain how they knew.) But the security service continued to have an interest in organisations such as the Coordinating Council for Colonial Student Affairs, the West Indian Students Union and the activities of future political leaders including Kwame Nkrumah and Forbes Burnham, and of Malayan students during its long colonial war.[53] Though the files get thinner it seems reasonable to assume that, throughout the cold war, the soft diplomacy of welcoming students was balanced by a security watch for subversion.

Until 1967, when the Commonwealth Relations Office was merged with the Foreign Office, and the Colonial Office was discontinued, the three shared policy on overseas affairs. There had been a decisive shift of policy with the passage of the Colonial Development and Welfare Acts from 1940. They made development funding available from British government sources throughout the colonial empire where, previously, each colony was expected to meet its needs from its own revenue. More scholarships were provided for the colonies (see Chapter 8). In contrast with earlier caution about university capacity, the head of the welfare and students department at the Colonial Office argued in 1948 that 'I cannot recommend that we suggest any limitation of admissions to Universities and Colleges on political or social grounds'.[54] By 1949 there were 1,389 students on Colonial Office scholarships alongside a further 2,088 who were privately financed. The Colonial Office did not see these as large numbers when Nigeria had a population of 24 million and only 718 students.[55] Funding for education in the interest of development increased so that, by the early 1980s about 8,000 trainees came to Britain each year under the government technical cooperation programme.[56] The Colonial Office saw a continuing role for British universities:

It is essential that the people of territories advancing politically and socially should be given the opportunity of training for posts of high responsibility and posts in the professional and technical fields. If political advancement takes place without corresponding educational advancement the result would be disastrous, and until the Colonial Universities are fully developed, and indeed to some extent after their development, the only way of getting quick results is to train as many qualified candidates as possible...in Britain in particular. It is inconceivable that this flow could be stopped – indeed in many territories there is considerable pressure of public opinion on the Colonial Governments to accelerate it, and criticism of the Director of Colonial Scholars because he cannot gain admission for all students who desire to enter British Universities.[57]

Its interests were practical and instrumental. The Colonial Office drew a distinction between scholarships carrying privileges, status and a 'mark of esteem' and those which were 'specifically designed to enable men and women to qualify for appointment to the higher grades of the public service'. It supported only the second type, including a variety of programmes and specialist courses that followed the well-established precedents of those for the Indian Civil Service and colonial administrators.[58] The Robbins committee reported on 16 academic courses for overseas trainees, mainly in the social sciences, education and administration. Aid funds were used to set up specialist departments, such as the Institute of Development Studies at the University of Sussex and the Agricultural Extension and Rural Development Centre of the University of Reading.[59]

An occasional note of complacency crept into colonial and aid policy in the 1960s and 1970s, quite different from the expansionist tone of the late 1940s, with an assumption that demands on Britain for training might be expected to decline. A white paper in 1961 recalled the history of technical assistance, which went back to helping Peter the Great and to harnessing the Nile, Tigris and Euphrates. It was claimed that the 'United Kingdom contribution to education overseas has been in the past, and remains today, outstanding'.[60] Following that proud history the Overseas Development Ministry argued in 1970 that 'the historically significant role we have played in the founding of a series of new universities overseas is now drawing to its close'.[61] Within five years it was expected that more students might in future train overseas, even with British funding:

We shall continue to offer training and further education in this country for those who require it and for whom the appropriate facilities are not available or cannot be economically provided nearer home. We may have to concentrate courses or training or research at particular 'centres of excellence' rather than picking up courses where they can be found and we are ready to encourage such centres overseas rather than always in Britain.[62]

This note of caution contrasts with comments that were coming from the Commonwealth. The continuing presence of a high proportion of Commonwealth students seemed to demonstrate the vitality of the links between British higher education and the Commonwealth. Alongside the developing Commonwealth countries, Australia and Canada still made heavy use of British universities for postgraduate education. Although there may have been other opinions in Australia, it was apparently with a straight face that the Oxford University registrar could report in 1948 to his Commonwealth colleagues, after a visit to Australia, that 'admiration of the British Universities is intense; and they are regarded by the young men and women as a sort of El Dorado':

> It is a commonplace that the most valuable features of life at Oxford and Cambridge are the contact of mind with mind in the intimacy of life in the College Common Rooms and in big departments and institutions. It is this kind of life which the Australian Universities cannot offer, and which chiefly attracts their students to the British Universities.[63]

Even a decade later Australia recruited 34 per cent of its university staff from abroad, with 20 per cent from Britain, evidently willing to abandon their chance of those English delights.[64]

The Commonwealth still had political salience in the 1950s. When in 1958 government wanted something positive out of a Commonwealth trade conference hosted by Canada, and disliked all the other Canadian proposals, it welcomed the idea of a programme of Commonwealth scholarships that were to sit alongside the Marshall scholarships. The programme was approved by a Commonwealth education conference in 1959 with its British element enacted in the same year, and the first scholars selected in 1960.[65] It was justified by government and universities alike on the grounds of its value to the Commonwealth. Civil servants argued that 'there would be great advantage if a form of words could be agreed between all Commonwealth countries which would link the scholarships with our aim of strengthening Commonwealth relationships generally'.[66] Eric Ashby, a former vice-chancellor in Belfast and a future one in Cambridge, saw the prime purpose of the scholarships as to 'consolidate the Commonwealth and in particular to establish a greater cohesion among the educated people in the Commonwealth', while from the University of Birmingham its vice-chancellor, Robert Aitken, explained 'that the main purpose of the scholarships was to strengthen Commonwealth cohesion'.[67]

Once the scheme was fully established it regularly brought between 200 and 300 scholars a year from both industrialised and developing

Commonwealth countries. Most went home once they had graduated, as they were meant to, but inevitably some stayed, particularly from the three industrialised countries. Evaluations suggest the plan had its biggest impact in supporting new universities within the developing Commonwealth. History confirms, however, that neither the plan nor the scholars achieved the elusive Commonwealth cohesion sought by its founding fathers.[68]

Policy was shaped by the decisions of universities and colleges, alongside government departments. They responded positively to requests from the Foreign Office and Colonial Office to ensure that places were available for overseas students. Even though its overseas numbers were relatively small, Aberdeen University, for example, offered places in 1946 for 40 students in arts, 15 undergraduates and five postgraduates in law with a priority for colonial students, and smaller numbers in divinity, sciences and medicine.[69] There was a willingness to support university development in the south. The physicist P. M. S. Blackett pointed out in a lecture at St Andrews in 1961

> that Britain has already a big stake in the higher education systems of developing countries. This role grew out of our past as a colonial power. It is essential that Britain should be prepared to continue and extend this rule in the future – if, and only if, the newly independent countries want us to do so.[70]

Responsibility to overseas universities was a common theme of the congresses of the Universities Bureau of the British Commonwealth (or Association of Commonwealth Universities as it became) where similar voices were heard from Britain and overseas. At the 1953 congress the vice-chancellor of the University of Panjab in Pakistan argued that 'Academic mobility is an important means to achieve a more uniform development of higher education in all parts of the Commonwealth. It is an important step for the promotion of Commonwealth solidarity and better understanding among its peoples'. A University of London professor of geography in turn thought it ought to be possible 'for an established teacher at every stage in his career, and for a candidate for entry into the ranks of the university teaching profession, to compete for an appropriate post in any university in the Commonwealth on level terms with any competitor'.[71] Student mobility was the other side of that coin of academic mobility.

International and colonial interests were expressed institutionally as well as rhetorically. Oxford set up an Institute of Colonial Studies in 1946. Oxford and Cambridge modified, but continued to run, their courses for imperial administrators even as students on them increasingly came from the overseas Commonwealth rather than from those intending to travel to it. (The Cambridge development studies master's course, which continues to this day, is a linear descendant of that course.) In the late 1940s London University considered the possibility of admitting as internal PhD students academic staff members at the university colleges associated with it in the Sudan, the West Indies, the Gold Coast, Nigeria and Uganda, alongside Exeter, Hull, Leicester and Southampton.[72]

Universities slowly, sometimes over slowly, adapted to the needs of their overseas students. Despite their long-standing preference for students who had completed a first degree at home, they were slow to adapt their practices to the needs of postgraduates. The Franks commission on Oxford University in 1966 found that conventional colleges were treating them poorly. It listened to Lord Robbins who argued that 'if we are to make our contribution to the intellectual leadership of the world, we must take graduate studies far more seriously than we have in the past' and agreed that Oxford had 'a special part to play in training postgraduates, both in view of the national pressures and, in particular of the increasing need for trained postgraduates to staff the new universities in this country and overseas'.[73] One step was to set up graduate colleges. Overseas postgraduate students at St Antony's, where they made up 70 per cent of the total, reported more favourably on their time in Oxford than overseas undergraduates.[74] But contemporary accounts, particularly by humanities postgraduates, reflect the Franks commission view. An English scholar told the Commonwealth Scholarship Commission:

> A word of advice, on the basis of my experience here, I should heartily dissuade any friend of mine from coming to Oxford to *begin* research in English literature. The research facilities and organisation of postgraduate studies in the English faculty lead the foreign student into a rather mole-like existence. There is little actual teaching, apart from obligatory classes in bibliography and the apparatus of scholarly writing. As a result, the graduate finds himself in splendid isolation in the Bodleian for most of the day and in his (usually grim) bed-sitter for the night.[75]

Durham had a similar collegiate system to Oxford with some of the same consequences so that it was 'sadly lacking in graduate facilities ... Whereas the Colleges tend to be self-contained units catering for all the need of undergraduates, the graduates are left to their own devices'.[76]

There were fewer comments like this from scientists, and they gradually became less common: university laboratories consistently offered clearer direction to their research students that were reflected in higher completion rates, for overseas as for home students. In seven universities 86 per cent of overseas PhD science students in the 1950s completed their course, as compared with 84 per cent of home students, while overseas arts students achieved only a 52 per cent success rate, compared with 61 per cent for home students.[77] Gradually changes in university practice, the development of middle common rooms, and the creation of postgraduate colleges and centres eased some of their social and academic difficulties, but completion rates in the arts and social sciences continued to lag behind those in science and technology.

Universities always had some concern for the welfare of their students. At the same time, over many years, overseas students came into a country in which discrimination on grounds of race or gender was legal, until the Race Relations Acts of 1965, 1968 and particularly 1976, and the Sex Discrimination Act of 1975. Landlords still could and did display signs reading 'No coloureds, no Irish'. Problems of discrimination and of accommodation were a common experience, as examined in Chapter 7. As the students were grappling with problems of accommodation and of prejudice, public and scholarly interest turned towards the difficulties they faced. In 1968 the National Union of Students set up a research unit to look at the experience of overseas students and the United Kingdom Council for Overseas Student Affairs was established as an information and welfare organisation. The 1950s and 1960s were marked by a new literature about overseas students, about immigrants and about the living conditions of both groups. Discourse had moved on from earlier concern about student problems – or students as a problem – or about their role in promoting trade or rejecting fascism, into one of sociology and welfare. There were surveys of students' experience by Political and Economic Planning (PEP), the National Foundation for Educational Research and the Fabian Society. Overseas research students produced dissertations on their contemporaries' experience and published them in book form. These works, like Carey's *Colonial students* in 1956 and Davison's broader *Black British* in 1966, were written within anthropological and sociological frameworks at a time when the academic study of sociology was expanding dramatically in British universities.[78] They can be seen as evidence of a changing public perception of overseas students which could in its turn influence the policy of universities as of government.

The tensions between financial constraints and the needs of home and overseas students were displayed – rather than resolved – in the development of policy on student fees, numbers and quotas in the 1960s and 1970s.

After the war, universities were funded partly by block grants and partly by student fees. The latter steadily decreased in real terms so that by 1959 they were so low that government had no difficulty in arranging that, for home students on a grant, fees would be paid directly to their university without any parental means test.[79] The Robbins committee found that fees meant met only 11 per cent of university costs, compared with 32 per cent in 1937. The committee looked at the possibility of significantly increasing fees but instead made the less radical recommendation that they should be increased to meet at least 20 per cent of university expenditure although 'Some of us would prefer to see the proportion greater'.[80] Government took no notice. The consequence was that all university students received a government subsidy, flowing from the block grant. Home and overseas students were subsidised in exactly the same way. In drawing new attention to the subsidy the committee nevertheless argued that:

> In our judgment this expenditure is well justified. It is a form of foreign aid that has a definite objective and yields a tangible return in benefit to the recipients and in general good will. It is, however, an open question whether aid is best given by subsidising fees; and it is a further question to what extent Parliaments of the future will permit it to grow without limit.[81]

That question was to lie dormant for three years.

While it might influence fees, government had only limited powers to control student numbers. Universities guarded their autonomy and made their own admission policies, with the result that government could recommend but could impose neither quotas nor limits. Government had not much more control over public-sector colleges. As they began to target courses to the increasing numbers of overseas students, the

Department for Education and Science was alarmed to find that colleges had no legal power to do this and ought only to be teaching national citizens.[82] Meanwhile in an Alice-in-Wonderland twist the British Council was encouraging colleges to run just such targeted courses for overseas students.[83] No action was contemplated as, while the department had powers of compulsion, it had none to prevent a local authority from 'doing that which it ought not to be doing but is doing'.[84]

Lacking powers, and concerned about costs, government and universities tiptoed towards a policy of limiting overseas numbers. In 1963 the Robbins report noted that these had long been at their steady 10 per cent and took this as a planning guideline which had the support of the Foreign Office, the Department for Technical Cooperation, education departments and the British Council.[85] But the University Grants Committee, conscious of the demand of home students, took a more cautious view and assumed that 'in the emergency period up to 1967–68…priority should be given to the increase in the home demand…and that a corresponding proportionate increase in the intake of overseas students could not be expected'.[86] Despite their best intentions the number of overseas students rose by 30 per cent in five years between 1961 and 1966.

Having failed to control numbers, government now tried to do something about costs. By the mid-1960s, in order to hold down budgets as government tried to stave off devaluation, the Department for Education and Science saw that it could ease its problems by introducing a differential fee for overseas students, thus reducing their subsidy. It argued that fees were absurdly low and that 'we get some benefit, no doubt, from educating these students but the fact remains that it is given at a tenth or less of its cost'.[87] The Treasury welcomed the idea despite reservations by the Foreign Office, the Commonwealth Relations Office and the Overseas Development Ministry, and anticipated objections by universities and from overseas.[88] Differential fees were duly introduced – though on a modest scale at £250 as compared with a home fee of £70.

The decision provoked a reaction that may have been stronger than the department had allowed for. The Conservative opposition made the most of the argument in Parliament, though conveniently forgot what they had said in due course. Universities objected that they, like the Foreign Office, had not been consulted; the vice-chancellor of the University of Bradford spoke for many in calling it a 'serious defeat for the universities in the United Kingdom'.[89] The minister thought they overstated their case:

I have been profoundly shocked by the near-hysterical reaction of some of the university critics. The Vice-Chancellor of Manchester said:

'this is an evil decision; what is at stake is our idea of the university'. The Vice-Chancellor of Sheffield said it would affect Britain's position as a world leader in advanced education. The Vice-Chancellor of Liverpool called it inhuman, foolish and autocratic. Others have spoken of our returning to the Middle Ages. Incidentally, no one would guess, listening to these papal edicts, that the vice-chancellors were strongly in favour of increasing all students' fees, for overseas as well as home students.[90]

Despite his profound shock the government came under stronger attack in the House of Lords with an accusation that it was adopting a discriminatory policy. Lord Robbins suggested to the minister, who came from an Irish family, that the policy was like a theatre proprietor who 'decided that all those noble Lords whose antecedents were on the opposite side of the Irish Sea were to pay an entrance fee twice or three times as high as they paid before'.[91] Peers, vice-chancellors and the bishop of Chichester together argued the cause of students from developing countries. Lord Taylor recalled meeting a Nigerian student studying in Moscow because, as he explained, 'The University of Moscow not only gives me free education but pays me a small salary on which I can just live'. 'What a sensible policy on the part of the Russians! But what a silly thing for us not to continue to do as we have done!'[92] Lord Gladwyn used his authority as an ex-ambassador to question the Education Department's arithmetic, point out that the presence of students from abroad 'is widely regarded as valuable' and 'fosters a sense of international community on both sides', and warn 'that we may well over the years be losing many thousands…of potential trade missionaries who, if they are happy in this country, will exercise a very important influence in their own countries in favour of importing British goods'. He went on to ask, 'Why, in any case, we should want to diminish the numbers of students coming from Common Market countries at a moment when we are moving heaven and earth to get into it, I find quite difficult to understand. Were the Foreign Office consulted on this point?'[93] While he was not speaking for the Foreign Office, his voice echoes some within it who thought it 'unfortunate that Sir Herbert Andrew [permanent secretary Department for Education and Science] should have plunged in without any consultation with the Overseas Departments'.[94]

As internationalism was part of the air they breathed, and there was an assumption that neither academic nor political barriers should impede the flow of university staff members or students, the introduction of the differential seemed particularly repugnant. John Carswell, who was then head of the universities branch of the Department of Education and

Science, explained the strength of universities' reaction in terms more measured than those of the debate at the time:

> I do not think it [the department] fully understood how deeply international affiliations matter to the universities and those who work in them. Those affiliations spring from the fact that knowledge and inquiry in any subject are valid regardless of the geographical origin or location of the knower or inquirer, and this is expressed not only in the presence of students and staff from overseas in a nation's universities, but in innumerable institutional and personal links throughout the world. ...
>
> A second reason for the affront caused to the universities was the unilateral character of the decision. True, the Government and the UGC had always had a voice in the level of fees, but constitutionally it was a matter for universities alone, something which needed the approval of each individual university senate. Yet in this case their approval was taken for granted, and if withheld would carry a financial penalty. Several universities took their stand on this issue and for a time refused to charge the increased fees.[95]

The arguments about fee levels were about money. When challenged on the wisdom of the policy in the same debate, the minister interrupted to explain: 'My Lords, may I clear up that point? The reasons for this step are financial.'[96] But the financial reasons were always intertwined with those about overseas student numbers.

The arguments now went back from fees to numbers. Though the introduction of a differential was seen at the time as a defeat for the universities, it turned out to be a pyrrhic victory for government as a means of holding down numbers. They rose again to reach almost 20,000 by 1971. With other priorities, and despite their earlier protests, the Conservative government of 1970–74 left fees well alone, retaining both the differential and the level at which fees were charged. On its return to office, the Labour government of 1974 was ambivalent about fees policy. It steadily increased fees, as rapid inflation eroded their value, while narrowing the differential between home and overseas students which it was concerned might be seen as discriminatory under the Race Relations Act.[97] It toyed with the idea of abolishing the differential but concluded that it could only reduce but not abolish it.[98] Radical reform, of charging full cost fees to all students, was not feasible as some 30,000 home students who were not on mandatory awards 'would be put in a hopeless position'.[99]

Government now tried a different tack of imposing quotas along-side differential fees. It announced in 1976 that it could not 'accept the continued rapid growth in the number of overseas students' and the Education Department asked universities first to stabilise numbers at the current level and then for the numbers to fall. This request had limited success and, though initial entrants did fall, total numbers rose over the next three years.[100] The policy proved unpopular and its implementation clumsy. The Inner London Education Authority tried to fine two of its polytechnics £50,000 for exceeding their quota, was criticised in Parliament for doing so, and then let one of them off.[101] By 1978/79 overseas fees had risen to £940 for undergraduates and £1,230 for post-graduates (see Table 5.4). The increases were not quite as dramatic as they seem: if the 1967 fees of £70 and £250 had had simply been raised in line with inflation, they would by 1978 have reached £221 and £791.

In a speech to the World University Service Shirley Williams, as secretary of state for education, made it clear she did not know what to do. Under the title 'Overseas students are valuable assets to social and cultural life of Britain' she explained:

So we face a twin problem: increasing pressure on our resources coupled with the indiscriminate nature of the tuition fee subsidy. What are we to do about the pressure? Control by quotas is unpopular with me as with the universities, the National Union of Students or anyone else. Control by the purse is no less unpopular again with me as much as with anyone else, for I see nothing of value in trying to price tuition out of reach of those who can least afford to pay for it. So what are we to do? It is well known, certainly to this audience, that I want to see a

Table 5.4 Home and overseas annual university fees (££), 1967–79

	Undergraduate		Postgraduate	
	home	overseas	home	overseas
from 1967	70	250	70	250
1975/6	140	320	140	320
1976/7	182	416	182	416
1977/8	500	650	750	850
1978/9	545	705	850	925
1979/80	595	940	890	1,230

Source: R. Bristow 1979 *Overseas students and government policy, 1962–1979*, n.p.: 18.

more rational system, I want to see the £100 million tuition fees used positively to help selected groups of overseas students, in place of the present indiscriminate system, if system is the right word to apply to the present practice.[102]

Resolution of her problems was to await the election five months later, and her replacement by a Conservative minister.

University philosophies, of holding open university doors and welcoming the ablest students regardless of nationality, did not sit easily with developing immigration policies or with the various attempts to restrain overseas student numbers. They may have been doomed for that very reason. The arguments were to be re-echoed in the new debates about student fees in 1979.

Policy and practice, in the 35 years after the war, were driven by demand and by a broad internationalist consensus. The demand flowed along well-established channels, with a steady proportion of students from the Indian subcontinent and from North America, and along newly important channels. Oil wealth and the pursuit of economic development brought students greatly increased numbers of students from Africa and Asia. That pursuit helped the numbers in science and technology to rise at the expense of those in the humanities.

Universities and government departments spoke the language of internationalism. The Foreign Office continued to value students as potential friends of Britain. The Commonwealth was still politically important with many Commonwealth files crossing the prime minister's desk – 20 per cent of the total in 1965, more than any other category – while universities themselves talked of Commonwealth cohesion.[103] Students from the Commonwealth continued to dominate the numbers and did so even as the wind of change blew through Africa and beyond and brought the colonial empire to its rapid end. Universities and colleges tailored courses to the needs of overseas students and, more slowly, worked out better ways of supporting postgraduates. They paid increased attention to student welfare. The language of internationalism was always tinged by the accents of the cold war: the Commonwealth was a potential bulwark against communism, overseas student programmes were seen as competing with those from the east, while communism among colonial students became the same bugbear as subversive nationalism had been among their Indian predecessors.

There were, however, growing tensions between internationalist principles and domestic economics and politics. While the Foreign and Commonwealth Offices echoed vice-chancellors in welcoming overseas students, the Department for Education and Science had to foot the bill and to ensure that overseas students did not overload the system or jeopardise places for home students. Governments were never satisfied with the outcome of their various attempts to balance the needs and costs of home and overseas students by means of fees and quotas. Along with these tensions, there were incipient ones, too, with domestic policies of immigration. The 1960s had proved to be a decade not of growing permissiveness but of increasing control for individuals hoping to travel to Britain to work and study.

Other changes were for the future. Just as the end of empire changed the pattern of Britain's international relations without immediately changing the flow of students, so British accession to the Common Market in 1973 was slow in its effects. European numbers in British universities, which have repeatedly risen and fallen, were to wait before increasing, well after British accession.

6
Into the Market Place, 1979–2010

The election of Margaret Thatcher in 1979 and Ronald Reagan in 1980 changed transatlantic assumptions about economics and politics, bringing a new respect for the market and new restrictions on government activity. The 1980s also brought to Latin America the worst recession since the 1930s and to Africa a decade in which the educational advances of the previous ten years went into reverse. But on a longer time scale all this was to be dwarfed by political transformations unthinkable at a time when the Soviet Union was entrenched as one partner in the cold war stasis, dictators were in power in much of Latin America, and apartheid South Africa glowered unrepentant in its laager. Two groups of foreign students symbolise the changed world that was to follow: in 1992 the first organised group of Russian students since Catharine the Great arrived in Britain, to be followed four years later by the first Commonwealth scholars from South Africa since 1961.[1] Policy towards students from abroad was shaped by these changes, by changes in British higher education and changes in international thinking about the purposes of higher education.

In 1979 British universities had 290,000 full-time students while another 76,000 were following degree-level courses in polytechnics. Overseas students made up 11 per cent of the university total with about half of these from the Commonwealth; only one in ten of the overseas total was from Europe. There were still some 28,000 students from overseas on lower-level courses despite the changes in immigration policy that had cut their numbers.

The new government brought new policies for higher education. Until 1979 universities benefited from a cross-party consensus that their numbers and budgets could expand, effectively unchecked, as increasing numbers of qualified school leavers demanded university and college places. In a break with this convention, in 1981 government announced cuts to universities' recurrent grants that varied from 6 to 44 per cent. The cuts were followed by cash limits, an instruction to become more efficient, a further reduction in real terms expenditure in the mid-1980s, and a reduction in target student numbers from the UGC. As a result university numbers faltered, rising by only 1,100, or 0.3 per cent, between 1981 and 1986. A government green paper in 1985 forecast that 'demand for full-time courses is likely to stay fairly constant or to increase up to 1990 and to fall after that by about 14 per cent by 1996'.[2] While university numbers were being held back, the polytechnics told a different story. They were funded on a different basis with unit costs that were, and were expected to be, lower than those for universities. Their full-time advanced students, on degree courses and their equivalent, had grown from 21,800 in 1965 to 87,300 in 1981. In the next five years, as university numbers were held back, they grew to 110,500, an increase of 27 per cent, and continued to rise, reaching 187,700 in 1991.[3]

Government policy then changed direction. The earlier predictions of flat student numbers now proved wrong: 'It all ended in tears, and was, amazingly replaced overnight by a policy with almost all the opposite emphases'.[4] A new white paper in 1987, new projections, and a new minister allowed the higher education system to respond to demand and university numbers again rose rapidly from the late 1980s to the mid-1990s. The same white paper argued that it was no longer appropriate for polytechnics to be 'controlled by individual local authorities' and that they should be given a measure of independence and funded through a polytechnics and colleges funding council.[5] Five years later, as they were exploring with the Department for Education just what their status meant and how it might develop, the secretary of state surprised them by announcing that they would all become universities. Within a year, 40 had adopted university titles and university numbers rose from 415,000 in 1992 to 845,000 in 1993.

University numbers then grew even more rapidly in the 1990s so that full-time students of the, now combined, higher education system exceeded 1.25 million by 2001. At the same time expenditure per student was steadily reduced. In 1987 government sounded almost triumphant, arguing that 'the productivity of higher education as a whole has increased greatly since 1979' with unit costs falling by 5 per cent in universities and 15 per cent in polytechnics.[6] Funding per student continued to decline and fell a further 35 per cent between 1989 and 1997, a policy to be described by the next government as amounting to 'decades of under investment'.[7] One observer's productivity improvements are another's funding crisis and by 1996 there was bipartisan support for a new enquiry into higher education and its funding: the Dearing committee was set up by a Conservative secretary of state in 1996 and reported to his Labour successor a year later. Its report looked ahead to further increases in numbers and recommended that 'over the long term, public spending on higher education should increase with the growth in Gross Domestic Product'.[8] Early in the new century, 43 per cent of the age group in England were entering higher education: government compared this with the 6 per cent who had gone to universities in the 1960s, announced that 'British universities are a great success story' and set a new target of a 50 per cent participation rate. To repair the funding gap universities were enabled to charge fees of up to £3,000 per course, which would be paid back by graduates through a student loan scheme.[9] Expansion continued and meant that by 2010 higher education had grown four-fold in 30 years with over 1.6 million students in institutions of higher education of whom 365,000, more than 20 per cent, were from overseas, with three out of ten of these from Europe.

University expansion responded both to demand and to changing perceptions of the value of higher education. In 1987, with 14 per cent of the age group in higher education, government thought it was acceptable to keep numbers steady, though also to 'study the needs of the economy so as to achieve the right number and balance of graduates'. In contrast, by 2003 no less than 'national economic imperatives' justified the new 50 per cent target for higher education.[10] This shift in thinking was part of a global phenomenon. By the beginning of the new century, economists were talking of education as a factor of production alongside land, labour and capital. The World Bank found a new interest in education and the development of human capital, arguing that education was a cornerstone of its work. International statistics illustrate the trend. In France, the proportion of the age group in tertiary education went from 40 per cent in 1990 to 56 per cent in 2007; Italy's figures went from 32 to 68 per cent. Figures for women rose faster than for men. Perhaps more remarkable, by 1990 India had reached the kind of ratio achieved by Britain in the 1960s. Figures for India then rose from 6 to 12 per cent, though with women still under-represented, and for China from 3 to 23 per cent. By 2010 China had over 31 million students in tertiary education and India over 20 million.

In 1979 overseas students felt the cold touch of austerity even sooner than university bursars.

The new government came into power with a pledge to cut public expenditure and a determination to do so quickly. Within two weeks of the election the chief secretary to the treasury had prepared a list of proposed cuts of £750–800 million only to be told by the prime minister that these were quite inadequate and a further £500 to £600 million should be cut. Ministers 'took note, with approval, of the summing up of their discussions by the Prime Minister' and were sent away with a fortnight to cut their budgets more severely.[11] As differential student fees had been in place for over ten years, and attempts to hold back overseas student numbers had failed, the Department for Education and Science saw the introduction of full-cost fees as an attractive way of cutting its expenditure. It expected a 'strong reaction from student and race relations bodies in this country, and heavy criticism from overseas' if fees were more than doubled, but this looked a better way of saving money than introducing fees for 16- to 19-year-olds, or halving school transport, or cutting expenditure on under-fives, all of which would also require legislation. The education secretary also needed to protect spending on schools in order to meet a commitment to maintain and improve standards.[12] By the late summer, and without consultation with the Foreign Office, the Overseas Development Administration – no longer a ministry but part of the Foreign Office – or universities, the decision had been taken to require overseas students to pay full-cost fees.[13] In October the cabinet concluded that it 'had already taken the most politically-sensitive decision on education, when it was agreed to tackle school meal charges and transport'.[14] Overseas student fees were not in the same sensitive class.

Changes to student fees were announced in two stages. A 22 per cent increase of fees for 1980/1 was formally announced in July 1979 followed in November by confirmation that full-cost fees would be charged from the following year. Both moves attracted criticism, from within government and without, and within a year two separate House of Commons select committees had set up enquiries into them. Within government, the Department for Education was warned in August that increased fees would cause problems for universities and in October that they were 'bitterly hostile to the policy of charging full cost fees and that "politically all hell will break out on the campuses" if the Government decided to go ahead'.[15] The Foreign and Commonwealth Office was concerned about the 'potentially damaging foreign policy implications of the decision' and regretted that they had been neither consulted nor alerted before the matter went to cabinet. (They could have noticed as the proposals were included in a document circulated before the cabinet decision but no one in the Foreign Office was 'deputed to read the details of other Departments' proposals'.[16]) The chief education adviser to the Overseas

Development Administration was put uncomfortably on the spot when he had to pretend to the foreign affairs committee that the department had prepared a paper on the policy's consequences.[17] A diplomatic colleague fared little better, and in ducking questions from the committee had to shelter behind the convention that MPs cannot ask officials of one department about the policy of a different one. Back in the office he recorded a comment by the chairman of the committee that his sheltering 'indicated that no work had been done in the FCO of a likely decision to raise fees before it was taken (which is of course true)'.[18]

The policy was even less popular outside government. Within a year Neil Kinnock could tell the House of Commons, from the Labour benches, that

> It is apparent that the policy has not a single friend. We hear nothing but continual criticisms – some extremely bitter and loud – of the Government's policy from the Royal Commonwealth Society and the British Council to the Association of Navigation Schools, from the Committee of Vice-Chancellors and Principals of the United Kingdom Universities and the Committee of Directors of Polytechnics to every university, polytechnic and college of higher or further education, every education trade union and every students' union. Disagreement with the Government's policy is not limited to those sources. We have also heard criticisms from Conservative students, just as we have heard them, in a courageous and direct form, from Conservative Back Benchers.[19]

More pithily the bishop of Oxford noticed that 'It is a comparatively rare issue that drives the House of Bishops and the National Union of Students, not to mention the principals and vice-chancellors, to make common cause'.[20] The House of Lords debated the issue twice, and the House of Commons once, and heard a set of arguments against the policy, deployed with particular strength in the House of Lords, well populated with past and present university chancellors and vice-chancellors.[21] They saw overseas students as potentially valuable friends and trading partners: Lord Alport cited the example of the vice-chancellor of Peking Technological University who had trained at City and Guilds, possibly outshone by Lord Hatch who remembered Julius Nyerere at Edinburgh and Lord Boyle who had met Tom Mboya in Kenya and heard about his time at Ruskin. Moving from influence to trade, Keith Hampson explained in the House of Commons, and from the government benches, that he had been urging Chinese businessmen in Hong Kong to buy British goods and argued that:

There is a direct and specific gain to this country in having Hong Kong students here. ... The bulk of students coming to Britain from Hong Kong for higher education go into engineering. They do not go back to Government service or white collar jobs, as is so often the case in this country. They go into industry and commerce and, therefore, have a direct impact on investment. In our own interests, it is important that the Chinese leaders in that colony have a British bias when they come to decide on investment and purchasing.[22]

For their part, universities saw the increased fees as a threat to their international character, a point tacitly accepted by government, and to student numbers. It was assumed that increased fees would deter students and so jeopardise the existence of some specialised courses and damage research. The policy was also seen as threatening university contributions to international development. In defending it the overseas development minister, Baroness Young, reminded the House of Lords that despite the 'hard reality [which] must also intervene' Britain was bringing in some 15,000 students under various aid schemes.[23]

Cold-war arguments were also brought forward. In their first debate the Lords heard how the Bishop of St Albans [Robert Runcie] had met large numbers of Commonwealth students in Belgrade, Sofia, Bucharest and Moscow where they found themselves 'among proponents of Marxist-Leninist Communism, with an avowed aim to convert the world to their way of thinking and acting'.[24] When they came back to the question in their second debate Lord Gladwyn warned that if priced out of Britain 'the bright boys of the future will have been trained in Moscow or in East Berlin, if not, of course, by our main competitors'.[25] Kinnock claimed in the Commons that 'while the Prime Minister is rattling her sword against the Red menace that allegedly threatens us in every continent, the Secretary of State for Education is acting as the registrar for the Patrice Lumumba university in Moscow'.[26] Christopher Price, a moderate Labour MP, referred to 'the menace of the Russians in the Indian Ocean' and warned that the majority of Mauritian students, who had previously come to Britain, would 'now be trained in the Soviet Union. ... no decision could have been more effective in promoting the Soviet cause in the Indian ocean than this decision on overseas students' fees'.[27]

Only two noble allies came out to support the government. Noel Annan, vice-chancellor of the University of London, had been almost alone in backing Crosland's introduction of differential fees in 1967. He was now joined by John Vaizey, a maverick and a pioneer of the economics of education, who had left the Labour Party out of admiration for Thatcher and her policies, and never minded upsetting fellow academics. He – correctly as it turned out – explained to the peers that 'the most extraordinary thing is that every time the fees have been raised the number of students has increased. I can only conclude that higher education is what economists call the superior good: as the price rises so does the demand, rather as it does for old masters'.[28] Annan had no objection in principle to differential fees or to quotas at undergraduate level, and accepted government's need to cut expenditure. But while offering a measure of support to the embattled government position, he was deeply concerned about the combined effect of reductions in university grants and of full-cost fees on institutions like the London School of Hygiene and Tropical Medicine, the Royal Postgraduate Medical School and the School of Oriental and African Studies, and warned that the university was in a disastrous plight which might force it to close the three schools.[29]

For their part, universities saw any governmental attempt to control their fees as a threat to their autonomy, though this was in practice overcome by passing recommendations, which were not directions, through the University Grants Committee. (They went through the consortium of local authority associations to advise polytechnics and colleges.) A separate issue of principle was that any reduction in the flow of overseas students could weaken membership of the international university community.[30] But universities were worried by practicality as well as principle and, ignoring Vaizey's advice that higher fees would increase demand, assumed that their income could fall dramatically away. Some, including the rector of Imperial College and the vice-chancellor of Essex University also feared that universities were as a result already recruiting students, from the United States and elsewhere, who were not up to academic standard.[31]

Attacks on the policy continued, from home and abroad, though with little immediate concession from government. Within Britain, the Overseas Students Trust, set up in 1961 to support their interests, launched a series of policy enquiries and deployed arguments that concentrated on the economic benefits that overseas students brought to Britain.[32] Meanwhile the Commonwealth Secretary General picked up the old imperial argument about Commonwealth cohesion and warned that full-cost fees for Commonwealth students would weaken the Commonwealth as an institution. He duly established an international standing committee on student mobility which met seven times between 1982 and 1992 and steadily but unsuccessfully sought concessions from government; the title of its seventh report, *Favourable fees for Commonwealth students: The final frustration*, is both an epitaph and a summary.

In its formal statements the government was unmoved. A concession for Commonwealth students would have imperilled the whole policy as they made up some 55 per cent of the overseas total. It was, however, quickly agreed that full-cost fees would not apply to students from other countries within the European Economic Community. The Treasury originally thought that mainland Europe counted as overseas and that heavy criticism could be expected 'especially from the EEC, differential fees being contrary to agreed EEC policy'.[33] While this was policy, the legal position was still unclear in June 1980 when there was no directive yet in force on the subject.[34] But a series of pragmatic arguments helped Britain come into line with its European partners. A concession to mainland Europe would not be expensive: it was estimated at only £5 million against total expected savings of £100 million. Day-to-day politics reinforced the argument: Mark Carlisle, the education secretary, told Peter Carrington at the Foreign Office that the German ambassador had warned him the issue might be raised at an EEC summit and 'implied in the nicest way that this was rather a test of whether we were "good" Europeans!!'[35] The Foreign Office supported the European policy but would have preferred no concessions to be announced ahead of a formal community resolution as this would help it disarm criticism.[36] The education secretary was able to justify the European exception to the Commons:

> The reasons are simple and threefold: first, we are demonstrating our acceptance of the principle of student mobility within the EEC. Secondly, a draft resolution has already been tabled which will require individual countries to agree to similar fees being charged throughout Europe. Thirdly, ... we are operating on a reciprocal basis with Europe. It is the one area of the world that has more of our students than we have of theirs.[37]

And that for the time being was the limit to the concessions, despite the hard cases of the students from Hong Kong and the English-speaking Caribbean who would have to pay differential fees while the European exemption applied to those – all seven of them – from the overseas French territories of Martinique, Guadeloupe and Réunion.[38] Malaysia, with 5,000 students in Britain was sufficiently angered by the new policy, and by unrelated changes in stock market rules, to introduce a 'buy British last' policy which almost halved the number of new Malaysian enrolments.[39] The president of Nigeria made his case to the prime minister while visiting Britain in March 1981 but got no more than an assurance that Britain would 'have another look at the issue'.[40] Mrs Thatcher's unpopularity among universities led to a well-publicised decision by Oxford not to offer her an honorary degree.

Universities adjusted to the new regime. In 1967 when differential fees were introduced, some universities had initially refused to implement them. They could not afford to do so this time. Oxford feared that full-cost fees would reduce its overseas students by 40 per cent and by 1981, in order to maintain its income, had agreed to increase fees above the minimum laid down by government. Cambridge did the same. Initial figures confirmed the universities' cause for alarm at the prospect of losing students and the income from their fees: by February 1981 overseas undergraduate figures were down by 12 per cent and postgraduate by 11 per cent.[41] The fall continued so that by 1982 university overseas numbers had dropped from 31,500 to 26,900, reversing a trend that had continued since the war. While other universities were protesting, the London School of Economics, which appropriately enough understood the economics, reacted differently: in February 1980 the *Guardian* reported 'High pressure "salesman" aims to recruit students' as its dean of graduate studies set off to America on a recruitment drive. Salesmanship did the trick and LSE announced three months later that it had signed up an extra 200 to 300 students and, by the end of 1981, that its overseas numbers were up by more than a half, making up 40 per cent of student numbers.[42]

Other universities quickly followed LSE in recognising the benefits of expanding overseas student numbers. Under the new policy it brought them an income from fees that were outside the control or restrictions of government and the University Grants Committee. Active recruitment became a priority. By 1983 numbers were again rising and a year later had regained and gone beyond all the lost ground. Overseas numbers then rose more rapidly in the late 1980s to reach nearly 61,000 in 1991, an increase of more than a quarter in five years (see Figure 6.1). While overseas polytechnic numbers were always lower then those for universities, by 1991 another 24,600 were on advanced polytechnic courses.

The controversy about their fees brought overseas students new public attention and, a rare event, a formal statement of government policy towards them. The two main political parties had both seen the earlier policy, of charging fees at below full cost, as a blunt instrument, benefiting

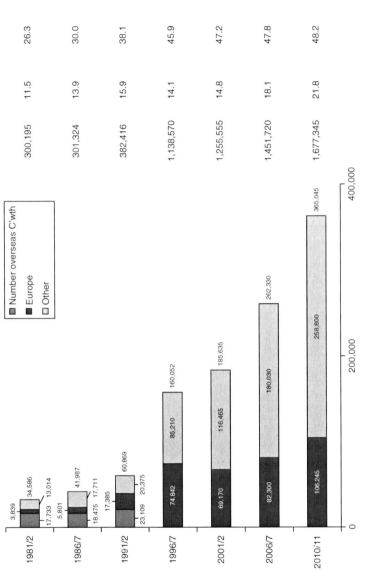

Figure 6.1 Home and overseas full-time university enrolments, 1981–2010

Sources: 1981–91: *UGC University statistics*; 1996–2010: *HESA statistics.*

the affluent and mediocre as well as the brilliant and poor. Both parties wanted to target finance towards those who merited it, although they may have differed on the definition of merit. Government initially gave a lukewarm response to a report from the Overseas Students Trust which set out a case for easing the policy but in February 1983 described it as 'a comprehensive and constructive contribution'. Meanwhile there had been moves within Whitehall to find a way of moderating the policy. With its continuing doubts about the policy, the Foreign Office compiled a list of 18 countries where there was a case for concessions. (As they included India, Pakistan, Bangladesh and Egypt concessions could have reached countries with one in five of the world's population.) Countering Soviet intentions was important in India, Pakistan, Nepal and Jordan while special cases included Cyprus, Hong Kong and Malaysia.[43] It could quote ambassadors and high commissioners to justify its affection for overseas students. They included the high commissioner in Lagos who argued that 'our predominant hold on the commercial life of this country has rested on our ability to influence the hearts and minds of successive generations of Nigerians' through its influence on Nigerian education and 'the despatch of promising students to complete their education in the United Kingdom'.[44]

Meetings between civil servants narrowed down the list of deserving countries to Cyprus, Hong Kong and Malaysia. Cyprus had British military bases and, on a visit to Britain, the president of the Cypriot House of Representatives had warned that 'all the eastern block countries were offering a generous number of scholarships and a growing number of their young people were being educated in those countries'.[45] Hong Kong, as a dependency, felt it had been badly treated and quoted the French overseas departments as its point of comparison. Malaysia had been both vociferous and effective in its pleas for special treatment. It was the only sending country for which Britain was the principal host and 'Most of the Rulers and a high proportion of professionals and officials have been educated here'.[46] Both Hong Kong and Malaysia were willing to explore the joint funding of some students.

There was now a rapprochement between Downing Street and the Foreign Office which was willing to release funds from its budget rather than that of the Education Department. In February 1983 the foreign secretary, Francis Pym, announced that it was 'in the national interest, both in the short term and in the longer term, to provide more help to enable overseas students to come to this country for their further and higher education'. Without suggesting that the original policy had been misconceived, he softened its effects at a cost of £46 million over three years. The money was to be split six ways. First, there were to be more funds for Hong Kong, with the costs shared between government and the colony. Then the Commonwealth Scholarship and Fellowship Plan would get some more. Alongside it a new scholarship programme, later named Chevening awards after the foreign secretary's country house, was introduced with 'the object of attracting students who will not only benefit themselves but whose study and experience here will be of advantage to this country'. (Ambassadors were to enjoy these as it gave them modest opportunities for patronage.) Fourth, Cyprus and Malaysia would get some help. Fifth, technical training was not forgotten as the Overseas Development Administration's technical cooperation and training programme was to be expanded. Nor were the rich forgotten: the sixth beneficiary was the British Council with extra funding to recruit more students who could pay their own fees.

Pym's speech got a relatively warm response, with particular support for the expenditure on Cyprus and Hong Kong. The opposition raised questions about the extent to which any of this was new money and one Labour MP criticised the total as 'niggardly'. There was a begrudging reference to European students who paid home fees while two MPs waved warning red flags at the danger, which the funds might help avert, of Cypriots going to Moscow for their training accompanied by potential lawyers from the middle east and the Commonwealth.[47] In one immediate welcome for this 'Pym package': the Malaysian prime minister announced he would visit Britain and might relax the 'buy Britain last' campaign.[48] Malaysian student numbers began to rise again in 1984. Pym took the opportunity to outline government policy on overseas students which was elaborated two years later by Tim Renton, a junior minister in the Foreign Office.[49]

Renton emphasised three points already made by his senior: that government 'accepted the need for a consistent and intelligible policy towards overseas students', that generally they should pay the full cost of their education, and that the main way of implementing policy would be through 'support targeted [sic] at particular groups of students in the national interest and in the interest of the students themselves'. In his fuller elaboration Renton took as his starting point the main foreign-policy aims of maintaining security, promoting national prosperity and supporting 'international arrangements for the orderly and peaceful conduct of trade and relations between states'. Within that context he set out in order his arguments for welcoming overseas students. The value of 'international scholarly exchange' came first, with a recognition that the presence of overseas students benefited British universities and that 'Britain has much to offer students from many overseas countries'. There was also 'a moral obligation to help the Third World countries'. Next he cited economic and commercial benefits, flowing from students' expenditure while in Britain and their buying British after returning home. He then talked about the political benefits of making long-term friends, with a reminder of the 'great efforts that the Soviet Union and Eastern bloc countries make to attract Third World students'. With hindsight his examples of long-term friends, Mugabe, Banda and Buhari, might have been chosen more carefully. He described this as a focused policy, consistent with full-cost fees, and an advance on the earlier practice of heavily subsidising students 'in a haphazard and indiscriminate way'.[50]

The debate about fees, the Overseas Students Trust report, and the statements by Pym and Renton mean that in the early 1980s university and government policy was clear, explicit and documented. As its policy was framed in terms of government expenditure, the Foreign Office had little to say about overseas students who were paying their own way. At the same time it tacitly reaffirmed its faith in scholarships as a tool of soft diplomacy through its Chevening scholarships, designed not to attract the poorest, or the ablest, or to reinforce the Commonwealth but to seek long-term national benefits or influence. It had little to say in response to allegations that the changed policies would bring fewer students from poor countries and more from rich. Government still wanted to control the number of home students going into universities, as most of their costs fell on public funds, but accepted that if universities were to recoup all the costs of students from abroad, then there need be no restrictions on the numbers they recruited, especially at postgraduate level. Overseas student numbers could be left to the institutions and to the market.

The policy remained in place, without any public restatement, for the remaining decade and a half of conservative governments. While they developed, announced and published policies on immigration and on higher education there was no further statement on the international role of higher education. 'While some other governments have produced documents expressing their view that [higher education] is an opportunity to "internationalize" the student population...the British government has never seen the need'.[51]

Government's views on the purposes of higher education and on university priorities came to bear on policy towards overseas students. The universities' first job was to produce an educated workforce. They were also now expected to compete and to demonstrate that their staff's entrepreneurship was as brilliant as their scholarship.[52] Economic arguments, and respect for the market, came with new boldness into the literature. Thus, while the education white papers of the 1980s and 1990s made at most passing reference to international market opportunities, by 1996 the higher education funding council was referring with pride to the winning of overseas research contracts worth £200 million.[53] Universities made their point through their recruitment policies, while private interest groups like the Association of Recognised English Language Schools argued that education was a valuable export business. The Dearing report, having looked at the direct economic benefits of higher education went on to argue:

> The other increasingly important economic contribution of higher education is as a generator of foreign exchange earnings. The UK remains one of the most popular destinations for overseas students, who bring with them, not just the fees they pay to higher education institutions in this country, but more general spending power used in the UK economy. Recent estimates suggest such spending exceeds £1 billion. There are also unquantifiable economic and other benefits for the UK in having people in positions of influence throughout the world who have a knowledge of, and links with, the UK. Such people are likely to look naturally to the UK as a potential trading partner or for investment opportunities.[54]

Despite Renton's placing of academic internationalism at the top of his list, economic arguments about the values of overseas students were taking pride of place by the 1990s.

While policy was being nudged towards the market, it was now shaped more by university practice than by government decision. The policy of charging full-cost fees, and the response to this by universities, turned out to have three unintended consequences. First, with a strong financial incentive, universities recruited increasing numbers of international students so that their proportion of the total began to rise. Second, the number and proportion of students from Europe, who paid only home-student fees, steadily increased while the terms of this intellectual trade changed. By the early 1990s Britain was receiving 32,000 European students but sending abroad less than 6,000 of its own.[55] Third, as they responded to market forces, and to demand for second as well as first degrees, universities increased the number and variety of master's courses designed to appeal to overseas students. Taught courses rather than research degrees came to dominate the overseas postgraduate community: in the early 1970s postgraduates were evenly divided between those on taught courses and those doing research degrees; by 1991 58 per cent were on taught courses, a figure that rose to 71 per cent ten years later.[56]

Universities put in place more vigorous policies to recruit overseas students. They created international development offices, followed LSE's lead in going out to recruit students, and paid new attention to student welfare. The British Council introduced an education counselling service to support them, with pilot projects in Hong Kong, Malaysia and Singapore. The service was set up in 1984, with 72 subscribing institutions; by 1998 it had 146 from higher education together with another 140 from other sectors of education.[57] In an international review the OECD found that within Europe, 'the United Kingdom was the first to take an explicit export and trade perspective on higher education, with clear objectives regarding the recruitment of fee-paying students'; by 2003 80 per cent of British institutions of higher education had 'targeted marketing strategies to recruit foreign students' as compared with a European average of 30 per cent.[58]

As they developed their strategies universities were successful in recruiting more students, helped by the recovering economies of the 1990s. After the initial fall in overseas numbers, by 1986 they had increased by almost a quarter in five years. There was then a dramatic increase in numbers in the early 1990s, bringing the total up to 160,000 in 1996, and then with a more moderate growth rate to nearly 186,000 in 2001. Along with these changes, the 1980s and 1990s saw changes in the numbers in polytechnics, and their successor institutions, and in the background of overseas students.

Numbers in the polytechnics and colleges recovered more slowly from the changed policy on fees and, following a decline, rose above their 1981 level only in 1989. As university numbers were held back, polytechnics could fill their places with national students, and there was less impetus to recruit overseas. The slow recovery may also have been a response to full-cost fees; once these had to be paid it was worth paying for university prestige (see Table 6.1). Overseas students in polytechnics were mainly on niche courses, developed because of existing specialisms and links: the city of Sheffield, for example, had a link with the Chinese steel town of Anshan which helped the polytechnic, later Sheffield Hallam University, to build up cooperation in metallurgy with China, and bring in students from there.[59] Programmes of this kind tended to be on a modest scale so that in 1992, as polytechnics changed their status, their full-time

Table 6.1   Categories of full-time overseas students, 1981–2010

Year	University under-graduate total	per cent of under-graduate total	post-graduate total	per cent of post-graduate total	total	Polytechnic and technical college advanced courses
1981/2	18,412	7	16,174	34	34,586	18,924
1986/7	20,519	8	21,468	39	41,987	14,466
1991/2	33,097	9	27,772	39	60,869	24,605
1996/7	110,877	11	49,175	35	160,052	
2001/2	105,625	10	80,010	43	185,635	
2006/7	137,105	11	125,225	52	262,330	
2010/11	187,225	14	177,820	57	365,045	

Sources: Universities – 1981–91: *UGC University statistics*; 1996–2010: *HESA statistics*; Polytechnics and colleges – 1981–6: *British Council statistics*; 1991: *Education statistics for UK 1993*.

overseas students made up less than 6 per cent of the total. After 1992, the former polytechnics were funded on the same basis as other universities: with their new freedom came a need to find a distinctive place in the university landscape. Many now saw the benefit of increasing their international numbers and launched successful recruitment programmes.

Universities continued to argue, as they had for decades, that overseas study was more appropriate at graduate than at undergraduate level. But they did so with little effect, and muted conviction where the financial benefit of recruiting undergraduates sat awkwardly with educational policy. Over 30 years there were always more overseas undergraduates than postgraduates and undergraduate numbers went from 6 to 14 per cent of the national total. Postgraduates were more important in proportionate terms. Overseas students made up 33 per cent of the postgraduate total in 1981 which rose to 57 per cent in 2010. British postgraduates were now in a minority.

Towards the end of the twentieth century Europe once again became a major source of overseas students, as it had been in the Middle Ages and during the Second World War. The process was driven by demand more than by university policy as, after 1979, universities' recruitment policies were directed most strongly towards full-fee students from outside Europe. Despite this, and in response to European demand, students from the European Community, and later European Union, went from 11 per cent of the overseas total in 1981 to a peak of 47 per cent in 1996 before falling away to 29 per cent in 2010. Greece continued to send large numbers of students but by the late 1980s Germany had joined the group of countries sending the largest numbers, to be followed by France. Alongside these

Table 6.2   Erasmus students, 1987–2010

	Outward	Inward
1987/8	930	1,080
1991/2	6,130	9,060
1997/8	10,582	20,770
2001/2	8,475	17,619
2006/7	7,235	16,508
2010/11	8,577	17,504

Sources: DFE *Education statistics* 1993 for 1987/8 and 1996 for 1991/2; EC – Directorate General for Education and Culture 2000 *Survey into the socio-economic background of Erasmus students*, Brussels for 1997/8; ec.europa.eu/education/erasmus/statistics_en.htm from 2001.

students the Erasmus programme, set up in 1987, began bringing students into Britain, generally for periods of between three months and a year (see Chapter 9). Only 1,000 students travelled to Britain in the first year but by 2010 Erasmus brought over 24,000. (Their figures, shown in Table 6.2, are additional to those in Figure 6.1.) The programme was always more popular in continental Europe than in Britain so that Britain consistently received about twice as many students as it sent abroad.

Most Erasmus students were from a fairly prosperous background. Whereas many earlier foreign students had travelled in order to get a valuable qualification, this was less important for the Erasmus group where surveys showed that improving their knowledge of a foreign language and simply living in a foreign country were markedly more important.[60] A Polish student summed up his experience in London:

> I believe that the Socrates Erasmus students exchange programme is an excellent possibility for every learner who wants to discover new academic environments, broaden the knowledge of different nationalities and improve the standard of a foreign language. I assume that I succeeded in all these fields...I am especially proud of the huge progress in my level of English (particularly spoken English) and making friends with people all over the world.[61]

As the proportion of European students rose, so the Commonwealth proportion fell. In 1981, students from the Commonwealth made up half of the overseas total, but by 1991 they had fallen to 38 per cent; after this date, in a recognition of political realities, statistics seldom use Commonwealth students as a category but the figures suggest they had dropped to 28 per cent by 2004.[62] The figures also reflect the end of the informal empire so that Egypt, Iraq and Iran no longer appeared among the top eight sending countries (see Table 6.3).

Asia now came to dominate the figures, with the most dramatic changes coming from China. In 1981 only 163 students from China came to Britain, although there were 3,600 from Hong Kong. By 2001 there were nearly 21,000 Chinese students, a figure that had more than tripled by 2010 when China headed the list of sending countries. Despite the fall in the proportion of Commonwealth students, south Asia continued to send large numbers of students as they had earlier in the twentieth century Taking the figures for all students in higher education, India, Pakistan and Bangladesh taken together were the third largest source of students in 2001.[63] Numbers from south-east Asia were consistently high with Malaysia remaining among the five largest sending countries from 1971 to 2001.

The proportion of women students rose. In 1981 they made up just over a quarter of overseas full-time university students: by 2006 the proportion had risen to 48 per cent. The latter total conceals significant differences, with women forming more than half of the total from Europe, North America, Australasia and, by a small margin, South America. Men were most over-represented among students from the middle east (70 per cent) followed by Africa (60 per cent) and Asia (54 per cent). These proportions also varied with the level of the course being studied so that women made up 45 per cent of overseas postgraduates but slightly over 50 per cent of undergraduates; for students from the other countries of the European Union the figures are 53 per cent and just below 50 per cent. Women often took up more than half of all Erasmus places. The figures suggest that constraints on studying abroad were now no greater for women than for men, provided the female students came from the industrialised north.

In terms of discipline, over these same 30 years, there was a decline in the proportion of students in engineering and technology, matching the collapse of British industry, and a slight fall in the sciences. Proportions in medical sciences stayed fairly steady. Numbers increased most rapidly in business studies (see Table 6.4). This proved to be even more popular outside Europe than within so that, by 2006, almost a third of post-graduate students from outside Europe were on business studies courses, twice the proportion from the European Union.

While Oxford, Cambridge and London continued to attract large numbers of overseas students, the expansion of other universities and colleges, and their careful international marketing, meant that increasing numbers went to other universities. By 2006 Oxford and Cambridge took just over 4 per cent of overseas students and London 11 per cent,

Table 6.3 Top eight sending countries – universities, 1981–2010

	1981/2		1986/7		1991/2		1996/7		2001/2		2006/7		2010/11	
	Country	No.	Country	No.	Country	No.	Country	No.	Country	No.	Country	No.	Country	No.
	Malaysia	5,077	Hong Kong	4,579	Malaysia	4,759	Greece	21,737	Greece	28,585	China	49,595	China	67,325
	Hong Kong	3,576	USA	4,187	USA	4,353	Malaysia	18,015	China	20,710	India	23,835	India	39,090
	USA	2,352	Malaysia	3,669	Hong Kong	4,307	Ireland	15,572	Ireland	13,235	Ireland	16,255	Nigeria	17,585
	Nigeria	2,041	Greece	1,643	Greece	3,854	Germany	12,582	Germany	10,960	Greece	16,050	Ireland	16,855
	Greece	1,551	Singapore	1,591	Germany	4,021	France	12,101	Malaysia	10,680	USA	15,955	Germany	16,265
	Iraq	1,270	Nigeria	1,489	France	2,613	USA	9,448	USA	9,985	Germany	14,010	Malaysia	13,900
	Iran	1,126	W Germany	1,363	Singapore	2,574	Hong Kong	7,767	France	9,940	France	13,070	France	13,325
	Singapore	877	Norway	1,101	Japan	1,522	Spain	6,945	Hong Kong	8,870	Malaysia	11,810	Greece	11,630

Note: Figures are for full-time GB students to 1991, then for all UK students

Sources: *UGC/DES University statistics to 1991; HESA statistics from1996; HESA press release for 2006, 2010.*

Table 6.4 Overseas full-time university students' choice of degree subjects, 1981–2010

	Percentages						
	1981/2	1986/7	1991/2	1996/7	2001/2	2006/7	2010/11
Humanities	10	13	12	19	15	15	20
Education	6	4	3	3	2	2	2
Social studies	23	28	19	8	14	14	9
Business			10	17	20	27	29
Science	19	18	15	13	16	17	16
Technologies	28	23	20	20	17	16	16
Agriculture, forestry, vet	2	2	2	1	1	1	1
Medical and health	9	7	7	7	8	7	7
Other	3	3	12	11	7	1	–
Total	100	100	100	100	100	100	100

Sources: Statistical bulletin 9/83 (1981), 11/89 (1986) 21/93 (1991); *HESA statistics* (from 1996).

down from 20 per cent and 22 per cent in the 1920s. Edinburgh, which was receiving over 10 per cent of all overseas students 85 years before, was down to less than 2 per cent of the total. Overseas postgraduates, however, had become even more important for these universities, making up 58 per cent of the postgraduate total at Oxford, 55 per cent at Cambridge and 45 per cent at Edinburgh.[64]

British schools and language schools continued to recruit internationally. After the rapid growth in overseas numbers in the 1970s described in Chapter 5, the numbers in independent schools stabilised at around 14,000 in the 1980s but then rose again to reach a new plateau of around 20,000 to 24,000 in the new century (see Figure 6.2). The proportion of overseas students, which had risen to exceed 3 per cent in the 1970s, rose and remained above 4 per cent from the 1990s. The overall figures conceal marked differences: it was reported that at the high status girls' school 'Half of Roedean's intake comes from outside Britain. It requires pupils to learn Mandarin, to help Chinese newcomers feel welcome'.[65] The geography of these enrolments changed. Numbers from Africa and America declined, with American enrolments in 2007 less than half their level in 1981. Between a quarter and a third of the students came from Europe in the 1990s and 2000s and there were changes within Europe so that by 2010 Germany had become he largest provider of European

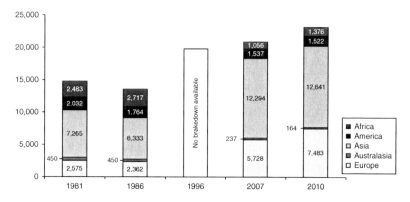

Figure 6.2   Overseas pupils in independent schools, 1981–2010

Source: Independent Schools Council *Annual censusNote:* proportions for 1996 are for new entrants, not total.

students with Russia in second place. As with universities, Asian students came to dominate the figures. There was a fall in the number of students from Iran with the change of regime, from 1,050 to 450 between 1982 and 1983. Despite that reduction, total figures for Asia almost doubled between the mid-1980s and mid-2000s. Hong Kong had a long tradition of sending school children to Britain: in 1980 there were reported to be 4,000 primary and 4,000 secondary school pupils from Hong Kong at British schools, though a proportion of these must have been from expatriate families. China then joined Hong Kong in sending increasing numbers of students. By 2010, with 8,500 students, students from Hong Kong, China and Taiwan made up 37 per cent of the total.[66]

Over the long run, the schools show similar trends to those of universities. The imperial and quasi-imperial links that brought school children to Britain fell away so that, in schools as in universities, the developing economies of southeast and east Asia came to drive student numbers. Schools, again like universities, moved closer to continental Europe while a remarkable recent change meant that 'Britain is also a great magnet for Russia's elite, who like to buy expensive properties in London and to send their children to smart private schools'.[67]

Language schools also prospered. Here, numbers are more difficult to interpret as they come from an organisation, English UK, which represents many but not all of the schools. Statistics before 1997 are meagre as they were jealously guarded by English UK's predecessor organisation. In terms of total students, numbers had reached 205,000 by 1997, then fell to 156,000 in 2001 but rose again, reaching 267,000 in 2006 and 381,000 in 2010. Most of these students were in Britain for a short time, with an average of just over six weeks for adults and three weeks or less for children. In 1997 students from Europe made up over 60 per cent of the study-weeks, a figure that fell slightly to 50 per cent. Italy generally provided the largest number of students. Between a fifth and a third of the total came from east Asia where in 1997 Japan was the largest source of students, later to be overtaken by South Korea.[68] By the present century language schools were seen as being of economic importance as part of Britain's educational exports. With various cautions about the uncertainty of the figures, their fee income was estimated at £689m in 2002/3 which had risen to £880m in 2008/9, by which time language students were estimated to be spending over £1 billion to meet their living and other costs.[69]

Beyond a concern to restrict expenditure, the Conservative governments of the 1990s seemed generally content to let overseas student policy drift. They were mildly sympathetic to Europe and, in response to a European memorandum of 1992 'the Department of Education intoned that "the UK Government's aim is to embed the European dimension in the daily practice of all higher education institutions" without being very specific about the means'.[70] More surprisingly Britain took the lead with France, German and Italy in signing the Sorbonne declaration in 1998 which was intended to lead to increased harmonisation of degree structures. But while government felt no need to revise the Renton statement of 1985, it continued to develop its policy on the minority of students which it was itself funding. In 1989 it set out its priorities for these in subtly different terms from those used by Renton four years before. Where he had put 'international scholarly exchange' first, the specific aims of policy were now, in order, to:

– win influential friends overseas by enabling future leaders, decision makers and opinion formers from all walks of life to study in the UK;
– help the development of manpower skills and resources in developing countries;
– promote the security and prosperity of the UK by cultivating good political and commercial relations with other countries.[71]

The implosion of the Soviet bloc meant that the Foreign Office could now be relaxed about competition for students from the east.

Other political changes brought the Foreign Office new friends to influence: in 1987, as apartheid was fracturing, a British Undergraduate

Fellowships Scheme was set up to bring disadvantaged black South Africans to an A level bridging course and to British universities and polytechnics. In the same year a Sino-British Friendship Scholarship Scheme was established with funds from Britain, China and Hong Kong to support China's civil modernisation programme. By 1995 government was funding 450 Chinese students on scholarships and nearly 200 through the Overseas Development Administration.[72] These new schemes existed alongside the Foreign Office's own Chevening awards, prized by its mandarins:

> Chevening is highly regarded by many within the FCO, and especially by Heads of Mission. Heads of Mission have an unparalleled overview of what is effective in their country, are frequently directly involved in promoting scholarships to a wide variety of audiences, and are likely to be in contact with the most successful Chevening alumni. Some Heads of Mission describe Chevening as the Post's *most* important activity, and the majority compete fiercely for access to scholarships resources. They argue that scholarships are helping the UK build a powerful network of long-term friends, and that this is having a tangible impact on UK interests.[73]

Given that high regard, Chevening awards remained in place, and continued to be funded, even as other schemes fell away.

Overseas development policy moved in a different direction when in 1993 the Overseas Development Administration closed its technical cooperation and training programme which, in the later 1980s, had brought more than half of all the government-supported overseas students to Britain – 12,000 out of 22,750 in 1988/89 – at a cost of £72 million out of £111 million.[74] Unusually, economy was not the motive. At this time the Overseas Development Administration was moving away from financing individual projects towards funding national programmes in agreement with overseas governments. As decisions were decentralised, so developing countries were told that, if they wanted to fund training in Britain, they should meet the costs from their general allocation of funding. British universities and colleges could no longer tap the Overseas Development Administration to finance a course designed to meet overseas needs. These were now provided only where a university was convinced of the existence of a market. A side effect of the decision was to make expenditure on the other scholarship schemes more obvious. In 1996, when the development budget was being cut, the Commonwealth Scholarship annual budget of £13.9m looked more exposed than when it was a small fraction of total scholarship funding, and was cut as part of a reduction in overseas aid.[75]

Britain continued to train overseas cadets at Sandhurst, some 4,230 of them between 1947 and 2010. Its alumni included six heads of state, with four from the middle east, the sultan of Brunei and the grand duke of Luxembourg.[76] It recruited overseas cadets within the defence engagement strategy defined as 'the means by which we use our defence assets and activities short of combat operations to achieve influence' in the interest of British prosperity, influence and security.[77] By the twenty-first century Sandhurst had only about 70 spare places a year, half the number available in the 1950s, and they went to a changed group of countries. The Commonwealth declined in importance with Commonwealth cadets forming over half of the total from 1947 but only a third in the ten years from 2003. With the exception of Nigeria, which steadily sent cadets, the Commonwealth cadets increasingly came from small states: Jamaica, Brunei, Belize and Singapore head the recent Commonwealth list. India sent its last cadet to Sandhurst in 1955 although Bangladesh and Pakistan continued to send small numbers. With the Gurkha connection Nepal remained in the list. There were, unsurprisingly, few women, less than 2 per cent of the total, with the largest contingents from Brunei and Jamaica where they made up 12 and 10 per cent of their totals.

Cadets from Asia dominated the numbers at Sandhurst, as among overseas university students, but principally because of the oil states of the middle east; their cadets rose from 24 per cent for the whole period to 39 per cent of the total from 2003. China, which had sent cadets to Sandhurst between the wars (see Chapter 4) only resumed doing so in 2007 and in numbers completely dwarfed by those of its university students. Only 4 per cent of overseas cadets came from Europe and, with the exception of those from Malta, most of these were from ex-communist countries in eastern Europe: cadet training was not part of the revived British closeness to Europe suggested by university numbers. Apart from the particular case of states too small to provide all their specialised military training, oil rather than the Commonwealth or European affinity now took military cadets to Britain.[78] As with their predecessors, overseas cadets' experience was mixed. Like university students, those from the tropics suffered from the cold. It is claimed that similar proportions of British and overseas cadets passionately disliked Sandhurst, seen as an unpleasant but necessary means to an end. Levels of tolerance seem to have changed little. Foreign cadets were described by their British contemporaries in the 1990s as floppies, explained either as 'Fun-Loving Overseas Persons Particularly

Interested in Exercises', or on the grounds that 'when the going gets tough, they tend to go all floppy'.[79]

Overseas student numbers grew more rapidly in the new century, increasing at around 40 per cent in five years, almost doubling between 2001 and 2010, and reaching 262,000 in 2006 and 365,000 in 2010. This reflected both university activity and deliberate policy introduced by the Labour government of 1997.

While the market was still seen as important, the new government re-emphasised the value of overseas students for soft diplomacy. Policy came from the top with an announcement in 1999 of a prime minister's initiative to increase the number of overseas students, with students from China to rise from 5,000 to 20,000.[80] In a world that had emerged from the cold war, and in which the BRICs – Brazil, Russia, India and China – were seen as future economic giants, Britain wanted to increase student enrolment from both India and China. Following the original target, the second phase of the prime minister's initiative, running from 2006 to 2011, was designed to attract an additional 70,000 international students to higher education and an additional 30,000 to further education; while doubling the number of countries sending more than 10,000 students per annum to the UK.[81] Government also saw overseas recruitment as bringing direct benefits to British universities and British research. It introduced a new scholarship programme of Dorothy Hodgkin awards in 2003, open to developing-country doctoral students, and aimed to:

> Provide the UK's best universities, and consequently the UK science base, with access to a pool of first-rate students with a variety of outlooks.
>
> Improve the profile of the UK as an outward-looking, technologically-advanced country.
>
> Help to equip developing countries with a pool of highly skilled people who can make a significant difference to the pace of development of those countries.

It was also hoped that the programme's alumni would be able to foster long-term British scientific collaboration with overseas partners. The largest number of students came from China, followed by India, Iran, Russia and Mozambique. Half of the costs were met by the research councils and half by private-sector sponsors. By 2009 it had brought more than 500 PhD students to Britain.[82] Alongside the new programme, Marshall and Chevening awards continued and the Commonwealth Scholarship Commission gained increased funding in 2003 and 2006.

The renewed welcome for overseas students continued to be expressed in the language of markets and competition. David Lammy, minister for higher education, argued in 2010 that 'the global education market is rapidly evolving, and the forces driving it and determining who succeeds are no longer entirely focused on traditional student recruitment'.[83] The British Council, set up to promote education and culture, now spoke the same language, claiming that 'research highlighted Education UK as the most visible among competitive brands'.[84]

While the prime minister, the Foreign Office and the universities were prepared to sing the praise of overseas students, discordant notes could also be heard. Although students were in principle welcome, the Home Office wanted to restrain immigration and saw policy on visas as a way of doing so. (It also wanted to ensure visa prices were high enough to meet the cost of issuing them.) During the 2000s fees for student visas steadily increased while new restrictions were imposed on the length of time students could remain in the country after graduating. Despite an early statement by the prime minister on easing visa restrictions, the cost of a student visa rose from £36 in 2002 to £99 and subsequently to £145 in 2009; a visa renewal fee, needed by students who did not complete their dissertations on time, was introduced in 2003 at a cost of £115 which was also to increase and bore more heavily on students with dependants who would each need the document.

Financial pressures were next exerted on Commonwealth scholarships. The scholarship commission modified its selection procedures in 2001, requiring its developing-country scholars to demonstrate the relevance of their course of study to national developmental needs. Earlier generations of the commission argued that they were not capable of making that kind of decision and that questions of relevance were the responsibility of nominating governments. Its developing-country awards now clearly meshed with the priorities of the Department for International Development. But its awards for the industrialised Commonwealth, where applicants had to demonstrate potential for leadership, were now at greater risk. In a round of spending cuts in 2008, the Foreign and Commonwealth Office protected its own, Chevening, awards, but cut off Commonwealth awards for Australia, Canada and New Zealand, along with the Bahamas, Brunei, Cyprus, Malta and Singapore. A small set of awards were continued with funding from individual universities and their parent department, of Business Innovation and Skills.

The government changed in 2010. Planned cuts in expenditure, and a new regime of university funding, left the income from overseas students of continuing importance to universities. But the government also had a populist and anti-immigrant tinge. Home Office policy now gained ascendance over foreign-policy interests, reflected in an announcement by the home secretary that:

> We cannot go on like this. We must tighten up our immigration system, focusing on tackling abuse and supporting only the most economically beneficial migrants.
>
> ... the majority of non-EU migrants are, in fact, students. They represent almost two thirds of the non-EU migrants entering the UK each year, and we cannot reduce net migration significantly without reforming student visas. ...
>
> As with economic migration, we will therefore refocus student visas on the areas that add the greatest value, and in which evidence of abuse is limited.[85]

In its domestic policies government went on to increase fees, for home and therefore for European students, which now generally reached £9,000 a year.

The late twentieth and early twenty-first centuries saw major changes in the numbers of overseas students, in their distribution, in policy and in the factors that were pulling and pushing them. Numbers increased, so that, as the number of home students rose, overseas numbers did so even more rapidly, going from their historic 10 per cent of the total to 20 per cent, with overseas postgraduate numbers exceeding 50 per cent. The Commonwealth had fallen away as a driver of student mobility to be replaced by the expanding economies of Asia. More students came from Europe, not only to British universities but also to its schools; in the 2000s Germany sent students in proportions not seen for a century. Students increasingly came to study business rather than technology. The gender balance had changed with women still a minority over all but exceeding men among some groups of students. Foreign and defence policy still drew military cadets. Well beyond the age of empire, the strength of the English language drew students of all kinds and English schools retained an international prestige.

Policy shifted as well as numbers. With the end of the cold war it no longer drove recruitment policies. The neoliberal principles of the new government in 1979 led it to a respect for market forces which was to influence educational policy and much more. Once the indiscriminate subsidy of overseas students was removed, universities accepted the logic of the market and recruited overseas students more vigorously than ever before. Principled objection to differential fees fell away. Public statements on international students were increasingly couched more in terms of the market than of internationalism. At the same time, the expansion of higher education, at home or abroad, was reinforced by new convictions about its importance for economic growth.

Contradictions and ambivalence continued to shade government and institutional policy. Some government departments wanted to welcome overseas students, others to hold down the numbers of those who might become immigrants. British higher education was seen as offering benefits to the developing world while it also wanted to attract, and sometimes keep, the ablest students from the south. University teachers could find respect for the market an awkward bedfellow for their well-established academic and internationalist principles.

Part II
Perspectives

During the eight centuries in which foreigners travelled to study in Britain their lives were shaped by the policies and practices of their host institutions – universities and schools – and of the governments of their day. As the last five chapters have shown, policy has seldom been explicit and often neither clear nor consistent. It has been made both by the state and by individual institutions, sometimes in harmony though sometimes with dissonance. It has been moulded and remoulded by ideology and by the institutional values of the universities that provided a home for most overseas students. Until the Reformation, the ideological unity of Catholic Europe, though fractious at times, was mirrored by an assumption that universities had an international and universalist function. For more than three centuries ideological divisions then determined who should study in northern Europe and what religious tests should be applied as they did so. From the seventeenth to the twentieth centuries, the expansion, politics and values of the empire called British universities and schools to service as students from the West Indies, the colonies of settlement and above all India began to dominate overseas student numbers. Post-imperial preference survived the end of the empire, bringing a large proportion of students from the Commonwealth and the English-speaking world. In the late twentieth century a new respect for the market, first demonstrated by government and then embraced by universities, sent academics out on recruitment campaigns in pursuit of foreign enrolments, seen as a valued source of income. All down the years there were tensions within policy, alike on the part of institutions and of government, with a welcome for students matched by doubts, often following from students' foreignness. Contrasts between the demands of the market and respect for long-established university values of scholarship and internationalism are only the most recent manifestation of this long history of tensions.

The changes in ideology and practice that are central to the story of foreign students marched hand in hand with changes in geography. Student mobility in the Middle Ages was essentially a European phenomenon. Exploration and the empire then redrew its boundaries. British universities moved closer to continental Europe just before the First World War and did so again with renewed energy towards the end of the twentieth century. By 2001 European students outnumbered those from the Commonwealth where, 30 years before, they had formed less than half the Commonwealth total. They were accompanied by steadily increasing numbers from the developing world and especially from Asia.

In their concentration on numbers, patterns of movement and changes in policy, the previous chapters have left aside four issues of interpretation – description, economics, comparative politics and outcomes – addressed in the next four.

Student voices were heard only intermittently in the last five chapters and deserve more attention. Overseas students' expectations and experience affected the quality of their lives and, in turn, had a bearing on the development of policy towards them. Chapter 7 seeks to redress the institutional bias of the narrative chapters with a description of students' varied hopes and everyday lives – from John of Barbara who rejected coming to Britain because it was too cold and wet to Cornelia Sorabji who found 'kindness and spoiling' and companionship in Oxford to Vladimir Nabokov who 'was quite sure that Cambridge' did not affect his soul. Another chorus of voices that needs to be heard is that of the paymasters, recorded in Chapter 8. This allows a calculation of the cost of studying in Britain and helps the development of an economic explanation, alongside the political and individual ones, of the decisions by families and funding agencies to pay for foreign study. These decisions in their turn provoke questions about the extent to which British experience is unique or one instance of a general process. Chapter 9 seeks answers by looking at the drivers and determinants of policy within other industrialised countries. It sets out international numbers and explores the changing political assumptions lying behind the recruitment of international students. To complete the examination of the British and comparative record, the final chapter summarises the discussion of politics, experience, economics and international practice, and moves on to examine the outcomes which students expected or achieved from studying in Britain.

7
Student Experience

The annals of Cambridge explain how in 1217 clerks loyal to the son of the King of France were excommunicated and expelled.[1] In Oxford Robert of Ireland, arrested in the 1240s for burglary, was only one of the Irish who got themselves a reputation for violence and disorder.[2] Sadly, but characteristically, the records give us only the English side of the stories. For many centuries we hear about the experience of foreign students through the writings of their hosts so that they are actors on the university stage with muffled voices coming from a part written for them and not by them. Almost all the voices are male although there were also always parts played by women.

The muffled voices become clearer as the years go on and tell us something about foreign students' relations with the British, about their academic experience and about their other activities. Students varied in the extent to which they were tolerated, scorned or welcomed, and in their reactions to these processes. Finding accommodation often presented particular difficulties, as did sex and its presence or absence. All of these changed over time and all were influenced by issues of class and race. Academic experience may be easier to describe – though many writers tell us more about their private life and its pleasures than about their work – and at least the records show how foreign students performed academically. For the rest, students told us in different periods how they rowed, played games, glided on university rivers, or simply spent their spare time in conversation. In different periods, too, some of them played political roles and, while these changed, they repeatedly tended to arouse controversy and distrust.

The medieval student enjoyed valuable privileges. He was likely to be subject to the discipline of the university and its chancellor rather than that of the town and its mayor. If he was a clerk, then canon law applied rather than civil law. He was likely to be exempt from the dues that added to the cost and difficulty of travel. While disputes between town and gown, in both Oxford and Cambridge, go back to the Middle Ages, the student was more likely to be involved in confrontations among students than between students and townsmen or town authorities. Students did not become militant in the way that they did in some of the continental universities. Their privileges meant that 'they had little motivation to do so. In the English universities the masters' guilds afforded adequate protection for the undergraduate body'.[3] The result was that university life was one of occasional turbulence rather than continuous riot.

Conflicts of interest, between town and university, and conflicts among students did, however flare up from time to time. Cambridge saw brawls in 1270 and more serious disturbances at the time of the Peasants' Revolt in 1281. Conflicts between northern and southern students at Oxford in 1274 led to 50 people being tried for homicide. Repeated riots followed, notably on St Scholastica's Day in 1355. The small minority of Welsh students, like the Irish, gained a reputation for lawlessness, as documented in the English records. In 1388 Welsh students at Oxford attacked students from the north of England and drove them out of town; a new fight the next year went on for four days.[4] The Welsh played a part in armed assaults, murders and thefts while disputes between the Irish and Welsh played a part in tensions between rival halls at Oxford.[5] The Irish reputation was such that they were banned from England by Henry V in 1413 and Henry VI in 1422, although university students were exempted from this ban.[6]

There were both national and local attempts to relieve tensions between universities and burgesses that affected foreign as well as home students. In 1231 a royal decree from Henry III reminded the mayor and bailiffs of Cambridge of their responsibilities:

> You are aware that a multitude of scholars from divers parts, as well from this side the sea as from overseas, meets at our town of Cambridge for study, which we hold a very gratifying and desirable thing, since no small benefit and glory accrues therefrom to our whole realm; and you among whom these students personally live, ought especially to be pleased and delighted at it.
>
> We have heard, however, that in letting your houses you make such heavy charges to the scholars living among you, that unless you conduct yourself with more restraint and moderation towards them in this matter, they will be driven by your exaction to leave your town and, abandoning their studies, leave our country which we by no means desire.

To bring rents down to a reasonable level he directed that these should be determined jointly by town and gown with valuations by 'two masters and two good and lawful men of your town assigned'.[7] The creation of a rent tribunal did not resolve matters and further measures were to follow. After a series of disturbances, and judicial enquiries into them, the university and the borough agreed in 1270 on a joint structure to keep the peace, which involved scholars from outside England as well as scholars and townsmen from within. Each year a *Magna Congregatio* or Black Assembly was to be appointed with ten townsmen, five scholars from each English county, and a further three from Scotland, three from Ireland and two from Wales. The assembly continued to meet until at least 1533, though it gradually became symbolic rather than an instrument of government.[8]

Despite measures of this kind, tensions between home or foreign students and local citizens were long to continue. Universities across Europe had an interest both in keeping the local peace and in asserting their authority. They had a common code of behaviour, with four prohibitions. Students were not to bear arms, they should not wear fashionable clothes, they should not insult or attack fellow students or teachers and they should avoid 'contact with women of all kinds'.[9] Colleges and universities were able to enforce these prohibitions – or at least to try – with the powers they acquired from popes and kings and gradually extended as they attempted to control not only their own students but also trade within their towns. 'The chancellors had at their disposal an awesome collection of penalties that could be imposed upon masters, scholars and townspeople.' For the students, the penalties could range from fines, to cutting down on food, to expulsion. Corporal punishment was used from the fifteenth to the sixteenth centuries.[10]

Student life before the Reformation, as after, was dominated neither by riot nor by codes of behaviour but by the need for accommodation and by the demands of the working day. Foreign monks and friars were at an advantage over others from abroad where they could expect their local convent to provide housing. For the rest, students were crowded together in rooms, generally for two to four people, and with space for a bed, a seat, a table and a bookshelf. Only the bedstead was usually provided so that, in a practice that was to endure sporadically until the twentieth century, students had to buy the rest for themselves.[11] Accommodation was likely to be overcrowded, dirty and unhealthy at least in low-lying Cambridge which had perennial drainage problems.[12] In both Oxford and Cambridge colleges and halls grew in the fourteenth century so that an increasing proportion of students could at least hope to find a room in one of them. Walter de Merton founded the first college in Oxford in 1264; within a century it had been joined by another half dozen in each of the English universities. The colleges, somewhere between a manor house and a monastery, grew to become teaching institutions rather than simply residential halls, and enjoyed a prestige denied to scholars outside their walls.[13] But few foreign students became college members: only 50 of 901 non-English scholars in medieval Oxford did so. Of 198 recorded Welsh students only 24 were college members, with the Irish, continentals and Scots faring even worse, though both the Irish and Welsh seem to have found reasonable accommodation in halls.[14]

Medieval students did not leave us memoirs to describe their working day. Teaching, in England as on the continent, was dominated by lectures and disputations. Lectures were devoted to explaining and elucidating an authoritative text, with an emphasis on the transmission of an inherited body of knowledge in the traditions of scholasticism. Disputations were formal and public occasions with debates between university teachers or regent masters, often backed by bachelors as respondents and disputants. Students also used texts, probably writing notes during lectures, and the presence of bookshelves in their rooms suggest that they had some of their own books, even before the invention of printing.

Both English universities became known for the quality of their teaching. Oxford developed a reputation for its Aristotelian logic in the thirteenth century and by the fourteenth both Oxford and Cambridge had a high standing among their European peers.[15] In the fifteenth century the fresh winds of humanism were blowing through the scholastic quadrangles (see Chapter 2). Scholars from the continent, and visits from Greek scholars, brought new ideas and by the end of the fifteenth century at least a handful of English scholars were, for the first time, able to read Greek.[16] While English universities were slow to change their methods of teaching they were by this time well placed to change its content in the new intellectual world of the sixteenth century.

The medieval records, with intermittent accounts of affrays and diatribes against gaudy clothes, confirm that the prohibitions on weapons, fighting and ostentation were only partially successful. So too with women. As they were likely to be sinful, or the cause of sin, many colleges imposed bans on their presence or allowed them only into public rooms. Some required all servants to be male, which made for difficulties as laundry work was a female occupation. One way of avoiding predatory laundresses was to ensure they were off the premises and that laundry was passed to them through an intermediary, while another was to insist they should be too old or too ugly to be alluring. Other than laundresses, some colleges would allow visits by a mother or a sister, but only to the hall or another public room, and then in the presence of a chaperone. Status might bring exceptions to the rules: at Cardinal College in Oxford the dean was allowed to entertain any female guest, even if she were not a relative.[17] These regulations would have borne as heavily upon foreign students as on local.

Inevitably prostitution flourished and, in another source of potential conflict between town and gown, the universities acquired powers to control it, which they retained for centuries to come. Until 1894 Cambridge University was able to lock up any woman suspected of prostitution; Evelyn Waugh, a good observer though not an academic lawyer, claimed that Oxford still had and used its powers in the 1920s.[18] They were ineffective. In the thirteenth century a bishop complained that some Oxford students were whoremongers while in the fifteenth an enquiry found that prostitution was well organised with scholars as pimps as well as clients. A rector from Ireland was imprisoned and a scholar in priest's orders was alleged to have had liaisons with nuns at the nearby Godstow nunnery.[19] 'Despite the best efforts of the English authorities to drive it out, prostitution was a tenacious reality that survived to satisfy the deep-seated needs of at least a minority of scholars who were ordinarily deprived of the company of women in a natural setting'.[20]

The Reformation, and the demands of government under the Tudors, brought changes to the university curriculum, functions and students (see Chapter 2). While tensions between university and town authorities remained, riots were a thing of the past. Disputes in Cambridge were now not about rebellion and rent but about the order of precedence between the mayor and the vice-chancellor and about control over the price of candles.[21] But, even after the Reformation swept away the benefits of clerical status, scholars continued to enjoy privileges which now reflected class rather than religion. Universities were never for the poorest in society so that anyone who had entered a university, surmounting the barriers of cost, religion and at least minimal schooling, looked like a person of some standing. Over the centuries there was often a contrast between the ascribed status of foreign students, as university members, and that of immigrants, even from the same territories, who tended to be at the bottom of society in terms of class, status and power. Overseas students' apparent class shaped their relations with the British.

Those relationships were also affected by attitudes towards foreigners, outsiders and immigrants, where England had a less than welcoming reputation from at least the sixteenth to the nineteenth centuries.

Visitors and students were likely to encounter, at best, English coolness. There were riots against foreigners in London in 1517 and expulsions in 1554. Foreigners living in England were classed as denizens with more limited rights than citizens. When the French physician Samuel Sorbière visited England in 1663 he found that a visitor was likely to be greeted as 'French dog' at Dover and be ignored by other travellers: 'They took no more notice of me than they would of a package of merchandise.' His awareness of 'English contempt for and indifference to foreigners' was reinforced by his complaints, echoed by other visitors, that the scholars he met in Oxford and London used a version of Latin which he could not understand.[22] Naturally there were both individual and general exceptions to the English coolness and the religious politics of Europe intermittently encouraged immigration (see Chapter 2). But a welcome could not always be assumed.

The English coolness and insularity long remained. By the nineteenth century Lewis Farnell, who later became its vice-chancellor, commented on Oxford's

> almost entire absence of foreign students in my early days [in the 1870s]. The Oxford of the eighteenth and the nineteenth centuries, when the colleges were becoming close and exclusive societies, had lost the international character that it possessed in the Middle Ages and which my own college... still possessed under Elizabeth and before the Civil War. ... We were secluded in a lovely park of our own, very happy to be so, but no doubt very insular and narrow.[23]

Undergraduate writers at this time illustrated that narrowness by identifying foreign students as a threat to their way of life. An Oxford voice warned about 'Transatlantic freshmen' in 1861. In Cambridge, the abolition of religious tests in 1871 prompted a warning cartoon with the vice-chancellor and his entourage, all depicted as foreigners, parading past the Senate House with a pagoda in the background, and a protest in verse:

> In an ancient and grave University
> All at once there appeared a diversity
> Of Turks, Greeks, and Jews,
> Hottentots and Hindoos
> Which altered that grave University.[24]

The racist assumptions that accompanied and followed the expansion of the empire provided a ready justification for xenophobia if one was needed.

Despite the insularity and racism, some at least of the students found a welcome. The eighteenth-century scholars from the West Indian plantocracy were probably indistinguishable from their English contemporaries. Charles Bristed commented on the ignorance of America displayed by many of his fellow students but added that only once, at an undergraduate drinking party, 'did I come near to getting into any difficulty on account of my country'.[25] Bristed was white but there were similar stories from black and Asian students. William Wells Brown, an escaped American slave who visited Edinburgh medical school in 1851, saw 'among the two or three hundred students, three coloured young men, seated upon the same benches with those of a fairer complexion, and yet there appeared no feeling on the part of the whites towards their coloured associates, except of companionship and respect'.[26] In Cambridge a future archbishop of Canterbury, then a pale slim undergraduate, came out on the side of an African student:

> On a certain Degree day in 1850 or thereabouts, a West African undergraduate named Crummell, of Queens', a man of colour, appeared in the Senate House to take his degree. A boisterous individual in the gallery called out, 'Three groans for the Queens' nigger'... A pale slim undergraduate... shouted in a voice which echoed through the building, 'Shame, shame! Three groans for you, Sir!' and immediately afterwards, 'Three cheers for Crummell!' This was taken up in all directions... and the original offender had to stoop down to hide himself from the storm of groans and hisses that broke out all around him.[27]

J. R. Maxwell, a black Sierra Leonean who went to Oxford in 1876, saw 'Oxford days as the happiest days of his life and never forgot the kindness he received there from tutors and students, in contrast to the sarcasm shown by Englishmen towards natives in West Africa'.[28] In an enthusiastic guide to English universities for Indian students, Samuel Satthianadhan pointed out the advantages of the college system and contrasted this with the need to live in lodgings if studying in London. Within a college, he claimed, the Indian student 'moves without any feeling of awkwardness or restraint in the company of young English gentlemen'. This meant that: 'There are no invidious distinctions of rank or race, the reverence with which men regard wealth or status being counteracted by the admiration they entertain for the aristocracy of moral or intellectual excellence'.[29] A slightly later account of Japanese students by the dean of Peterhouse in Cambridge suggested that they probably 'like the society in which they find themselves, as it is certainly true that the society likes them. English undergraduates welcome them to their rooms and parties, and in not a few cases to their homes'. At the same time, with reserve on both sides, 'the friendships which the Japanese form at Cambridge, though natural and cordial for the most part, rarely develop into real intimacies such as are common-enough between our fellow-countrymen at the University, because few confidences are given or invited'.[30]

Racism and xenophobia, as well as insularity, were widespread in British society by the late nineteenth century and these views were carried into university and university life by students and academics. At the same time, they were neither universal nor universally applied. Class was often more important than race and class could almost be absorbed by osmosis from the river Cam or Isis. The formidable Indian student Cornelia Sorabji demonstrated how to use Oxford as a way round the constraints of race and gender. Despite being turned down for a Government of India scholarship – she was top of the examination list but a woman – she had the right connections in England to find an alternative scholarship (see Chapter 3). Her welcome by Jowett, the master of Balliol, astonished the warden of her own college:

> When he went, the Warden took me in her arms and said, 'My child, this is a great honour'. And in my ignorance I wondered if that were a traditional Oxford custom when aged cherubs with white hair were polite to foreigners.

She made the most of her time in England, meeting politicians, writers and artists who included Gladstone, Asquith, Bernard Shaw, Ellen Terry and Holman Hunt. 'It was a good life being up. Kindness and spoiling, feeling after one's powers, meeting people who thought, and people who talked clever nonsense: and finding companionship outside my family for the first time'.[31]

Student life was shaped by college and university policies as well as by national attitudes. Foreign students were a small minority and these policies followed from the universities' functions in society. From the sixteenth century onwards most students lived in colleges or were members of them. While this eased the problems of accommodation that had confronted the less fortunate medieval students, it made them increasingly subject to college discipline. This became stricter in the later sixteenth century. Just as the university relations with the state were clarified and codified under Queen Elizabeth, so the universities and colleges in their turn imposed a more clearly defined set of restrictions on students.[32] In both Oxford and Cambridge a new and expanded set of prohibitions for students banned football, the keeping of dogs, ferrets or more exotic animals including bears, swimming, frequenting taverns, gambling, smoking tobacco, long hair, exotic fashions or, at least in Oxford, keeping crossbows or fowling pieces.[33] The pursuit of virtue went alongside the banning of vice and, with many students destined for a life as priests or ministers, daily attendance at college chapel was a feature of student life, and remained so into the nineteenth century and even beyond.

Compulsory chapel and puritan prohibitions affected the daily lives of students but form an incomplete picture of what it was like. From the sixteenth century, student memoirs begin to fill it out. In 1552 John Conrad ab Ulmis, who had come from Geneva to study in Oxford, described his day:

> From six to seven in the morning he read Aristotle's *Politics* to gain both a knowledge of Greek and moral philosophy. The next hour he devoted to digests of Roman law and the hour following to reconsidering these readings. At nine he attended Peter Martyr's lecture. The hour from ten to eleven he passed on the rules of dialectics of Melanchthon's *de locis argumentorum*, and after dinner he read Cicero's offices, 'a truly golden book'. From one to three he wrote letters, as far as possible imitating Cicero. At three he learnt the institutes of civil law, which he read aloud and committed to memory. At four he read privately in the hall where they lived in the rules of law which he had heard previously, and learnt them by heart as he did the institutes. After supper he indulged in various discourse, either in their chamber or walking up and down in some part of the college where they exercised themselves in dialectical questions.[34]

The records do not show how far his Calvinist sobriety was the norm, but it fits with other accounts of the time. Scholars may have written for effect, emphasising their reading, though remembering their rations. An eighteenth-century student at Caius College, Cambridge,

> described his day as follows: he generally rose at 5, read for an hour, took a walk, and came back for chapel at 7. After that came breakfast followed by 3 ½ hours reading from 9 until 12.30, then dinner, followed sometimes by a visit to a friend's room, a dish of tea, and a glance at the newspapers in a coffee house, followed again by chapel at 6, a walk and supper.[35]

But it was not all sobriety and he also explained how in the summer of 1767 he had been 'somewhat more gay and idle than I should have been this last fortnight, in making parties to go on the water and in riding out to Newmarket and the country round about in little one-horse chaises'.[36] Despite the earlier ban on weapons, shooting of wildfowl was now popular, especially in the fens round Cambridge. Conversation, regular chapel and occasional lectures, together with regular meals appear to have dominated the life of a Scottish student who arrived at Oxford in 1791:

> We occupy, each of us, our separate apartments, and lock ourselves in at night. At seven o'clock we repair to prayers…That detains us half an hour, after which most of us choose to talk till 9 o'clock, at which hour a George (that is to say a round penny roll) is served up, with a bit of butter on a pewter plate, into each of our chambers where we provide our own tea and sugar.…From this time till 3 we do as we please, unless there be any lectures to attend; but at three, the trumpet's martial voice proclaims the hour of dinner, to which we all repair in the Common Hall, after having ordered, on our way through the kitchen, whatever part of the bill of fare we may choose.[37]

Little had changed by 1859 when William Everett arrived in Cambridge from the United States, although he makes more reference to his tutor and to lectures. He was also more critical of the catering which he claimed was run by college servants who would take food away before it was finished in order to serve it again the next day. On a typical day his college servant would have lit his fire before waking him at six thirty. Breakfast arrived at nine, as did his friends as it was a social meal, after which he might go to lectures, visit his tutor, or consult old examination papers in the college library. From two to four he walked with friends, then dined, went to chapel and read *The Times*, before working for two hours from seven to nine then going out for tea, bread and jam, and whist with his friends.[38] His account fits closely with that given by Satthianadhan though by 1890, the date of his guide, chapel was required only several times a week and there were lectures not exceeding three a day. Afternoons were 'entirely given up to sport' which for him, and for other writers of the period, included walking. 'A Cantab never fails to take his two hours exercise per diem'.[39]

These sober college accounts tell only part of the story. In eighteenth-century Oxford drunkenness among undergraduates was exceeded only by that among fellows. William Shenstone, who arrived there in 1732, soon came across several groups of scholars. Having abandoned one group who read Greek and drank water, and left the 'low company of west-country lads, who drank ale, smoked tobacco, punned, and sang bacchanalian catches' he joined a more gentlemanly group who treated him 'with port-wine and arrack punch; and now and then…would conclude with a bottle or two of claret'.[40] More than a century later, though English universities were becoming more serious and at least contemplating reform, the American Charles Bristed found in the 1840s that his contemporaries expected to get him drunk. They apparently failed as he had a strong head. He went on to contrast undergraduate wine parties, described by Thackeray as 'thirty lads round a table covered with bad sweet meats, drinking bad wines, telling bad stories, singing bad songs over and over again' with a more elegant 'Trinity supper party – a perfect symposium: good dishes and wine, an entire absence of display, and the genial conversation of clever men'. Despite the geniality and cleverness they proceeded to drink the one Australian present under the table.[41] While there were still bans on contact with women, wine and song were a consistent part of student life alongside work.

Much of the work was of limited interest. From the mid-seventeenth to the mid-nineteenth century intellectual ferment was to be found outside the English universities – in the Royal Society founded in 1662, and in Edinburgh at the time of the Scottish Enlightenment (see Chapter 2). Theology, law and medicine had atrophied at Oxford and Cambridge with teaching, such as it was, concentrated on the arts.[42] Examinations were something of a formality but, to do well in them, students needed to find a private tutor, operating outside formal college and university structures, and find money from their budget to pay him (see Chapter 8).

Universities long continued their attempts to control the sex lives of their scholars and fellows, just as they had in the Middle Ages, with complicated rules and mixed success. The Reformation swept away the bans on marriage which had applied to all clerics, including those in universities, only for Queen Elizabeth to react against married priests and married academics.[43] In 1561 she published an injunction to keep women out of colleges where wives, children and nurses had moved in,

> whereof no small offence groweth to the intent of the founders and to the quiet and orderly profession of study and learning.…her majesty…therefore expressly willeth and commandeth that no manner of person, being either the head or member of any college or

cathedral church within this realm, shall from the time of the notification hereof in the same college, have or be permitted to have within the precinct of any such college, his wife or other woman to abide and dwell in the same.[44]

For the next three centuries, colleges in England and Ireland tried to legislate for the absence of women. Generally, university and college staff had to be single though they were free to marry once they left their academic post. Loopholes abounded. In some cases the heads of colleges, but nobody else, could marry. Leaving room for informality, the relevant statute at Trinity College Dublin required fellows to resign if the board were formally notified of their marriage.[45] In eighteenth-century Oxford, where fellows were also required to resign on marriage, 'there appears to have been a widespread ignoring of the statutes, with Fellows' wives of long standing being known to the college without any action being taken'.[46] The prohibitions were gradually abandoned in the nineteenth century. Bristed commented on the oddity that 'in America you may not marry but your tutor can; in England you may marry and he can't'.[47] They never applied in London and academics were allowed legitimate wives at Oxford and Cambridge from 1878. Women were admitted as students in both ancient universities and in London from the 1870s, and could attend lectures and take the same examinations as men, although they were not formally allowed to graduate at Oxford or Cambridge until the next century.

For the male students, the formal assumption and polite fiction was that, apart from the married minority, they led celibate lives. For some this was only a fiction and, as foreign students tended to be older than the English, chastity may have been as rare as temptation was common. German visitors commented on the beauty of the women and on the fact that they kissed strangers at a time when continental visitors expected them to shake hands. Nikolaus von Popplau in 1484 had found them both beautiful and lascivious; later visitors like Samuel Kiechel who came to England in 1585 at the age of 22 confirmed their reputation for beauty. The beauty, and the lasciviousness if it was accurately reported, would have had an appeal for the aristocratic young men who were sent to England in the late sixteenth century to acquire 'polish and knowledge of the world' at a time when German universities catered mainly for theologians, lawyers and doctors.[48]

There were abundant opportunities for students to widen one aspect of their knowledge of the world. Alongside more acceptable relationships, prostitution continued to flourish despite all attempts to control it. An Oxford satirist in the early eighteenth century warned of 'Kidnapping females' who threatened 'the almost universal Corruption of our Youth'.[49] In the next century Bristed was criticised for the openness, or the salaciousness, with which he described the 'state of morals and religion in Cambridge' in his volume of advice for other American students. He attributed this in part to the English class system which was reflected by 'the low estimate which men in the upper ranks of life form of women in the lower' where working-class women were treated as if they 'were expressly designed for the amusement of gentlemen'. He failed to persuade two of his companions, whose status as MAs would have allowed them to do so, to take 'two ladies of the town...and make them go away under pain of the *Spinning House* (the Bridewell or House of Correction for such characters)'. He criticised the university for failing to control 'the notorious prostitutes, of whom there are nearly a hundred at the lowest estimate' and condemned as hypocrisy the way in which colleges provided testimonials of good character for students who were going on to enter the church despite a record of 'open acts of profligacy and disorder'.[50]

The universities may have failed to control illegitimate relationships but had their own rules for legitimate ones. There were restrictions on female visitors and requirements for chaperones. Cornelia Sorabji remembered

> one occasion when Richard Burn (later Sir R. Burn I.C.S.) and my brother, both of Balliol, took some of us from Somerville out on the river, making our chaperones – the Warden and the wife of a Don – tow the boats! They'd had a bet about this, the College rules of the time about 'River Chaperones' being very strict. The incident was commemorated in *Punch* – 'Uses of Chaperones on the River'.

Out of term, and outside Oxford, things seem to have been less strict. She later herself learned to row which meant that in her last Oxford summer she, her brother and two friends (also apparently brother and sister) could spend three days rowing down to Reading, staying at inns overnight, with the women rowing, 'our training requiring that they should sit together at the steerage ropes, criticizing, or chaffing or frightening us – an arrangement which suited Bonté and me admirably'.[51]

Chaperones went out with the nineteenth century, or soon after. The new century was to bring far more dramatic changes to the life of foreign students, some of them foreshadowed by the growth in their numbers between 1880 and 1900 (see Chapter 3). As with their predecessors, their lives were influenced by the welcome they received and their relations with the British, by their accommodation, by their academic experience and by their non-academic interests including politics, sport and sex.

Some were welcomed for what they brought. J. J. Thomson, Rutherford's tutor, emphasised in his memoirs how Cambridge benefited from overseas students:

> The advantage gained by our own students by their intercourse with men of widely different training and experience, of different points of view on political, social and scientific questions, of very different temperaments, can, I think, hardly be exaggerated. They gain catholicity of view and some of the advantages they would get by residence in the universities from which the research students came.[52]

Rutherford was fortunate and for others first impressions were at best muted. K. P. S. Menon, who was later to be an Indian diplomat and government minister, arrived in Oxford in 1918 and found

> Our first view of Oxford was far from impressive. An old, drunken coachman drove us through squalid lanes, full of butchers' shops and breweries. The streets were forlorn and empty and the lights were shrouded, lest some German bomber should spot the city from above. Occasionally, an old man, half-drunk, could be seen loitering along, singing wearily to himself; occasionally, a maimed soldier with his arms round an ungainly woman's waist. Then we entered a fine broad street, the magnificence of which merely accentuated our sense of desolation. Soldiers and old men again – maimed, half-drunk, mournful.[53]

More than 50 years later, Brian Gould who had arrived from New Zealand at the age of 23, was disappointed by the scruffiness of Piccadilly Circus while a compatriot warned that 'taking a person from a country such as New Zealand with almost a surfeit of natural beauty, and sending them to a place such as Battersea is bound to have a profoundly disturbing and depressing psychological effect'.[54] Neither London nor Oxford raised the spirits of Mandy Merck who came from America with high hopes after reading *Brideshead revisited* 17 times:

> I got off the plane at Heathrow and into a train for Didcot, Reading, then Oxford. I was very surprised and dismayed. The Thames Valley did nothing for me ... Then getting to St Hugh's, which is not a pretty place, and thinking, 'This isn't so great'. Trying to have lunch in the buttery, 'This is really not so great'.[55]

Britain was slow to ensure that students were met and welcomed. The Lee-Warner committee on Indian students in 1907 (see Chapter 4) was disturbed that 'extremists of Indian politics' greeted new arrivals from India, plied them with the dangerous journal *Indian sociologist* and ran a lodging house that they could use.[56] Once the Indian Students' Department was established in 1912, it began to ensure there was a welcome for its students and within two years had established hospitality committees round the country.[57] In its turn, the British Council took on a general responsibility for the welfare of overseas students, so that after the Second World War there was a good chance that students would find someone looking out for them, at Tilbury, Southampton, or Heathrow. But all this took time. Until 1950 the 'vast majority' of students from the colonies 'had no special friends or organizations to help them settle in on arrival and … were suddenly confronted with the difficulties of arriving in a strange country, including the problems of finding suitable accommodation'.[58] Little was done to meet, welcome, or induct trainee nurses who, while they often had hostel accommodation, might still leave Mauritius on a Monday and be working on the wards of a Manchester hospital on Wednesday.[59]

Any welcome was tempered by the continuing English reputation for coolness. In the 1920s a Canadian Rhodes scholar identified the problems this could cause for a foreigner:

> My love of Oxford and England was not blind. … Most Rhodes scholars would … gladly go home at the end of their first term. One knows no-one. There seems to be no possibility of knowing anyone. The men on your staircase do not speak to you. … Many Rhodes scholars give up the struggle and say the Englishman is not worth knowing and from then on consort only with their own nationals or with other Rhodes scholars.[60]

Thirty years later overseas students in Oxford 'felt that they were being lumped together by the English into a class of their own – classless but somehow inferior', but that the national indifference was worse.[61] That indifference was ubiquitous, reported by white students from New Zealand and North America as well as being a fact of life for those from Africa, Asia and the Caribbean. An Indian student in London realised in her first term that

> with the English you have to have some passing of time. … The English find it extremely difficult to make the effort, to make the first move,

even if they want to. They find it difficult to do that with each other, it's not only with people who come from elsewhere.[62]

Nor was this just an English phenomenon. An African student in Glasgow in the 1950s reported similar problems of isolation and coldness. The majority of his fellow students came from schools in and around the city and already knew each other: 'Thus the overseas student has either to walk alone or try to fit himself to any group that will have him'.[63]

Many students did make friends, discovering that friendship could exist alongside the English coolness. Class, and status within the university, could counterbalance foreignness or race. Before the First World War Prince Yusupov was unusual, not just in his enormous wealth but also that he could claim that on arriving in Oxford in 1909 'within a few days I knew almost everyone in college'.[64] A decade later, though his countryman Vladimir Nabokov claimed never to have warmed to Cambridge, he wrote lyrically about punting on the Cam with his friend Violet and, while she apparently kept her distance, made no suggestion that he was friendless:

> I had no interest whatever in the history of the place, and was quite sure that Cambridge was in no way affecting my soul, although actually it was Cambridge that supplied not only the casual frame, but also the very colours and inner rhythms for my very special Russian thoughts. [65]

Another decade on, another exile, Dmitri Obolensky remembered how

> Before long I found myself having an absorbing social life. Being invited to numerous parties by undergraduates and dons was a novel and exciting experience. The feeling that I was liked and appreciated added to the many attractions of Cambridge. Had I then been familiar with Vladimir Nabokov's autobiography *Speak memory* I would probably have wondered how the author…could so signally have failed to enjoy himself.[66]

Students from outside Europe were as positive. Among Indian students, both K. P. S. Menon, who wrote of a 'positive sea of friendship', and M. C. Chagla, who were at Oxford soon after the First World War, spoke of their many friends there, though both mainly quote the names of others from south Asia.[67] Solomon Bandaranaike found it took time to get acceptance from his peers and even his Eurasian contemporaries. He changed all that by making a name for himself in the Oxford Union.

> With the establishment of my position at the Union, and my recognition as one of its foremost speakers, a new world had opened up to me. Gone were the days when I wandered with shame about the dark and dingy outer halls of Oxford. I had gained entrance to the richest inner chambers of 'Varsity life.... Young men no longer hesitated to greet me and walk along with me, who would have evaded me furtively before. What snobs the majority of Englishmen really are! But what proved most amusing was the conduct of one or two Burgher lads, who made a point of avoiding their dark-skinned Ceylonese friends through fear of being dropped by their English acquaintances. These now thought that they had nothing to lose by recognizing me. My victory, I felt, must indeed be complete.[68]

Despite the victory he could not escape prejudice and thought that it had prevented his becoming president of the Union.[69]

Bandaranaike was able to use class, derived from his privileged background, and status within Oxford, to master the English system. Others saw how the class system was embedded in England's older universities and reacted against it. The Canadian socialist and Rhodes scholar David Lewis 'found it objectionable that a healthy young man like myself was not required to wash his own dishes, sweep his own floors or make his own bed' at Oxford in the 1930s. He failed in attempts to stop being addressed as 'sir'.[70] In the same way, 20 years later, Brian Gould was 'shocked by the pervasiveness of the class structure. I found it embarrassing to be looked after by a grown man (a "scout") whose job it was to make my bed, until I dispensed with his services.' He was at the same time realistic in recognising that Oxford endowed him with a privilege to take him through life: 'In English society, getting a good Oxford degree is almost like a magic talisman. It wards off evil spirits and is as effective as abracadabra at opening doors'.[71]

The apparent coolness and indifference of the British was not simply class – or race – prejudice. But race and class were part of it. As Indians formed the largest group of non-white students before the First World War, much of the discussion of prejudice was about them (see Chapter 4). Attitudes changed slowly but after the First World War it was claimed that the Indian military record had reduced prejudice.[72] Although the Lytton committee recognised that there were still problems in Oxford and Cambridge in the 1920s, the atmosphere seems, from memoirs, to have become happier by the 1930s: J. D. Shukla commented that in the late 1930s 'It was so pleasant to be in Oxford' while in 1935 D. F. Karaka became the first Indian president of the Oxford Union.[73]

While Indian students attracted the greatest publicity before the First World War, by the 1920s overseas students from other parts of the world were gaining attention and sometimes meeting hostility. Egyptians were often lumped with the Indians by critics of overseas students and both groups were classified as 'oriental' by Oxford University, while Europeans, Americans and Australians were put in the separate 'overseas' category. Palestinian Jews were overseas, Palestinian Arabs were oriental.[74] (There may well have been as much anti-semitism as colour prejudice: David Lewis, who was Jewish, exposed the views of one Rhodes trustee who told him 'he understood why Hitler wanted to eliminate my people'.[75]) While Egyptians had their share of opprobrium, Edward Atiyah, a Syrian Christian, educated in Egypt and with Egyptian friends, was extremely happy at Oxford in the early 1920s:

> Not even at the beginning did I in any way feel that I was a stranger, nor was I ever conscious of a racial prejudice against me. On the contrary I encountered kindness and friendliness everywhere. By my friends in College I was treated in every respect as one of them, and my identification with the English people was now complete.[76]

Among Asian students, the Siamese from today's Thailand were seen as welcome and well behaved. Imperial College commented warmly on its Chinese students.[77] In Cambridge, Japanese, Siamese and Chinese students were better received than Indians where 'The latter were reported to be regarded as "black men" and the others merely as "yellow men"'.[78] For much of the twentieth century the degree of prejudice, or the warmth of welcome, towards overseas students was a function of the darkness of their skin.

Students from sub-Saharan Africa were often therefore less fortunate than those from Asia. In 1929 Hanns Vischer explained at the Colonial Office, where he was advising on educational policy, that African students saw the 'different treatment meted out to Indians, Egyptians and men from the Near East and they object to it. ... The fact is that the English home, often open to Indians and others, is closed to the African negro'.[79] A year later Sir Michael Sadler, the master of University College Oxford, who had a reputation as an imaginative and liberal educator, was 'doubtful if a negro would be really happy in College life ... [although] they are doing all that they can to admit the proportion of Oriental students that can be assimilated'.[80] Cambridge told the Colonial Office in 1938 that 'all Colleges were reluctant to accept coloured students and…all would feel more difficulty in accepting Africans than others'.[81] Women may have had a better time of it than men. There were then nearly as many 'girls who are sent to England to qualify as nurses, midwives or even doctors' from the colonies as there were men but they were reported to suffer 'from fewer disabilities whilst in England than the men, and are cared for adequately by the institutions to which they are sent'.[82]

Life was easier within universities than outside, often easier for students than for immigrants. In Oxford in the 1920s there was prejudiced amusement and geographical ignorance rather than hostility:

> There were very few, if any, Negro undergraduates, but Asiatics abounded, and these were usually referred to as 'black men' whether they were pale Egyptians or dusky Tamils. There was no rancour in the appellation; it was simply that these exotics seemed as absurd among the stones of Oxford as topeed tourists in the temples and mosques of the orient; there was no hint of deliberate personal contempt; still less of hostility. It struck us as whimsical to impute cannibalism to these earnest vegetarians. We may have caused offence.[83]

Racial prejudice survived the Second World War, with some loss of vigour. Whereas between the wars African and Caribbean students had difficulty in finding restaurants that would accept them 'except as members of a jazz band', by the mid-1950s this was reported to be no longer a problem.[84] Despite that advance, a survey of colonial students in the early 1950s found that nearly three-quarters of Africans had personal experience of colour prejudice; smaller numbers of students from Asia and the Caribbean also reported prejudice.[85] A follow-up survey, ten years later, found that about half of all students from east Africa believed 'themselves to be victims of some form or other of discrimination'.[86] While the two surveys (which are not strictly comparable) might suggest prejudice was declining, other evidence shows the reverse. Immigration became a charged political issue in the 1950s even before the Commonwealth Immigrants Act of 1962 changed the legal status of actual and potential immigrants.

Trainee nurses saw discrimination as a regular part of the job and 'only one in ten said they had never experienced what they interpreted as unfair treatment from a senior nurse'. One explained how: 'You are new on the ward and don't get shown around and then someone else comes on – English – and they are told everything. It's the same old thing – colour'.[87]

Concern about racial tensions became a repeated theme of reports by Commonwealth scholars in the 1960s. In 1965, for example, two scholars studying in London reported on 'students being manhandled by a group of white boys in places like railway stations' and 'a few sudden and shocking behaviours from strangers'. One doctoral student from Northern Rhodesia studying in Glasgow commented:

> Talking about the racial problem in this country, my personal impression is that the situation has worsened since I came here last year, in fact one can almost 'see' it deteriorate every day. It is no doubt part of the general wave of discontent about the immigrants from other countries, and since people in this country do not bother to take the trouble of drawing a line between the ordinary immigrant worker and the 'so-called' students the situation is hitting us more.[88]

Prejudice was never universal. Students repeatedly commented that while it was a standard feature of British life, it was rarely encountered in college or university. Small colleges were likely to be more friendly than large, while institutional policy could make a difference as the University of London Institute of Education and the London School of Economics demonstrated, developing relatively easy and unprejudiced relations with their large numbers of overseas students.[89] There was friendliness too. When east African students in the 1960s were asked about the qualities that most impressed them, considerateness or friendliness came top of the list among students in Scotland, with many in London reacting in the same way.[90] Despite their experience outside college, Commonwealth scholars commented that 'it is a great relief for us to see that the universities with their affiliated institutions are totally free of such racial prejudice'. One scholar from Basutoland, familiar with South Africa and Rhodesia, even commented on the lack of prejudice in Northern Ireland alongside its 'quaint oratory'.[91]

Racial discrimination became illegal with the Race Relations Act of 1976 and overt prejudice declined, without entirely disappearing, so that it was unusual for a Commonwealth scholar to be reporting in 1982 that a fish and chip shop in Glasgow had refused to serve him. He explained that his British friends 'were very much embarrassed and kindly shared their fish and chips with me. I am not reporting this because I was offended. No. ... But I think it is important to be aware of such incidences'.[92] While, even in 1993 Commonwealth scholars were reporting 'disturbing, though few, instances of racial abuse' and it seems that overt displays of prejudice slowly ceased to be a regular part of daily life.[93]

For much of the twentieth century students, regardless of their background often had problems with accommodation, with race more important than class in compounding their difficulties. It may have been easier in the early years of the century, and in the provinces than in London. When William Macmillan arrived at Oxford from South Africa in 1903 the college porter found him digs.[94] Yusupov and Bandaranaike were more fortunate as they began their Oxford careers living in their colleges although in his third year Bandaranaike had to 'tramp round trying every house which had a board up "rooms to let". I usually received the answer that the rooms had just been booked by someone else, or more frankly, was told that they did not like to have Easterners'.[95] Medical students in Edinburgh faced problems of accommodation in 1907, which appear to have continued after the First World War, although the Lytton committee sniffily commented that 'Scottish Universities are apparently unconcerned to know how their students live or what they do outside the University buildings'.[96] Even 32 per cent of the relatively privileged Rhodes scholars reported problems with accommodation.[97]

It was worse in London and worse for black students. (It could sometimes be difficult for northern Europeans. When Pyotr Kapitsa arrived from Russia in 1921 he found that London landlords turned him down if he wore a cloth cap but accepted him in a suit.[98]) Studies of student experience from the 1940s to the 1960s repeatedly tell the same story. In 1948:

> Many colonial students at British universities and colleges are living in slums and deriving the worst possible impressions of the British way of life. That, in plain language, is an epitome of the evidence given by a spokesman for the Colonial Office at a recent Press conference in London.[99]

It was not a new problem. The Lee-Warner committee recognised its existence but concluded that the 'provision of residential hostels and the organisation of recreation, hospitality and social intercourse should, we consider, be left entirely to private enterprise, and should not be the concern of Government'. The Victoria League, set up in 1901 to support colonial interests, had premises in Cromwell Road and some students were looked after by the Northbrook Society, founded in 1879, which itself opened a hostel for overseas students in 1910. Gradually more hostels were provided. By 1939, London had an Indian students' hostel run by the YMCA with funding from Indian provincial governments, a West African Students Union hostel and one run by the Student Christian Movement. In the 1940s the Colonial Office accepted that it needed to provide more accommodation and, by 1950, had set up a colonial centre and a women's hostel, both in London . It then passed over responsibility for the hostels, and for student welfare generally, to the British Council in 1950.[100] Over the next two decades individual London colleges added to the amount of accommodation by building their own student hostels.

The building of hostels specifically for overseas students was initially seen as controversial and even undesirable, separating foreigners from the civilising influence of their hosts. Nor were hostels universally welcomed by overseas students. Indian students suspected that the India Office was keeping an over-close watch on them in any accommodation funded by government and preferred the Indian YMCA. Similarly the West African Students Union opposed the establishment of Aggrey House, opened in 1935 with funding from the Colonial Office, that brought with it suspicions of surveillance.[101]

Despite the controversy, students with college or hostel accommodation were at an advantage and those outside them faced greater difficulties. They were most severe for those from outside Europe. Loughborough did not want to treat colonial students 'differently from other non-European overseas students'. The more fortunate students had study bedrooms but others were in dormitories (unheated) or superior dormitories (heated) and it was reported that 'although the authorities manage occasionally to place a coloured student in a dormitory it has not been found a happy arrangement'.[102] In London in the early 1950s Carey found that 'with the exception of a small minority who live in hostels for the whole of their stay, most students feel that the accommodation problems are among the most unpleasant features of their stay'. When they found accommodation many black students thought the price was inflated because of the colour of their skin – a colour tax. A survey of landladies, registered with a student accommodation agency, found that 82 per cent would accept students from the United States and the 'white dominions', 70 per cent continental Europeans, 26 per cent 'lightly-coloured non-Europeans' and 10 per cent 'Africans and other Negroes'.[103] The earlier of the two PEP surveys of 1955 and 1965 found that the new colonial student's search for accommodation brought 'him into contact, at the earliest occasion, with the worst possible aspect of his relations with the British people'.[104]

Little changed in the next ten years. Landladies were often at best insular, at worst prejudiced. Students who did not have temporary accommodation on arrival were 'most exposed to the discriminatory practices of some landladies and the bitter experience of rejection on the door-step of possible lodgings. And when they do find accommodation, "for many the conditions are truly appalling"'.[105]

It took several decades and action on several fronts to resolve the problem. Building more hostels was part of the solution. The race relations legislation, which made it more difficult for landladies to display and act from prejudice, formed another part. Yet another was a change in attitude on the part of universities. In the last two decades of the century they paid greater attention to student welfare and housing, for their increased numbers of overseas students who were now paying full-cost fees. At Nottingham University, for example, where there had been no one point of reference for overseas students and for the university's international activities, an international office was established in 1982 in order to fill that gap. By the 1990s, as the Erasmus programme was bringing increased numbers of students to Britain, accommodation difficulties were well down the list of problems for students. Three-quarters of the Erasmus total had sorted out their accommodation in less than a day while only 15 per cent saw accommodation as their most serious problem in Britain. Confrontations with landladies were almost a thing of the past for these students of whom 65 per cent were in university halls or residences and 32 per cent in apartments with other students.[106]

Once overseas students had achieved a modus vivendi with their host society, and found somewhere to live, they could begin to work. For some, even after the Second World War, university life was little more demanding than it had been for their predecessors a couple of centuries before. Brian Bamford arrived from South Africa in 1951 as a law student on a Rhodes scholarship and described his Oxford day. After breakfast he would spend half an hour at the porter's lodge with post and newspapers before going to one or two lectures and having an extended mid-morning coffee break. Lunch was a formality 'both on account of the shocking food and because rugby practices began promptly at two o'clock'. Rugby occupied his afternoons but he had tutorials twice a week between 6 and 7 p.m. He and his friends did not distinguish themselves at these. 'It was not that we did not work, but merely that we were still too close to school, where an essay is something superficial, either to enjoy or benefit from an hour which is ideally one of give-and-take'.[107]

He may have been exceptional and life may have been easier for lawyers than for scientists. Michael Berridge, who went on to a distinguished career in biochemistry, recalled arriving as a graduate student from Southern Rhodesia in the 1960s and finding it was

> every bit as hard as I thought it was going to be, to be honest ... Well, the other two [postgraduates] were Cambridge graduates and they knew their way around the department ... and I was still looking around for apparatus and not really knowing what I was doing. I learnt very quickly.

Similarly a New Zealand pharmacologist of the early 1990s found that: 'It was hard work ... Three years is quite tight to come from abroad and be expected to do a PhD and have it written up, completed and examined.' Hard, determined and successful work was a feature of many students' lives, documented by tutors as well as students. Tutors who supervised Commonwealth scholars, recruited competitively on academic merit, repeatedly commented on 'outstanding' students, or 'one of the best of the class' and even 'the most organised student I have ever known'.[108]

The statistical record confirms the impression that a fair proportion of overseas students were hard-working and successful. They often had a better record at postgraduate than at undergraduate level. In the 1920s Indian doctoral students had higher completion rates at both Oxford and Cambridge than those for their own graduates. At three London colleges, University College, the London School of Economics and Imperial College, the overseas figure was 77 per cent while the home-grown students managed only 53 per cent. Indians studying for doctorates at Oxford performed better than Oxford graduates over the whole period from 1917 to 1959.[109] In Edinburgh in the 1920s 'of the overseas postgraduate, one seldom hears anything but appreciation here: he brings and carries away friendly feelings, and his influence tends towards the development of an international friendliness'.[110] The pattern continued after the Second World War. Commonwealth scholars who arrived in Britain in 1984 achieved postgraduate completion rates of between 70 per cent for doctorates and 95 per cent for master's degrees while a further study in the mid-1990s reported rates comparable to those for home students funded through the British research councils. The research council figures then improved so that by 2008 Commonwealth scholars had fallen behind. Scholars in the sciences performed better than those in the humanities and social sciences, reflecting the pattern among students as a whole, regardless of where they came from.[111]

In contrast with the comparative success of the postgraduates, a larger proportion of overseas undergraduates in Britain found study a struggle. There was steady criticism early in the century of potential students from India who arrived with inadequate preparation (see Chapter 4). Nearly all needed 'help beyond that which is given them in the ordinary course by the authorities of the School or University at which they study or is available in handbooks'. When Edinburgh's overseas postgraduates were performing well its overseas undergraduates had a graduation rate of only 56.5 per cent in the faculties of arts and sciences, and in medicine of 60 per cent where home student rates were 92 and 81 per cent. The principal attributed the difference partly to a false expectation that Edinburgh degrees were a soft option, partly to language difficulties, but mainly to undergraduates' being inadequately prepared and sometimes too immature.[112]

Undergraduate pass rates in London in the 1950s were lower than those for home students. Full-time colonial students doing a BScEcon at the London School of Economics achieved a pass rate of 60 per cent, at the first try, as compared with 77 per cent for all students.[113] Students outside universities seeking lower-level qualifications also tended to have poor results. Progress was particularly slow and difficult for the west Africans who arrived in London in the early or middle 1960s and combined work and study. Despite their hopes of studying and returning home, 40 per cent of those surveyed in 1970–2 had already been in Britain for eight years while only one in four was able to study full time.[114]

A steady minority of overseas students, including both the more and the less privileged, found their course was disappointing or unsatisfactory. A quarter of all Rhodes scholars 'had problems with the course they had chosen'.[115] Commonwealth scholars in the 1960s repeatedly criticised their teaching and complaints were most marked in the humanities at Oxford and Cambridge (see Chapter 5). Woodville Marshall, who came from Barbados to do a doctorate in history, found no one in Cambridge who could effectively supervise him and relied on advice by post from historians in the Caribbean. As he needed to spend most of his time in the archives in London he then ran into difficulties with the university authorities who thought he had spent too few nights within the specified distance from the university church.[116] A survey in the 1980s of study fellows funded through the government technical cooperation and training programme, working at all levels from technicians' courses to postgraduate degrees, found that while over 90 per cent were satisfied with their programme, only about a third had been able to specify their own training needs or felt they had sufficient advance information about their course.[117] Towards the end of the twentieth century, Erasmus students from southern Europe reported difficulties with quality and standards when they travelled north.[118]

Alongside the disappointed and the ill-advised there was a steady line of criticism, often from good scholars, of the quality of teaching that overseas students found when they arrived. Robert Oppenheimer moved to Cambridge from Harvard in 1925 and described his early reactions to a friend studying at Oxford:

> I do not think that Cambridge can be quite so bad as Oxford. But the excellences here are just as fantastically inaccessible, and there are vast, sloppy strata where there is nothing, absolutely nothing, to be found... Most of the scientists are frightful. But all of them are uncommonly skilful at blowing glass and solving differential equations, and the academic standard here would depopulate Harvard over night. ... I am having a pretty bad time. The lab work is a terrible bore, and I am so bad at it that it is impossible to feel that I am learning anything.[119]

Another contemporary, from Newfoundland, found that most of the lectures he attended at Oxford were 'very inferior' to what he had been used to at McGill.[120] Ten years later, in the same spirit, an Indian student found that 'the value of my stay at Oxford was the texture and experience of living in a social and economic order that enjoyed real freedom. Intellectually I got very little out of Oxford, less so than from St Stephen's [Delhi]'.[121] Among overseas students in Oxford, well after the war, 'there were very strong criticisms of the syllabi, especially in Law, English, History and Modern Languages'.[122]

Academic experience was inevitably mixed. Where there are statistics, favourable results outweigh unfavourable at least for postgraduate students; more anecdotes are positive than negative. At least until the 1970s, twentieth-century students saw academic problems as less significant than those caused by coolness towards strangers, hostility towards non-Europeans and the shortage of accommodation.

There continued to be more to many student lives than academic work. Sport was important for some where Rhodes scholars set a benchmark. Bamford was not alone in spending every afternoon in playing rugby.

Rhodes would have approved. By 1991 30 per cent of Rhodes scholars had played some sport for Oxford University while 61 per cent had played regularly or occasionally at their college, only slightly less than the 66 per cent who got a first or second class BA.[123] Between the wars sport was consistently encouraged. Scottish universities explained that they wanted overseas students to 'play their part in the social and corporate life of the College' through sport and the India students' department found in 1923 that:

> It was everywhere emphasised that Indian students who are prepared to do this, especially those who take an active part in the University games and athletics, find no difficulty in mixing freely, and making friends with, their fellow students, and at Edinburgh one of the Professors spoke with real appreciation of students who had joined the harriers or who played good tennis.[124]

For many students domestic, national, or in its day colonial politics were more important than sport. For some, as for Bandaranaike, this was a matter of plunging into student politics at the Oxford or Cambridge Union societies where Waugh found that 'these emergent politicians [from Asia] made themselves at home and introduced a vehemence that was normally lacking in our debates'. Reaching high office could form the prelude to an active political life. The presidency of the Union, which had eluded Bandaranaike, offered politically successful students kudos that they might not achieve through other routes. David Lewis, who was to return to a life in Canadian politics, felt that he could not compete with more athletic Rhodians in the early 1930s so asked the warden of Rhodes House if becoming president would do instead.[125]

During the colonial period the politics of liberation were more important than student politics and these tended to bring students into confrontation with authority, with suspicion on both sides. While the Lee-Warner committee in 1907 worried about those who carried on 'constant advocacy of pronounced opinions on political and social matters' while holding aloof from college sport, *The Times* warned that Indian students 'frequently found their chief zest, outside the range of their studies, in political discussion in which emphasis was laid on the imagined "wrongs" of India'.[126] For their part Indian students found that 'Scotland Yard dogs their footsteps' and the *Manchester Guardian* wrote in 1910 of 'the evil consequences of the social suspicion, distrust, and cold-shouldering which in too many cases is the treatment received by our Indian fellow-subjects when they come here to share in the educational opportunities which all ought equally to enjoy'.[127] After the First World War there was an 'almost universal belief' that the Indian students' department existed 'to exercise surveillance over their political opinions'.[128] In 1934 a student magazine, *Student vanguard*, was (uncharacteristically) banned at the London School of Economics after alleging that tutors at Oxford and Cambridge were spying on their students and that a retired Indian policeman fulfilled the same function at LSE.[129]

While the Indian students of the early twentieth century were undergraduates first and politicians second, the accelerating pace of decolonisation suggests that it was almost the other way round for some of the first generation of African independence leaders. Kwame Nkrumah signed up to study anthropology at LSE in 1945 but switched to philosophy at University College and was admitted to Grays Inn in 1946. But in the same period, and with MI5 watching close behind, he was also active in the West African Students Union, in turn regional secretary and vice-president of the Pan-African Federation, attended the 6th pan African congress in Manchester, and was involved with the West African National Secretariat. Unsurprisingly he developed pneumonia (and was treated by Hastings Banda). A. J. Ayer, who was supervising his proposed thesis on knowledge and logical positivism thought 'he wanted answers too quickly. I think part of the trouble may have been that he wasn't concentrating very hard on his thesis. It was a way of marking time until the opportunity came for him to return to Ghana'.[130] Once he did so, he benefited from MI5's surveillance as its spooks were able, with more common sense than they are often credited, to reassure the colonial authorities that he was not a communist.[131]

Nkrumah may have been an extreme example of the politician marking time as a student whereas Tom Mboya, who spent a year at Ruskin College in the 1950s, successfully balanced intellectual and political activities. His education had been cut short, as his father could not afford to let him go beyond junior secondary school in Kenya, and he had qualified as a sanitary inspector. He made his way through the trade union movement and got to Oxford with a scholarship from the Workers' Travel Association to study political science and economics. And he made the most of Oxford in 'a year of unhurried thought' which 'gave me the time to read more, it taught me to look at books as a source of knowledge'. In contrast his weekends were more political and more cosmopolitan, often spent in London with Joan Wicken, then working for the Labour Party but later a key associate of Nyerere in Tanzania, or addressing meetings of organisations like the Movement for Colonial Freedom. With fellow overseas students at Ruskin he worked out the constitutional approach Kenya needed to take as Britain was flirting with a restricted franchise for its independence.[132]

Nkrumah and Mboya were only two of the many future political leaders who studied in Britain after the Second World War and sought to balance their formal and their political education. The alumni of the colonial hostel Nutford House included future leaders of Botswana, Guyana, Mauritius and Nigeria, all following in the footsteps of the earlier independence leaders of India.[133] Politics became a less consuming, or a less reported, activity for later generations of students. Commonwealth scholars from Southern Rhodesia during the illegal Smith regime were banned from political activity on behalf of Smith, but there seems no evidence and little likelihood that they would have wanted to proselytise for him.[134] (Many managed not to return home after graduation.) The press hinted that overseas students were partly to blame the student protests of 1968, themselves a pale reflection of *les événements* in Paris. Certainly there was vigorous activity among students of the social sciences at the London School of Economics and the University of Essex which had significant overseas numbers. But home-grown protesters were capable of taking the lead and foreign students, as contrasted with foreign influence, do not seem to have played a disproportionate part.

Academic work, sport and politics did not occupy the whole of every day. Until after the events of 1968, and the reduction of the age of majority from 21 to 18 in 1970, twentieth-century universities continued to interest themselves in student lives by night as well as day. Foreign students discovered the rules on arriving and found them irksome. Commonwealth scholars at Oxford, complained that for postgraduate students in their twenties requirements about dining and 'for those that "live in" about hours, are both onerous and pointless'.[135]

Rules about sex could be more onerous. They were imposed by colleges, universities and funding agencies and in some cases it took much of the twentieth century for them to be relaxed. From the outset Rhodes scholars had to be unmarried men, as women would be a distraction. Engagements came to be tolerated but at a distance: if there were fiancées they should live in London.[136] At St Catharine's College Cambridge in 1934 the rule book explained that

Gentlemen may entertain ladies in the rooms in college between the hours of 1 p.m. and 6 p.m., provided that they have signed a book which will be kept in the Porter's Lodge, and provided that at least one other gentleman or lady is to be present besides the host and his guest ... In exceptional cases permission to entertain a lady alone, or to entertain more than one lady after 6 p. m. may be obtained from the Junior Dean.[137]

The Rhodes trustees maintained their ban on marriage until 1959 when, with some reluctance, they agreed scholars could marry in their third year. Two years later they were warned that they were losing good potential scholars who could not face two years of celibacy, but stuck to their regulations. Meanwhile rules and assumptions about sex and gender were changing all round them, with contraceptive machines appearing in colleges in the 1960s, and Oxford and Cambridge colleges becoming mixed in the 1970s. Colleges lost interest in the sex lives of their students and stopped expelling or suspending those found in bed with a partner. But for their part, even after they admitted women as scholars, the Rhodes trustees kept their ban on married applicants until 1994.[138]

The rules on licit and illicit sex had two points of origin. One lay in the assumption that colleges had a quasi-parental responsibility to enforce a moral code over students below the legal age of majority: in its Latin prose Oxbridge saw itself as *in loco parentis* over those *in statu pupillari*. For overseas students from outside Europe the other starting point was a shared suspicion of sex across racial boundaries and its consequences. K. P. S. Menon encountered the suspicious myth in 1905 when it was suggested that his brother should be sent to England to study for the bar:

There was only one danger, my father was told: English girls were vampires and would gobble up any young foreigner, and my brother would not be willing to be gobbled up. So it was decided that he should be married before he left for England, and he accepted this condition. He married the charming daughter of the Peshkar, or District Magistrate, of Kottayam and sailed for England three days later.[139]

The shared suspicion was common in Britain where it acquired another twist to embrace class as well as race. In evidence to the Lee-Warner enquiry in 1908 the chaplain of Balliol warned that Indian students were quicker than the English to 'seek out low society' while

Dr Knight at Edinburgh University had also observed that, while students in general were often pursued 'by shop girls and women of that class', Indians in particular were singled out more than other students. He attributed this to the fact that Indian students were often regarded as princes…The landlady's daughter was often a snare.

While she might be a snare and the male foreign student a threat, the 'perception of the Indian student as a sexual predator' existed awkwardly alongside upper-class British doubts about the morality of lower-class women.[140] As the twentieth century went on, and increasing numbers of students from Africa and the Caribbean joined the Indians, so they too came to be seen as potential predators. One London landlady in the 1950s explained that she could not have a west African tenant because 'we have young girls here and the doors aren't locked' while another claimed 'I always say we should give Colonials a chance to learn our ways. Of course, I couldn't take Negroes. I am sorry for them, but I have my daughter to consider'.[141]

The constraints and complications meant that some students simply avoided having a sex life. Menon 'developed a healthy contempt for women, for though women had just been admitted to Oxford, they were there on sufferance. This superior attitude enabled me to remain a virgin as long as I was at Oxford' in the 1920s. He found that life 'was too full, too rich, too exciting for me to seek casual flirtation or to crave animal satisfaction' with the result that he felt ill at ease with girls when visiting a friend in Edinburgh 'who seemed to keep a regular harem'. Evelyn Waugh's recollection suggests he was not untypical and thought that only 10 per cent of his contemporaries had girlfriends though 'some had made a single, pleasureless, adventure with a prostitute abroad'. It is unclear why fornication had to be in another country but Menon also reported that 'before leaving Europe I, together with some of my companions, tasted the forbidden fruit that was on display in the markets of the Continent'.[142]

Licit relationships existed alongside the illicit and some of these went across race lines. Despite the national concern about mixed marriages, some Indian students married and settled in Europe in the early twentieth century. The Lee-Warner committee was told of landladies' daughters and drapery assistants who had married Indian students who either moved to India with them or had 'taken up practice in mining areas of Britain such as Durham or Wales'.[143] Despite the prejudices of the time, mixed marriages were not confined to foreign students with working-class wives: the two oldest children of the Indian nationalist W. C. Bonnerjee were educated at Oxford and Cambridge before the First World War, with the older marrying an English wife – the daughter of a congregational minister – and the younger an English husband – the son of a Bradford businessman – both of whom they had met as college friends.[144]

After 1945 students' sex lives became more open and better documented as, while causing new difficulties for the authorities, they also attracted the interest of sociologists. (In a contrast between differing scholarly traditions at least one American study of foreign students reported on their bowel movements but not their sex lives.[145]) Many overseas students – some of whom had served in the war – assumed that they were old enough to make their own decisions about sex, and for that matter class and race. By the 1950s most male colonial students were 'anxious to find girl friends and complain about the great difficulties this involves'. Not all did so. Some saw cultural and race barriers as too high; one Nigerian, for example agued that inter-racial friendships 'never came to anything. English people resent them and I would object to my sister going out with a white'.[146]

At a time when Oxford and Cambridge colleges were still suspending students with visibly active sex lives, it was somewhat easier in London. In the late 1940s, at Nutford House, which was for men, a rule 7 prescribed when and whether students could entertain women in their private rooms but, with many trainee lawyers among the residents, jurisprudence found ways round the rules.[147] Enterprise also found ways over class barriers so that one student from British Guiana

> has had a number of girl friends, all of whom have been of working-class origin. He discontinues his interest in these women if they do not show themselves willing to go to bed with him within a reasonable period of time: 'two or three weeks at the most'.[148]

Similarly a Trinidadian had several girlfriends though he did not want to marry any of them. He complained that the women he met through his political activities were not good looking while those at a social club

> tended to be unattractive or otherwise unsatisfactory. Nevertheless he has had sexual relations with several of the women he has met in this way. He has found that even women who are reluctant to be seen in public in the company of a coloured man, are 'glad enough to sleep with them, if this can be kept quiet'.[149]

Class both influenced and complicated students' lives. While 85 per cent of upper-class Indian students had friendships with someone of the opposite sex, only 53 per cent of middle-class students did so.[150] For colonial students, it was often easier to meet young working-class women from the continent than young British women. One social club in London was patronised mainly by continental domestic workers and colonial students who, because of their colour, were 'usually able to contact only women of a social standing and of an educational background below that acceptable to British students'.[151] But friendships across colour and class lines were not always acceptable to other students. At Nutford House,

> At the first dance, given a few weeks after the house was officially opened, an African student invited a maid and she attended – much to the surprise of the warden and most of the students. There was talk of taking disciplinary action against the maid and this in itself caused concern. But there was also the fact that some of the students were very class conscious and abhorred the development. This was particularly the case among West Indian men who had West Indian girlfriends.[152]

While friendship and sex were possible for male students from the colonies by the 1950s and 1960s it presented more difficulties for women. In the eyes of Braithwaite, a male observer from Trinidad, the racial history of the Caribbean meant that 'the question of relationships with European girls came up…in many cases immediately on arrival…the question of How soon a girlfriend?, or How soon sexual relations with an English girl? was an immediate obsession'. At the same time many students expected that they would marry a West Indian woman: 'some of the West Indian men solved the problem by having two girlfriends, an English girl with whom he slept and a West Indian with whom he carried on a somewhat platonic relationship'.[153] For their part, women student nurses found themselves isolated, with the isolation worsened by the behaviour of their male peers. Among Nigerian students 'the most disturbing experience takes place at dances when the African girls sit out most of the evening while the English girls enjoy the company of their male partners'.[154] A Sierra Leonean nurse confirmed that at college dances in London 'even coloured men prefer to dance with English girls'.[155] Friends of a light-skinned trainee nurse from the Leeward Islands found a way round the problem by introducing her as French or Spanish rather than Caribbean.[156]

Sociology has acquired new interests since the 1960s, and educational institutions have abandoned their belief that they should control and document their students' relationships. As a result we know less about the sex lives of later generations of overseas students. From a study of student mobility in 2002, for example, which has neither sex nor love in its index, we learn only that

> Sharing accommodation with local people signals a desire to immerse oneself in their life with the added bonus of constant language practice and of socio-cultural discoveries from the inside. However, relationships which are fashioned in this type of context are immediately set on a more personal footing and as such exposed to the vagaries of subjective affinities.[157]

The vagaries of subjective affinities have, indeed, played themselves out in the lives of overseas students. While students' everyday experience has hugely changed across the centuries, there has been some continuity among the themes that shaped their lives. Relationships with each other, and with the British, have always been important; the records suggest that they have often been less than cordial, but records concentrate on conflict rather than on quiet harmony. Accommodation presented its difficulties in the Middle Ages, which became less severe as pressure on the universities reduced from the sixteenth to the nineteenth centuries, only to re-emerge in the twentieth. Students' days became less controlled while some elements of the teaching day survived, with lectures retaining their place and seminars taking that of disputations. They contributed to the lives of their institutions and, where we have figures, performed acceptably in examinations, with postgraduate results better than those at lower levels. Women, for many years kept officially at arm's length, came into colleges and universities in increasing numbers from the nineteenth century. Religion, that for centuries demanded time and allegiance, became less important while for many the ideology of politics in turn grew in its importance. Sport, once discouraged, later encouraged, had a constant appeal for some. Rules and prohibitions about sex remained in place for more than seven centuries and were steadily relaxed only in the last 50 years. Rules generally proved irksome at some institutions and for some students.

For the most part the everyday life of overseas students attracted little attention from policy-makers until the twentieth century. Their lives were influenced by national law and practice with migration law of steadily increasing importance as the twentieth century went on. Changes in the law on discrimination brought benefits for many in the

1970s. They were expected to behave like British gentlemen even if they encountered coolness or suspicion because they turned out not to be. Loyalty was required, in religion from the fifteenth century to the nineteenth century, and in politics in the nineteenth and twentieth. It was sometimes found lacking. Attitudes and practices shifted when overseas students were valued and seen as offering benefits either to institutions, or to the national or, in its day, imperial interest. More deliberate policies followed: affiliation agreements, allowance of advanced standing, specialist courses and, crucially, student hostels all changed British institutions and improved the lives of overseas students.

Student lives were also dominated by money, and its scarcity, the theme of the next chapter.

8

Poor Scholars and Endowed Scholars

Students have always complained of poverty. In the Middle Ages they used standard letters drafted by professional letter writers and sent them to their parents, guardians or patrons.[1] In the twenty-first century Commonwealth scholars set up a website to make their case. At the same time students' lives have often been privileged with their bills paid by somebody else – families, employers, institutions and scholarship agencies. Any exploration of why they did so needs to start by looking at the cost of being a student and at changes in the costs over time. Money was the fuel that drove the model of student mobility and the lubricant that helped students to travel.

Almost from the foundation of the English universities some students already received grants which suggest how much their education was costing. Henry III (1216–72) made royal grants of between £5 and £10 to a small number of favoured scholars. These were either kinsmen or students whose families he wanted to influence, and look generous in comparison with others.[2] Records survive for three students at an Oxford hall in 1424 which show that an undergraduate commoner, W. Clavyle, had total costs, including food and drink, rent, clothes, lecture fees and the cost of travel from home, of about £2 13s 0d a year. A contemporary named Okeford apparently managed on £1 12s 0d while another, Robert Canon, had costs of about £2 0s 3d, with the differences explained by differing expenditure on food and drink. Rent was a small proportion: Clavyle and Okeford were charged only 6d a year for their rooms, which were usually shared, with two to four students a room.[3] Some costs were slightly higher: at Merton College, Oxford, they were about £2 5s 6d for the 36 weeks of the university year, rising to £2 12s 6d by the end of the fifteenth century while a student at King's Hall in Cambridge was likely to spend £7 a year.[4]

The cost of education, as of everything else, rose in the sixteenth century so that by about 1600 students living frugally, or as batteliers who acted as servants to other students, would need £20 a year, which rose to £30 by 1660.[5] Fellow commoners, who had a higher status, had costs estimated at £30 to £35 in the 1590s, rising to £35 to £45 by 1610.[6] Costs at the Inns of Court were of the same order. They were about £30 at Grays Inn around 1600 but continued to rise so that by the 1620s students at the Middle Temple found it difficult to make ends meet on £40 a year.[7] Status naturally influenced cost. In the mid-1650s Lord Brooke managed to get through £450, though this was exceptionally high as it was estimated in 1687 that a nobleman could live at Christ Church for £120 to £200 a year.[8] Costs continued to rise, though more slowly, into the eighteenth century while these class differentials were maintained. The cost of supporting a commoner for a year rose from £50 in 1720 to between £80 and £100 in 1750.[9] By 1795 £300 was seen as too little for a fellow commoner.[10]

By the mid-nineteenth century costs had stabilised and remained at about the same level of between £150 and £250 until the 1930s. Annual totals at Cambridge in 1865 varied between '£125 for the economical and £250 for the indulgent' (who might treat themselves to another meal after dinner, served in the afternoon and likely to include up to two pounds of meat).[11] When the Indian government created scholarships in 1886 these were worth £200 a year, with another £100 for kit and passage, while the Gilchrist trust, which offered them for 'deserving natives' increased them in 1890 from £100 which had proved too low a figure.[12] Estimates of the cost of going to Balliol College, Oxford, in 1881 were at £187 5s 6d a year together with a one-off cost of £63 8s 0d.[13] At about the same time the National Indian Association put the total cost for three years at Oxford, Cambridge or London at £750 with initial expenses of £85.[14] Some awards were more generous, some less: Rhodes were set at £300, though their scholars were expected to pay their own passages, while Great Exhibition scholarships were only at £150 in 1890.[15] Nor did students always find them adequate so that Prio Krishna Majumdar, who went to Birmingham University in 1904 to study mining engineering, eked out his scholarship by coaching other students.[16] He might have envied his contemporary Jawaharlal Nehru who had £400 a year from his family, but still ran up debts. Stipends, costs and difficulties continued in the same way into the 1920s and 1930s when Indian students generally found they needed about £200 a year, with slightly higher figures for Oxford and Cambridge.[17] Fees at Sandhurst were at a similar level. In the early 1920s they varied between £55 and £200 according to the status and military record of the cadet's father.[18]

Inflation, during and after the Second World War, makes the later twentieth-century figures look completely different. The Commonwealth Scholarship Commission, which kept its awards broadly in line with other government scholarships, saw the personal stipend for single scholars rise from £624 in 1960 to £1,320 in 1975, £4,632 in 1990 and £8,268 in 2005. In 1965 the average annual cost per scholar was £830, with fares – mainly then by air – at an average of £279 return. By 1979 the average cost per scholar was £4,760 with an average return fare of £840. Continuing inflation and the introduction of full-cost fees took average annual costs to £15,170 in 1993 and £19,937 in 2001. These figures conceal marked, and new, differences between fees which now varied according to the subject of the degree course. The precedent was set in 1981 when government recommended annual undergraduate fees for overseas students of £2,000 in the arts, £3,000 in the sciences and £5,000 in clinical subjects. With universities free to determine their own postgraduate fees, and rising university costs, by the 2000s annual postgraduate fees in medicine and the life sciences sometimes exceeded £20,000 while MBAs could cost double this. (The Commission gritted its collective teeth and paid up for good students in the life sciences but rarely if ever for MBAs.[19])

While these sharp differences by subject were new, there were always differences between universities. In the early nineteenth century, Duncan Dewar spent seven sessions at St Andrews at a total cost of £101, half what he might have spent in a year at Oxford or Cambridge, partly helped by his meagre diet of porridge.[20] A poor student at Aberdeen in the 1840s could manage on less than £20 a session, suggesting a total cost of well under £100.[21] By the 1930s, when Oxford and Cambridge cost between £200 and £300 a year, it was possible to meet the cost of fees, board and lodging in a hostel at Edinburgh for £180, while figures for Birmingham and Manchester were lower.[22] In the late twentieth century costs in London, followed by those in Oxford and Cambridge, were higher than those for provincial universities. By 2002 single students with Commonwealth or Chevening awards received an annual stipend of £8,760 in London or £7,296 elsewhere in the country. Students in Oxford and Cambridge argued that their living costs were higher than the average but without success and a review of allowances rejected their case for a third tier of allowances.[23]

It is difficult to compare the 1s 6¼d weekly living cost for Clavyle in 1424 with that of a Commonwealth scholar on £159 in 2005. Not only does inflation make apparent nonsense of the figures, reflecting the fact that wages increased 150 times between 1264 and 1954 and prices by a further 17 times in the next 50 years, but patterns of expenditure changed as dramatically: candles were a necessity in the sixteenth century and an important part of the Cambridge economy, while laptops had become necessary by the twenty-first. Some comparisons are, however, possible. Phelps Brown and Stokes have collected data on wage rates for building craftsmen and labourers in southern England from 1264 to 1954 which show the earnings for a working day throughout this period.[24] With their figures, and the available data on university costs, it is possible to calculate how many days a craftsman builder would have to work in order to pay for one year at university, giving an index for comparing costs over the years. These results are set out, for the thirteenth to early twentieth century, in Table 8.1. As the retail price index, and its predecessors, have been in use since 1914 and extended back to 1900, costs for the twentieth and twenty-first centuries have been converted to constant 2010 currency.

The limited figures available suggest that in the fifteenth century a year's study would cost the equivalent of about 100 days skilled work. The relative cost then rose so that within a century a skilled builder would need to work at least 400 days in order to support a university student, and considerably more to support a gentleman or aristocrat. The figures then show a remarkable consistency and suggest that, from the sixteenth to the early twentieth century, annual university costs could be equated to somewhere between 400 and 600 days work. University education was never cheap: a skilled labourer who wanted to send two sons to university for three years would need to spend all his earnings for ten years in order to do so.

Costs of £150 to £200 [2010£14,800 to £19,800] in 1910 then fell in real terms to a level of around £200 [£10,000] between the wars.[25] After the Second World War inflation took them to £625 in the 1960s but with the cost in real terms remaining at about [£10,000]. Real-term costs then increased by 50 per cent to exceed £1,400 [£15,400] in the early 1970s. Rising university costs and the impact of full-cost fees then brought further increases for overseas students from outside Europe so that total annual costs for a student rose from around £6,700 [£18,000] in 1980 to £25,500 in 2010.[26] (As craftsmen builders' wages were at £21,163 in 2009–10, a builder would then, despite the increase in costs, be able to fund an overseas student for a year with something over a year's labour.[27])

The costs for a foreign student always included three elements – board and lodging, university fees and transport. Although we cannot always

Table 8.1   Some university costs, c. 1240–2010

Date	Sum per annum	What it is	Days of labour	2010££
1216–72	£5–£10	Royal grant to student	400–800	
1424	£2.10.0–£3.13.6	Undergraduate expenses at Oxford	100–147	
Late 15th century	£2.5.6–£2.12.6	Cost for 36 weeks at Merton, Oxford	91–105	
1580s–90s	£20	Sufficient for lower grades living frugally at Oxford	400	
1660	£30	Cost for batteler to live comfortably at Oxford	400	
Late 1680s	£120–200	Cost for nobleman at Christ Church, Oxford	1,600–2,667	
1720	£50	Cost of supporting commoner at Oxford	545	
1750	£80–100	Cost of supporting a commoner at Oxford	800–1,000	
1863	£125–250	Cost from economical to indulgent at Cambridge	417–833	
1886	£200	Government of India scholarships + kit and passage £100	667	
1920s–30s	£200	Costs for Indian student, Oxford/ Cambridge slightly more	267	9,000
1963	£715	Average cost Commonwealth scholar – fare £185		11,902
1979	£4,760	Average cost Commonwealth scholar – fare £840 return		18,807
1993	£15,170	Average cost Commonwealth scholar		24,105
2010	£25,487	Average cost Commonwealth university staff scholar	14–15 months	25,487

Sources: 1216: Pegues 'Royal support', 462; 1424 and late fifteenth century: Evans 'Oxfor 501–3; 1580s–90s and late 1680s: Porter 'University and society', 87; 1660: Stone 'Educatio revolution', 71; 1720 and 1750: O'Day *Education and society*, 198; 1863: Searby *History Cambridge*, 80; 1886: Brown 'Indian students', 145; 1920s–30s: Mukherjee *Nationalism*, 1 1963–2010: ACU, CSC papers.

break down the total cost, the first of these has generally been the highest. Board and lodging made up more than two-thirds of Clavyle and Okeford's expenditure in the fifteenth century. In the mid-nineteenth century, when a student would need a minimum of £150 a year at Merton College, Oxford, university and college fees were about £25 a year and private tuition £30, suggesting that board and lodging made up nearly two-thirds of the total.[28] In 1960 the maintenance cost for a Commonwealth scholar was £726 [£12,844] while fees were £85 [£1,508] so that board and lodging now made up almost 90 per cent of the total.[29] Living costs continued to rise although student grants did not keep pace with inflation so that by 2001 a Commonwealth scholar received a stipend of £6,960 [£8,978]. By this time fees had increased so that they were only slightly below the costs of board and lodging for students in classroom-based subjects, who paid postgraduate fees of £6,895 [£8,894]. Fees for students of laboratory-based or clinical subjects, at £8,700 [£11,223] or £17,093 [£22,050], were now well above the cost of board and lodging.

Costs for tuition have been a permanent element in the total but seldom a simple one. Clavyle and Okeford spent about 20 per cent of their income on university teaching costs and on payments to the principal. When students came to take their degrees, if they did, they would incur further fees but, in the Middle Ages, these were set at a different rate for poor, middle-class and rich students. They were at their lowest for students taking a bachelor's degree and their highest for doctorates. The poorest students, and the richest, tended to avoid paying fees by concessions available to both groups.[30] The many students who did not take a degree avoided paying the graduation fee and meeting the cost of feasts for the university masters which were part of the expected package. While some of these costs dropped out of the equation, others came into it. By the nineteenth century, when feasts no longer had to be paid for, college teaching had become so inadequate that students at Oxford and Cambridge needed to pay for private tuition as well. Alongside their college tuition fees of £10 a year, they could therefore expect to pay around £50 a year to a private tutor.[31] Edinburgh had a different system, abolished in 1894, of individual payments of fees for lectures and fees to professors. Like the Oxbridge system this aroused controversy; the author James Barrie, who studied at Edinburgh from 1878 to 1882, wrote of 'the opening of the Session when fees are paid, and a whisper ran round the Quadrangle that Masson [professor of rhetoric and English literature] had set off with three hundred one-pound notes stuffed into his trouser pockets'.[32] But these were exceptions and expenditure on fees and tuition remained a minor part of total student costs until the late twentieth century.

The cost and hazards of travel had an influence on students' willingness to study abroad; there were more Welsh students in Oxford than in Cambridge because it was nearer.[33] Travel was hazardous by land or by sea so that, from its establishment, Trinity College Dublin attracted students from within Ireland as this avoided the perils of sea travel. This advantage was eroded, at least for the aristocracy, once steam packets were running across the Irish Sea.[34] But neither hazard nor cost was ever a complete barrier. Within continental Europe, where students would travel in groups and follow well-established trade routes, wandering scholars did so both before and after the Reformation (see Chapter 9). Until then travel was even more affordable for monks and friars who could rely on religious accommodation on the way. By the seventeenth century, while in real terms travel costs were high as compared with their later levels, the figures suggest that travel costs, while substantial, were lower than students' other costs. The fare between Dover and Calais was 5s 0d at a time when a student might need £20 to £30 a year; in 1655 five middle-class men travelled from Venice to London for £125 in total and many students would have travelled in less comfort and at less cost.[35]

Travel was cheaper by sea than by land. A passage across the Atlantic in 1650 would have cost about £6, amounting to between three and four months work for a skilled craftsman. Costs then remained at about the same level between the late seventeenth century and the early nineteenth. They then fell, in real terms, by as much as 80 per cent between 1816–21 and 1859–61 so that in the late nineteenth century steerage costs across the Atlantic were as low as £3.[36] Steamships and the opening of the Suez Canal together brought down fares from India. Towards the end of the century, a successful Indian barrister, W. C. Bonnerjee, was able to fund fares to school and university in England for seven children and could also afford an annual visit himself, and pay for the cost of a sea-going ayah when his children were returning.[37] Second-class fares – and students could have paid less than these – between Europe and India were advertised at £35 in the 1880s and £27 in the 1890s, which included wine at table if you travelled with an Italian line.[38] The sudden increase in Australian students towards the end of the nineteenth century was helped by the fall in sea fares. The twentieth century then brought further reductions, most marked as mass air travel replaced travel by sea. In 1960 a return fare for a Commonwealth scholar or fellow cost an average of £240 [£4,310].[39] Inflation brought an apparent increase to £840 by 1980 but a real reduction to [£2,806].[40] Fares continued to fall so that by 1988 return fares for Erasmus students travelling within Europe took up only 6 per cent of their total expenditure.[41] By 2010 the average air fare for

Commonwealth academic fellows had fallen to £885.[42] By the twenty-first century, while the cost of travel must have deterred some potential students, it was no longer an important part of their budget.

To summarise, until the late twentieth century board and lodging was likely to be the largest single item in a student's total budget, probably followed by the cost of travel, and with the cost for university fees and tuition as the smallest. Travel costs then fell while fees rose so that by 2010 fees for Commonwealth university staff scholars made up 46 per cent of their total costs against 50 per cent for maintenance and only 4 per cent for fares.[43] Fees made up an even higher percentage for students in the sciences or medicine. The changes, and the amounts involved, had implications for the three groups of people who found the money – students and their families, sponsors and employers, and scholarship agencies.

While it is difficult to determine the exact proportions of these groups, all the evidence suggests that individual students and their families usually met the costs of foreign study. This was true alike for the West Indian plantocracy in the eighteenth century, the black middle class of west Africa and medical students from America in the nineteenth, and the prosperous Indian middle class. In the nineteenth century, local income differentials were so great that 'at the top of the social pyramid, African and Indian elites often sent their children to Britain for schooling and higher education' and could afford to do so.[44] They did so before scholarships were widely available and continued to do so in larger numbers than the scholarship holders. Discussion of Indian students before the First World War was predominantly about these self-financed students. 'Indian', who wrote anonymously to the *Manchester Guardian* in 1910, referred not to scholarships but to the fact that his fellow students 'are sent here, at considerable sacrifice, by their parents'.[45] By 1921, while there were some 1,500 Indians studying in Britain, only 80, listed under the heading 'government scholars', were under the charge of the Indian Students' Department. By 1927 some 175 were on scholarships out of a total of 1,600.[46] Inevitably some students ran out of money, so that by 1921 322 from India had been helped by the Distressed Indian Students' Aid Committee.[47]

Students from the colonies showed a similar pattern to those from India. In 1929 the educational adviser to the Colonial Office knew of 125 self-supported young Africans at British universities, many of whose fathers had themselves been educated in Britain.[48] At this time the director of colonial scholars was looking after only 113 students, up from 30 in 1920.[49]

Family funds could stretch to school as well as university fees and, at least for some, needed to do so. There were few public schools in India, apart from those 'intended exclusively for the sons of Ruling Princes and Nobles'.[50] The education department of the Indian high commission saw this as a regrettable problem as it drove parents to send their children to school in England. The department looked forward to the establishment of 'more schools on the lines of the great English public schools' within India.[51] Families from the ruling class of the empire beyond India could afford to place their sons under charge of the director of colonial students; in the late 1920s he was looking after the young son of the Amir of Trans-Jordan, and the nine sons of the Sultan of the Unfederated Malay State of Kedah.[52] Less wealthy families found that scholarships met some, but not all, of the costs so that they had to find the rest: the Syrian student, Edward Atiyah, needed £250 a year on top of his £150 scholarship when he went to Oxford in 1922 (see Chapter 7).[53] Indian parents who wanted their sons to have a military career might be able to send them to Sandhurst, with a grant of £200 from the government of India, but would still have to find a further £477, and the cost of travel, to pay for the 18-month course.[54]

Privately funded students continued to form the majority of those from overseas after the Second World War, even though far more scholarships became available for the colonies. By 1948 there were thought to be more than 1,300 scholarship holders and more than 1,900 private students in the United Kingdom and Ireland while by 1955 the figure had risen to 10,200 of whom less than one-third were on scholarships.[55] Scholarship numbers then increased so that in the early 1960s the Robbins committee found that some 45 per cent of overseas undergraduates and 60 per cent of postgraduates were on awards, with the balance apparently self-financed.[56] It is likely that those dependent on their families and their own income formed a higher proportion of the total among students outside the universities. The overseas students studying part-time for school-level and professional qualifications in the 1960s and 1970s, who had arrived before the tightening of immigration restrictions, generally tried to fund themselves. Only 11 per cent were dependent on grants, loans or even families.[57]

Private and family finance continued to dominate in the late twentieth and early twenty-first century, even as university fees rose and student numbers increased. In 1997/8, among higher-education students from the Commonwealth, 68 per cent of those from rich countries were self-funded as were well over half of those from developing countries.[58] In

2004/5 almost two-thirds of all international students in higher education and four out of five undergraduates, were reported to be self-funded.[59] Erasmus students benefited from European Union funding but many of them also topped up their awards with their own money.[60]

Families who continued the centuries-old tradition of sending their sons (more often than their daughters) to schools in Britain, and the more recent one of sending their daughters (more than their sons) to language schools, also used their own funds to do so. Dillibe Onyeama who went to Eton in 1965 and claimed to be only the second African ever to go there, was one of these. His father had been educated at Oxford and put Onyeama's name down for Eton at birth when he was working as a magistrate in Mid-Western Nigeria. While he later became a supreme court judge, his public-sector earnings – or family wealth – were already enough to send his son first to a prep school, then to a crammer's and then to Eton, whose fees were £614 [£8,859] in 1967.[61] Expectation of long-term benefits, and the use of British schools as a route into university, continued to attract parents despite the level of school fees required. These fell in real terms in the late 1970s, when schools showed a temporary reluctance to match inflation, but then rose again later in the century (see Table 8.2). By the twenty-first century, parents convinced of the value of British schooling would have to pay school fees that amounted to as much as sending a child to university: assuming a parent paid about the same stipend as that received by Commonwealth scholars (£7,000) and overseas undergraduate fees also of about £7,000, the total university cost in 2001 came to £14,000 [£18,063] while the average cost for a boarder at a public school was £14,208 [£18,332].

Language schools made more modest demands on parental budgets, though mainly because students stayed there for weeks or months rather than years. In 1981 language students in Cambridge spent an average of £726 [£2,170] per head; those in Bournemouth in 1994 had bills of £783 [£1,215] for a four-week course.[62] Estimates by the Department of Business, Innovation and Skills, interested in the value of British educational exports, put the average tuition fees at about £1,000 [£1,100] in 2008 with the other costs of the same order of magnitude.[63] Parents, or others funding these students, also had to meet the cost of travel to Britain.

International study was never cheap but families' great expectations consistently took their children to Britain to study.

Alongside students who were paid for by their families, others had their costs met by an employer or a patron so that study in Britain came with

Table 8.2   Boarding school fees, 1966–2010

Date	Type of school	Annual boarding fee ££	Fee in 2010££
1966	Major boarding schools – average cost	545	8,583
1971	Major boarding schools – average cost	951	10,619
1976	Major boarding schools – average cost	1,598	8,978
1979	Major boarding schools – average cost	2,289	9,043
1980	Major boarding schools – average cost	2,744	9,185
1986	Headmasters' Conference Schools	4,593	10,501
1991	Headmasters' Conference Schools	7,869	13,180
1996	Headmasters' Conference Schools	11,598	16,983
2001	Headmasters' Conference Schools	15,105	19,489
2007	Independent schools	20,136	21,793
2010	Independent schools	24,009	24,009

Sources: 1966–80: J. Rae 1981 *The public schools*, London, 163; 1986–2010 ISIS/ISC *Annual census.*

the job. The motivations and expectations of patrons and employers were different from those of parents. As higher education was a necessity for the monastic orders in providing intellectual leadership to the church, the orders needed to support students as future members of this elite (see Chapter 2). They could afford to do so as, though individual monks and friars were sworn to poverty, the orders were emphatically not. They were mocked for their wealth and could readily fund their own students at both local and distant universities. Alongside this institutional funding for members of the orders, individual clerics could also fund themselves by obtaining a benefice – a paper responsibility for a parish which, more importantly, brought a salary.

With the Reformation this source of patronage dried up and Anglican clerics generally had to find their own funds, or seek a scholarship, in order to go to university. Many succeeded in doing so, enabling the universities to maintain their function of supplying the church with its clerics. The church then began to sponsor students abroad as well as at home as missionary agencies used their patronage in the late eighteenth and early nineteenth centuries to send catechists and potential missionaries or teachers to Britain for training.[64]

The state followed the church in funding students as the empire began to demand trained and qualified staff. Colonial authorities started to use the blunt instrument of scholarships in the hope that colonial or Indian subjects, chosen for their academic merit, would return home to the benefit of their fellow subjects. But in other cases staff were recruited first and then sent for training – patronage rather than scholarship. In the early twentieth century a small number of Indians went to study engineering at Cooper's Hill College. On qualifying they were expected to move into public works departments in India.[65] Once Indians were accepted into the Indian Civil Service, they too were paid for and sent as probationers to study at Oxford, Cambridge or Trinity College Dublin alongside their British peers (see Chapters 4 and 5).

From the late nineteenth century colonial governments sent students to Britain to train as doctors and to prepare them for work in technical or administrative posts. Patronage in the interest of the empire, and of colonial development, then expanded dramatically after the Second World War under the colonial development and welfare acts. The funds were 'designed to enable members of the public services to qualify for higher appointments' in administrative, professional and technical posts. Experienced civil servants were sent for two- and three-term courses, while others went on conventional degree courses or on specialist courses for police officers, prison staff, nurses, labour officers, tax and customs inspectors, and even trade unionists.[66]

These awards went on to become the technical cooperation and training programme, run to support overseas development. Its aim was not to provide scholarships for bright school and college leavers but to offer training that fitted with national priorities in 'developmental subjects' which excluded 'humanities, cultural subjects, fine arts etc, theoretical social science (except economics) and pure science'. Its budget expanded in the 1980s from £31 million in 1981 to £72 million by 1988.[67] Its students made up more than half of all those on government awards and its closure led to a major reduction in government expenditure on scholarships (see Chapter 6).[68]

Missionaries, engineers and administrators were all sent to Britain to study in the expectation that they would return and enter private or more often public service. Independent governments continued to fund students at university and other levels. Alongside students on more advanced courses, in 1975 overseas governments met the fees for 9 per cent of students in language schools while employers paid for another 19 per cent. Sponsored students from the middle east, on courses in technical English, made up an important part of these.[69]

British employers also used their patronage to bring students to Britain. The largest public scheme of this kind was probably that run by hospitals to recruit nurses between the 1950s and 1980s. Its costs, which were not gathered together, would need to be set against the value of the trainees' labour in any economic assessment. The Royal College of Nursing recognised that many 'came expecting to be learners and find they are labourers'. There was therefore 'an uneasy marriage of convenience between the nurses' desire for a valuable British training and subsequent qualifications and the National Health Service's desire to fill a manpower gap'.[70] While its trainee nurses came as students many of them remained as immigrants to the benefit of the hospitals that had recruited them.

Scholarship funds have often brought more students to Britain than employers or patrons. (Not always: mendicants in the later Middle Ages, nurses in the 1960s and 1970s, and technical trainees in the 1970s and 1980s, may have exceeded the number of scholarship holders.) Scholarships have been given for institutional, economic and political reasons and an analysis of these reasons sheds light on institutional and national policy.

Oxford and Cambridge colleges have awarded scholarships since the Middle Ages. They were rich enough to do so. Before the Reformation they received endowments, which enabled them to pay fellows and scholars, in return for the assurance of prayers for their benefactors; to this day they annually commemorate benefactors with celebratory dinners even if fewer of those dining now pray for them. In the fourteenth century, described as 'an age of ambition' colleges and universities 'were competing with warfare, marriage, and trade to be the best avenue of social mobility and thus to attract students'.[71] As they built up their wealth they used scholarships to attract poor but able students to support them in that competition, and provide a means of filling the ranks of the clergy. College endowment and landed property gave them the means to do so. These college scholarships effectively replaced monastic sponsorship as a route to education for both the clergy and the laity. Many were tied to specific localities or schools within England, which made them of less international significance than the old ties to the Catholic church. With time, some of the restrictions fell away so that institutional scholarships, designed to attract able students for academic reasons and in the interest of the individual college or university, helped bring some students from across borders as well as from the British Isles. Some twentieth-century scholarships can be seen as their linear descendants, designed to attract scholars whose presence would benefit learning within Britain. Academic excellence was one of the criteria for Commonwealth scholarships while the later Dorothy Hodgkin awards had as one of their aims the strengthening of British academic institutions. Colleges, universities and governments continued to use scholarships for their own academic and institutional purposes.

Colleges, like the monastic orders before them, pursued their own economic interests without formally setting these out as an objective. By the nineteenth century scholarship programmes were being set up with specifically economic aims. The Great Exhibition of 1851 came first. One of its themes was the support of British industry so that, once the exhibition had made a profit and left its trustees with the problem of deciding how to use it, they agreed on 'measures…which may increase the means of industrial education, and extend the influence of science and art upon productive industry'.[72] In 1889 the trustees set up a programme of science scholarships which were to be tenable at any university at home or abroad. They could be held for two years which might be extended to a third, and were 'limited to those branches of science (such as physics, mechanics, and chemistry) the extension of which is especially important for our national industries'. Scholarships were offered to students throughout the British Isles and to Australia, Canada and New Zealand.[73]

Most of the Great Exhibition scholars were British and the freedom to study anywhere meant that between 1891 and 1910 35 per cent of the total studied in Germany. From the start the trustees were also successful in attracting talented young men from the empire, including Rutherford in 1895 and Leakey from Kenya in 1928. The programme gradually developed a more imperial character. It was extended to India in 1937 and overseas scholars were then required to spend some time in Britain 'otherwise the award is of purely scientific value, and in no way contributes to the promotion of friendship between this country and the Dominions'. In response to a complaint in the 1930s that it brought New Zealanders to Britain who did not go home again, the awarding committee justified its policy as inculcating 'a feeling of *camaraderie* among scientists from the different Dominions'.[74] In 1945 it reiterated that it wanted to attract the best young postgraduate researchers from the dominions and India and argued that 'the need for treating the British Commonwealth as an entity with the maximum interchange of scientific workers between its constituent countries has been amply proved by the war' and should be preserved in peace.[75] A review of the programme's influence on Australian science in the early 1970s was reassuring: Australians had received 180 awards by 1960, around half had gone into industry and half to universities, and 'many members of the Australian Academy of Sciences had started their careers as 1851 scholars'.[76]

Economic interests have intermittently spurred scholarship activities since the launch of the 1851 programme. As set out in Chapter 4, the Board of Trade wanted to encourage overseas students in the 1930s, only to be rebuffed by industry's representatives. After the Second World War it succeeded, although on a modest scale through a programme designed to allow graduate engineers from abroad to work with British firms for up to a year. The programme was run in association with the Confederation of British Industry and by 1989, when there were 89 award holders, it had brought 2,500 engineers to Britain from some 70 countries. With an annual government expenditure of only £200,000 it was modest in scale as compared with the technical cooperation and training programme with its budget of £72m.[77]

Scholarship programmes have more often been launched for political than for economic reasons and these can be traced back at least as far as Henry III. His grants of £5 and £10, shown in Table 8.1, went to 'Instructus', a clerk to the Welsh prince Llewelyn ap Jorwerth whom he was hoping to influence and restrain, and to Guy, brother of the count of Auvergne, as he was making alliances with powerful barons in the south of France.[78] Ambassadors making Chevening awards have centuries of precedents to guide them.

The twentieth century saw the launching of more scholarship programmes for political ends with Cecil Rhodes in the lead. The bulk of his estate went to provide scholarships at Oxford for men from the colonies, the United States and from Germany. A contemporary account explains that the will was

> received with acclamation throughout the civilized world...for the striking manifestation of faith which it embodied in the principles that make for the enlightenment and peace and union of mankind, and for the fine constancy of Mr Rhodes's conviction that the unity of the British empire, which he had been proud to serve, was among the greatest of organized forces uniting for universal good.[79]

Scholarships were set up for three groups of students, from the colonies – Australia, Bermuda, Canada, Jamaica, New Zealand, Newfoundland, Rhodesia and South Africa – from the United States and from Germany. In an earlier draft of his will he had hoped that his educational bequest would help to re-establish the empire, bringing the United States back into its fold and, while the final version was not quite so bold, he still had clear and high hopes. The advantage for the colonists would be 'for giving breadth to their views, for their instruction in life and manners, and for instilling into their minds the advantage to the colonies as well as to the United Kingdom of the retention of the unity of the empire'. The American scholarships were intended to 'foster an appreciation of the advantages which…will result from the union of the English-speaking people throughout the world' and to foster an attachment to the United Kingdom. Germany got its scholarships in the hope 'that an understanding between the three great powers will render war impossible and educational relations make the strongest tie'.[80] The scholarships were for men who were not to be 'merely bookworms' but should have some educational attainments, enthusiasm for 'manly outdoor sports', 'qualities of manhood, truth, courage, devotion to duty, sympathy for and protection of the weak, kindliness, unselfishness, and fellowship' combined with 'moral force of character and of instincts to lead' as demonstrated in their school days.[81]

The Rhodes trustees succeeded in recruiting paragons of manliness and virtue and brought 7,000 to Oxford over the years. The terms of the will were adjusted from time to time, though with some difficulty, with changes to the geographical limits and to selection criteria. With time, selection became more diverse: the first black American scholar was selected in 1907 and, after a half-century gap, others followed from 1963. Women were eventually allowed (see Chapter 7). In recent years the Rhodes Trust has given more emphasis to the original concern for peace than to the hopes for empire. And, from their foundation, Rhodes scholarships attracted a prestige which other programmes could only envy, perhaps because they were the first of their kind, perhaps because their beneficiaries were healthy upstanding men, perhaps because they were a visible memorial to Rhodes' imperial ideas in a privileged university, perhaps because they started with such clear political aims.

Where Rhodes led the way with a political agenda, twentieth-century governments followed. The trail leads through China, America and Europe. In the early 1920s Britain followed an American lead, described in Chapter 9, in using indemnities from the Boxer Rising to provide scholarships for Chinese students in their and the British national interest. Bertrand Russell had told readers of the *Manchester Guardian* that the American programme meant that 'Young China, as a result, is predominantly American in training and sympathy'.[82] Scholarships might help Britain to compete at least in a small way.

The 1930s brought new scholarship programmes to counter Italian and German political offensives, as discussed in Chapter 4. The British Council began by providing bursaries for teachers of English but, by the late 1930s, provided university scholarships more generally and warned of the 'violently active cultural drive' in the middle east which included 'the provision of facilities for bringing students in large numbers to Germany, not only for their academic, but also for their technical and political education'.[83] The arguments were convincing enough for the Council's scholarship budget to be expanded to the point where, in 1944 it was provoking a demarcation dispute with the Colonial Office. It argued that the Council belonged 'in what might be termed "cultural subjects" such as music or the fine arts' and should be 'discouraged from assuming any responsibility for the higher education of Colonials in this country'.[84]

Political aims continued to influence scholarship policy after the war. The assumption that intellectual cooperation would bring political benefits lay behind the establishment of the Marshall and Commonwealth scholarships discussed in Chapter 5. It informed the Chevening scholarships introduced in 1983. Under the Labour government of 1997, recruiting more students from India and China was justified with political arguments about Britain's long-time relations with both countries. European politics drove the Erasmus programme (see Chapter 9).

Scholarship programmes, like other social institutions, often survive beyond their original purpose whether this was religious, educational, economic or political. Oxbridge colleges have continued to award scholarships without expecting regular prayers for their benefactors. Scholarships to mark the 1851 Great Exhibition are still awarded though hopes of sustaining British industry have faded. The Commonwealth scholarship plan has survived despite the Commonwealth's losing the cohesion it was expected to sustain. The various scholarship programmes together brought large numbers of students to Britain but, with no national register of awards or beneficiaries, data on them are scattered and exact figures on numbers or costs are not available. Some information on government-funded awards is brought together in Table 8.3. While they are incomplete – notably omitting the costs of nurse training where costs were met by individual hospitals – they are adequate to show how expenditure for colonial and international development rose during the twentieth century, but then fell towards

Table 8.3   Government support for overseas students, 1899–2010

Year	Number	Type of award	Cost £m
1899	c. 40	Students supported by colonial office	n/a
1966	1,750	Supported by overseas development ministry	n/a
	200	Supported by British Council	n/a
	4,000	Foreign governments and other non-private sources	n/a
1984/5	600	FCO scholarships and awards scheme	> 3
	700	Commonwealth scholarships and fellowships	> 8
	1,700	Overseas research students awards scheme	n/a
	400	British Council scholarships	3.5
	n/a	Marshall scholarships	0.75
	n/a	UN awards partially funded by British government	n/a
	16,000	total	>71
1988/89	12,000	Technical cooperation and training programme	72.00
	250	ODA shared scholarships	1.40
	950	Commonwealth scholarships and fellowships	10.21
	170	BRUFS for disadvantaged black South Africans	1.86
	120	Nassau fellowships	0.65
	620	Sino-British fellowships[a]	0.70
	1,737	FCO scholarships and awards scheme	8.99
	3,100	FCO fee support scheme (for Malaysia, Cyprus and dependencies)	3.84
	70	Marshall fellowships	0.83
	1,713	British Council fellowships	4.54
	1,900	Overseas research students award scheme	5.90
	44	Fulbright scholarships	0.29
	83	CBI scholarships	0.20
	22,757	total	111.41
1997		DfID	
		Commonwealth scholarships and fellowships	9.9
		Shared scholarships	2.0
		Chevening scholarships	12.0
		Prince of Wales scholarship at Atlantic college	0.165

continued

Table 8.3   Continued

Year	Number	Type of award	Cost £m
		FCO[b]	
		CSFP	2.50
		Chevening scholarships	13.0
1998/9	2,196	Students funded by FCO	39.0
2010/11	600	Chevening awards – FCO	14.5
	36	Marshall scholarships – FCO	2.2
	1,357	Commonwealth scholarships and fellowships funded by	
		Department for international development (DfID)	17.5
		Department of business, innovation and skills (BIS)	0.5
		Foreign and Commonwealth office	0.5
		Scottish government	0.07
	61	Fulbright awards (BIS meeting ⅓ cost with balance from USA)	0.6
	67	Scholarships for excellence (BIS with ½ cost from China)	0.7
	2,121	Total	36.57

Notes: a. Programme also had private funding.
  b. This report focused on DfID; the 1998/9 figure suggests it may have underestimated FCO spending.

Sources: 1899: 'Report of committee on scholarships funded by colonial governments', NA, CO 885/7/16; 1966: Cohen to Andrew, NA, FO 924/1560, 8.9.1966; 1984/5: T. Renton 1985 'Government policy on overseas students', 4–5; 1988/9: *HC minutes of evidence*, 1.3.1989, 3; 1997: ACU, W. Taylor 1997 *Scholarships and the DfID*,6; 1998/9: *Hansard HC*, 25.2.2003, col. 428W; 2010/11: CSC 52nd annual report and FoI requests British Council, FCO and BIS.

its end, with the end of the technical cooperation and development programme, descendant of the colonial development and welfare acts. They did so even as privately funded student numbers increased, despite rising costs.

Even with their limitations the data are good enough to sketch an answer to the basic questions: what did it cost, who paid and why did they do so?

Despite the apparent changes in cost, from £5 a year to £25,000, the necessary costs of university education showed considerable similarities from the thirteenth century until well into the twentieth. It was always expensive and always for the privileged, more so in England than in

Scotland. It is safe to assume that the costs of schooling, for the small numbers of children travelling to Britain, who would not have been content with dame schools, were also high. There were always, too, differences in the level of expenditure for students of different wealth, marked by the difference in status between the various categories of student at Oxford and Cambridge. These differences had their champions. The archbishop of Dublin spoke for them in 1852, asking 'Why should a man not be allowed a valet, or a horse, who has been always used to such luxuries, and to whom they are no more extravagant luxuries than shoes or stockings are to his fellow-students?'.[85] Although some overseas students – like Nehru and Yusupov – enjoyed their luxuries, most eked out a more modest living. For them, board and lodging usually took the greater part of their budget, though rent was modest in the Middle Ages, and could be pared to a minimum in nineteenth-century Scotland. The total needed for university and college fees was often lower than the cost of board and lodging, even though at times it was swollen by the need to pay for private tuition. But, until the late twentieth century, the figures repeatedly show that the cost of tuition was a modest proportion of the total – 11 per cent in nineteenth-century Cambridge, less than 10 per cent for a Commonwealth scholar in 1960. Travel costs must always have deterred some students, but declined in importance as shipping costs fell in the nineteenth century and air fares followed them down in the twentieth. A major change in the balance of costs came in the last third of the twentieth century: the total cost for an overseas student, even without the contemporary equivalent of a horse and a valet, more than doubled in real terms between 1960 and 2010 while the proportion of the student's budget needed for fees increased from about 10 per cent to almost 50 per cent. Savings in travel costs went some way to compensate for this, but not far.

Most of these costs were met by students' families who saw expenditure on a British education as a sound, lifetime, investment. From the seventeenth century families in the colonies of settlement could find the resources to pay for their children to study in Britain and from the nineteenth there were enough to see the advantages of doing so in west Africa and above all in India. The same calculations were made by the young west Africans who moved to Britain in the 1950s and 1960s, expecting to rely more on their own earnings than on their families.

The smaller numbers of students on scholarships benefited from the varied motives of those who established them. By later standards, modest numbers were endowed in the interest of religion, of education, and of the prosperity and reputation of individual colleges and universities. Larger numbers were then endowed, in the political and economic interest of the colonies, for the economic benefit of Britain and the empire, and for changing political motives. As the twentieth century went on, politics came to outweigh economics or the needs of development as a justification for expenditure on scholarships. The prime minister's initiative in the new century had political motives, seeking British influence in India and China, in a way that Henry III would have appreciated as he used scholarships in an attempt to placate the French and Welsh aristocracy.

9
International Comparisons

International students have never travelled along a single one-way street. The previous chapters have explored their movement to Britain and interpreted this in terms of individual motivation and of politics, ideology and economics. This chapter looks at those who went along other roads, examining how far the same kind of analysis fits the international record and what comparison with its peers or rivals can tell us about the British story. It begins by looking, as in the British chapters, at student numbers and changing patterns of movement, before relating those to the model of student mobility and to some of the tensions inherent within it. It goes on to examine changes since the nineteenth century, looking in particular at policy and practice in France, Germany and Switzerland, which had all become major players by the early twentieth century, and in the United States, the Soviet Union and Australia which joined them as the century went on.

From their foundation, medieval European universities attracted students from beyond their immediate region (see Chapter 2). By the late twelfth century Bologna had a rapidly increasing number of foreign students and they were already attracted to Paris and Padua.[1] Political and religious authorities both encouraged students to travel. The emperor Frederick I Barbarossa, in a constitution for Bologna issued in 1155, legislated for freedom of movement for professors and safety for students, even from debt collectors.[2] The Dominicans expected their members to travel, so that the order became something like a 'disseminated university'.[3] Civic authorities provided their own support; the citizens of Basle were assured in the mid-fifteenth century that if a university had a thousand students they would spend 200,000 ducats a year within the city.[4] With support from church, empire and city, universities were in their beginnings 'supranational centres propagating an international culture'.[5]

Despite that support, the Middle Ages were far from being a golden age of wandering scholars, always a minority of students. Travel was slow and dangerous. Wars within Europe, and the great schism (1378–1417) within the western church, hindered movement and reduced their numbers. As more universities were established in the fourteenth and fifteenth centuries, so each became more of a regional and less of a universal institution. Students evidently became poorer: in the fifteenth century the universities of Bologna, Avignon and Aix-en-Provence all reduced fees for poor scholars.[6] By the late fifteenth century three-quarters of all students went to a regional university, usually the one nearest to home, although even in the next century one student in four within the Holy Roman Empire attended more than one university.[7] While movement generally declined, universities that were particularly well placed to attract distant students provided exceptions. Some benefited from their reputation, as Padua did for medicine, and others from their geography, as Krakow did with a hinterland housing few other universities; it drew between 30 and 50 per cent of its students from abroad between 1400 and 1520.[8]

Towards the end of the fifteenth century the numbers both of students and of foreign students increased, to reach a peak in the late sixteenth and early seventeenth centuries. In post-Reformation Europe standard itineraries tended to include either Catholic or Protestant universities rather than being across the whole of western Europe. At the same time there were convenient exceptions. While the pope could flex his muscles – in 1564 Pius IV issued a bull restricting degrees to professing Catholics – universities found a way of weaving round external authority. The University of Padua did so after 1600 by issuing its own degrees instead of relying on imperial sanction. It was one of a number of universities, including Siena, Montpelier and Leiden, that accepted students regardless of their faith. Padua admitted Jewish students and allowed 80 to graduate there between 1517 and 1619, though they were charged registration fees at three times the normal price.[9] (Though there had been a Jewish community in Oxford in the thirteenth century, there was no question of Jews entering its cloisters as students, though the community was valued as a source of loans.[10]) Meanwhile numbers of students followed their religion rather than the law, crossing borders to study with their co-religionists. Despite bad roads, war, danger, religious differences and xenophobia, student mobility remained until about 1700 'an important and essential part of university history' when 'thousands and thousands of young people travelled all over Europe in search of knowledge, culture, adventure, safety, people of their own religion, and more prestigious academic degrees, or merely to ape the fashion of the moment'.[11]

Travel became more restricted in the Thirty Years' War (1618–48) and declined at the end of the seventeenth century, although there were always exceptions: at the University of Reims foreign students made up 60 per cent of the medical graduates in the early eighteenth century and 30 per cent at the end.[12] These were generally years when European university numbers tended to decline and new bans on foreign study were imposed by mercantilist monarchs.[13] By the end of the eighteenth century not only had travel become more restricted but universities themselves were struggling to survive. They were abolished by revolutionary France in 1793 to be replaced by Napoleon with a new system of education in 1808. In Germany universities in Mainz, Cologne, Bamberg, Dillingen, Duisburg, Rinteln and Helmstedt disappeared from the scene between 1798 and 1809. In Britain, as we saw in Chapter 3, universities remained at a low ebb till the middle of the nineteenth century.

The expansion of universities in the second half of the nineteenth century, in Europe and beyond, brought in its train an increased flow of international students. European university numbers increased dramatically in the 1870s, rising by 90 per cent in ten years in Britain and 61 per cent in Germany. They rose again in the 1900s with increases of 48 and 58 per cent. Across the Atlantic, United States figures rose 22 times between 1860 and 1930.[14] Foreign-student numbers rose even more rapidly. In Germany they went from 750 in 1860, or 6 per cent of the total, to exceed 7,000 and almost 11 per cent by 1911. While in 1900 Britain may, briefly, have been the most popular host country in the world, within ten years Germany had more foreign students. France showed a similar pattern: in 1899 its 1,600 foreign students made up nearly 6 per cent of its total, which rose to 15 per cent in 1916.[15] These proportions were exceeded within Switzerland, always more important than its size would suggest. It became a magnet for students from Russia, where restrictions on Jews, various non-Russian groups, and women drove the ambitious abroad. Russian women went to study medicine in Zurich where the first European woman with a licence to practise, Nadezhda Suslova, graduated in 1867. By 1906 over 90 per cent of the women in Swiss universities were from outside the country, with the great majority from Russia. Just before the First World War more than half of all Swiss students were from abroad.[16] Some figures for the late nineteenth and early twentieth centuries are in Table 9.1.

While many of these students crossed European borders to study, an increasing number came from America: some 10,000 of them studied in Germany in the nineteenth century, drawn by the reputation and rigour of its universities and by the doctoral programmes they had developed. (Unlike their peers a century later they were apparently untroubled by the

Table 9.1   Foreign student numbers in France, Germany and USA, 1860–1940

France			Germany			USA		
Year	No.	%	Year	No.	%	Year	No.	%
1899	1,635	5.7	1860–1	739	6.1	1921–2	6,488	1.0
1916	1,945	15.4	1880–1	1,129	5.2	1926–7	7,541	0.9
1920	4,887	n/a	1900–01	1,751	7.6	1930–1	9,961	0.9
1924–5	8,789	16.5	1911–12	7,088	10.7	1935–6	5,641	0.5
1930	15,198	n/a	1927–8	6,217	6.8	1938–9	8,000	n/a
1935–6	9,061	12.2	1930–1	7,422	5.7			
			1933–4	4,853	4.5			
			1937–8	5,158	7.9			

Source: Klineberg *International exchange*, 77, 113, 201 except for following: France 1920, 1930, Latreche *'Etusdiants'*, 138–9; USA 1938–9, IIE 1948 *Open doors*.

language although two-thirds of them came from families with Anglo-Saxon rather than German names.)[17] Some American observers saw this as a healthy sign: Daniel Gilman, who was president of Johns Hopkins University from 1875 to 1901 and had himself studied in Berlin, noticed early in the twentieth century that 'Very many of the foremost professors in American universities are the scholars of European teachers, especially German. Candidates for professorships are resuming the usage which prevailed early in the nineteenth century, of studying in France and Britain'.[18] As the First World War loomed, higher education blossomed and more foreign students were travelling than ever before, demonstrating host universities' renewed commitment to internationalism.

Between the two world wars student mobility, like higher education itself, reflected the political and economic changes of the time. Student numbers grew in the 1920s only to be held back in the depression of the 1930s. As before the First World War, most students travelled between industrialised countries and most European students travelled within Europe. In France, students from Europe made up between 75 and 90 per cent of the foreign total between 1920 and 1940. In contrast with the numbers of Indian students in Britain, France had few from the Maghreb where secondary education was limited – only 151 in 1931 – few from Asia, who never reached 10 per cent of the foreign total, and fewer still from sub-Saharan Africa.[19] European students dominated the German figures, with a significant proportion of those from neighbouring countries to the east and from German-speaking families outside Germany. Americans continued to make their way to Europe and did so in increasing numbers.[20] The United States also became a host country: although figures for outgoing students were not compiled, it seems likely that by the end of the First World War it was receiving more students than it was hosting.

Student movement within Europe and beyond was then transformed by the rise of fascism and Nazism. The students themselves could see what was happening. Those attending an international summer school in Geneva in 1928 noticed the 'Italians, young, alert, aggressive, [who] are sent by their government to preach the gospel of Fascism and distribute booklets in all languages justifying the work of Mussolini'.[21] By November 1933, ominously, the annual International Student Service congress opened in Germany but then moved to Switzerland where it went on to examine the problems of exiled and refugee students. Meanwhile both Italy and Germany were ready to attract foreign students in the interest of soft diplomacy. At a Congress of Asiatic students in Europe, organised in the same year by the *Gruppi universitari fascisti*, 500 students, from Egypt to India and Japan, were told of the Italian 'need for collaboration between Europe and Asia and of thus re-establishing after an interruption of nearly two thousand years, the Roman unity of the two continents based on mutual exchanges'. Germany announced that it would provide ten scholarships for Indian students in 1934–5.[22] In reality, the story of the 1930s is of repression, fear and flight for students as for whole populations. German and Austrian universities rapidly became a source of students and academics as refugees fled west. German loss was the democracies' gain. Ironically, the proportion of foreign students in German universities rose, as they enrolled decreasing numbers of their own citizens.

Higher education recovered rapidly after the Second World War and has expanded almost unchecked ever since. The numbers of foreign students generally kept pace with that increase and continued to do so into the new century: between 1999 and 2004 world numbers of tertiary students rose by 43 per cent as did the number of mobile students. Growth was not, however, even and there were marked changes in the patterns of student movement for both host and sending countries.

The most noticeable change was the new dominance of the United States as a host country. In 1935 more students went to France than to the United States but by 1950 the French numbers were less than half the American. The United States continued to be consistently the most popular country with the numbers of its foreign students outstripping the rest, decade by decade. America was so popular that from the 1970s to 1990s it received more foreign students than Britain, France and West Germany put together. Changes came in the 1990s and in different parts of the world. Australia had always been a minor player, hosting fewer foreign students than Switzerland in the early 1980s, but then launched an aggressive programme of student recruitment so that by 2000 it was the fifth most popular international destination. With its English-language universities it had moved into third place by 2008. Meanwhile, in the new century China took Australia's position as fifth in terms of popularity. It was now not only one of the major countries sending students abroad but also one that was attracting large numbers of them from outside its borders (see Table 9.2).[23]

While the United States came to dominate the world as a host for foreign students, Asia came to dominate it as a source. In 1970 Asian students made up 41 per cent of the international total within the most popular host countries, a figure that reached 47 per cent by 2010. By that time they made up 64 per cent of the Russian total, 70 per cent of

Table 9.2   Foreign student numbers in higher education in some countries, 1950–2(

		1950	1960	1970	1980	1990	2000	201
UK[a]	foreign	8,242	12,410	24,606	56,003	80,183	222,936	389,9
	%	8	10	n/a	n/a	n/a	n/a	n/a
France	foreign	13,510	27,132	34,900	114,181	136,015	137,085	259,9
	%	10	13	5	10	8	7	
Germany (W)	foreign	2,114	21,701	27,769	61,841	107,005}	187,033	200,8
	%	2	7	6	5	6}}		
Germany (E)[b]	foreign	n/a	829	3,350	7,106	13,343}	n/a	n/a
	%		1	3	2	n/a}		
USA[c]	foreign	29,813	53,107	144,708	311,882	407,529	475,169	684,7
	%	1	1	2	3	3	4	
USSR/Russia[d]	foreign	5,900	13,500	17,400	62,942	66,806	41,210	129,6
	%	< 1	n/a	< 1	n/a	1	1	n/
Australia	foreign	339	4,991	7,525	8,777	28,993	105,764	271,2
	%	1	6	4	3	6	13	
Switzerland	foreign	4,177	6,987	9,469	14,716	22,621	26,003	38,7
	%	25	33	22	17	16	17	
China	foreign	n/a	n/a	n/a	1,381	8,495	n/a	71,6
	%				n/a	n/a		n/

Notes: a. UNESCO figures are for all higher education so that these totals are higher than thos
universities cited elsewhere.

   b. East German figures are for 1957, 1969, 1980, 1988;

   c. UNESCO figures are calculated differently from those of the IIE so that there
discrepancies between the two sets.

   d. USSR 1980 figure is for 1978.

Sources: UNESCO *Statistical yearbook* 1963, 1972, 1983, 1993; UIS statistics; USSR figures for 1960
Pis'mennaia 'Migration', 73; East German 1957 figure from UNESCO *Basic facts and figures* 1960.

the American, and 80 per cent of the Australian. International student mobility was now dominated by movement from the developing to the industrialised world (see Figure 9.1).

The American figures illustrate the story: in 1970 students from Asia made up just over half of the foreign total, with the countries of the middle east to the fore. The change of regime then cut the flow of Iranian students so that by 1980 students from east, south and southeast Asia for the first time exceeded those from the middle east. From the 1990s east Asian countries were consistently the most important source of students. Over 60 years the only countries outside Asia to appear regularly in the United States list were its neighbours, Canada and Mexico (see Table 9.3).[24]

Although Asian students travelled to all continents, European experience was different from American. Students from within Europe made up half of all foreign students in France in 1950 and generally made up between 20 and 30 per cent of their total in the later twentieth century. While Germany often drew more than a third of its students from Asia – with Turkey and some German residents of Turkish origin included in the Asian total – it consistently drew over half of its foreign students from elsewhere in Europe. Switzerland, too, continued to attract its fellow Europeans, making up to about three-quarters of its total. Movement between European countries was already part of the normal pattern of university life even before the European Community launched its Erasmus programme.

Linguistic preferences and colonial legacies helped shape student movement to European universities. After the Second World War as before French, German, Belgian and Swiss universities attracted other European

Table 9.3   Top five source countries for foreign students in USA, 1950–2010

1950	1960	1970	1980	1990	2000	2010
Canada	Canada	Canada	Iran	China	China	China
4,498	6,058	12,595	47,550	39,600	59,939	157,558
China	China	India	Taiwan	Japan	India	India
3,549	5,304	12,523	19,460	36,610	54,664	103,895
Germany	India	Taiwan	Nigeria	Taiwan	Japan	S Korea
1,264	4,835	9,219	17,350	33,530	46,497	73,351
India	Iran	Hong Kong	Canada	India	S Korea	Canada
1,136	2,880	9,040	14,320	28,860	45,685	27,546
UK	Japan	Iran	Japan	S Korea	Taiwan	Taiwan
874	2,434	6,402	13,500	23,360	28,566	24,818

Source: IIE *Open doors*, various dates.

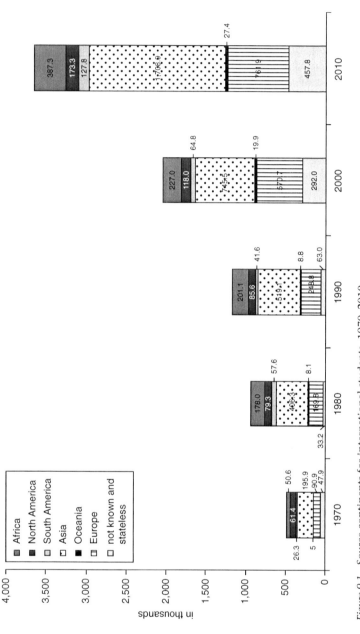

Figure 9.1 Source continents for international students, 1970–2010

Note: Figures from 1970–90 are for the largest host countries and therefore only some 90 per cent of the total

Sources: UNESCO Yearbook 1972, 1983, 1992; UIS database as at September 2013.

students because they taught in French and German. The shared use of French drew students from France's former colonies in sub-Saharan Africa and from countries making some use of French such as Lebanon and Egypt. More important for France were students from the Maghreb who now travelled to France in increasing numbers. Although Algerian numbers fell after independence as a result of a boycott, they later recovered; total numbers from the Maghreb grew rapidly from 1960, when they made up 5,184 or 27 per cent of the foreign students to 33,371 or 30 per cent in 1980 and still remained at 23 per cent in 2010 (see Figure 9.2).[25]

European student movement was not confined to the west. During the cold war, the universities of the eastern bloc continued to attract students from abroad so that two circles of European student mobility came into existence, with an ideological division between east and west to echo the earlier religious divide between the Protestant north and the Catholic south. The Soviet Union was the largest player and drew students from its European satellites, who made up 29 per cent of its foreign total in 1970, alongside students from Africa and Asia. Universities in Czechoslovakia and East Germany also ran programmes that attracted both international students and western alarm. The history of these students is very much part of the cold war (see below). With the collapse of the Soviet Union the number of foreign students in Russia fell in the 1990s. Numbers then recovered in the 2000s, increasing more than three-fold in ten years, with European students making up 31 per cent of its foreign total in 2010. Within a reunited Europe there was now again one circle of mobility.

Student movements, across boundaries and down the centuries, were shaped by politics, by university interests and by personal choice and have inevitably changed over time. The differences are at first more striking than the similarities between Erasmus's journeying between Paris, Cambridge, Turin and Basel in the fifteenth century, Léopold Senghor's travel from Dakar to the Ecole des Hautes Etudes in Paris in the twentieth and the movement of 57,000 undergraduate students from China to the United States in 2010. But there are commonalities among the factors pushing and pulling international students (see also Chapter 1 and Figure 1.1). Nineteenth-century students who were able to start their education at home, but found restricted opportunities at a higher level, included the Russian medical students who travelled to Switzerland and France in the late nineteenth and early twentieth centuries. They were

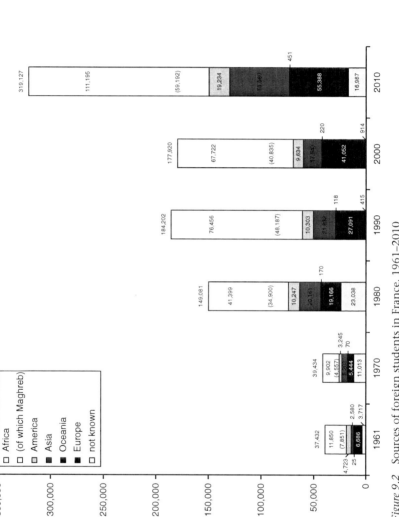

Figure 9.2 Sources of foreign students in France, 1961–2010

Note: The 1980 total is as shown in UNESCO's figures which appear to understate the number of 'not known' students

joined by American women who also had few opportunities to study at home. Medical education for women was repeatedly started and stopped under the tsarist regime while in the United States it was almost impossible for women to get clinical training before the 1890s.[26] Demand on a much larger scale followed the expansion of schooling in Asia in the late twentieth century, which meant that the demand for higher education, from the new and educated Chinese and other Asian elites, was greater than could be met locally or even nationally.

Local opportunities were, at different times, limited for reasons of religion, ethnicity or gender. Christian divisions restricted movement within Europe (see Chapter 2). Over many centuries, and in many countries, Jewish students had restricted access to higher education. They were among the Russian students in Zurich, affected by quotas within the Russian empire. Between the wars Jewish quotas in medical schools within the United States continued to drive medical students to Europe and in particular to Switzerland which had 493 American medical students in 1931, more than the number in Britain.[27] The flow of American medical students continued until new restrictions on foreign degrees sent them not to Europe but to branch campuses, set up by American institutions, in the Caribbean. (Even more remarkable the offshore Ross University of Veterinary Medicine was set up on similar lines in St Kitts, an island almost entirely lacking domestic animals.)

Many of those who travelled came from privileged backgrounds which meant that their families could afford to pay for them. In the late nineteenth century, with steamship travel available, prosperous American families sent their children to elite boarding schools in Europe almost as a finishing school.[28] The pattern continued. In the late twentieth century, children of the American privileged who did not have the necessary marks to get into their desired universities crossed the Atlantic to study in Europe, while English children who failed to get entry to Oxbridge travelled in the opposite direction in pursuit of the same dream of status: Ivy League colleges noticed the trend and began to recruit in British 'top independent schools'.[29]

Students were pulled as well as pushed. They included the medical students attracted to Padua in the Middle Ages, Leiden in the seventeenth century and Edinburgh in the eighteenth because of the quality of the teaching. The shortage of local alternatives sent students across borders: Swedish medical students went to Leiden for that reason. Institutional policies could help encourage foreign students. One of the reasons that Swiss universities welcomed foreign students was the lack of local demand which led them to recruit internationally in their own institutional interest. Students were also attracted where university study in a particular place brought kudos: from the early nineteenth century it took young men from eastern Europe to universities of the west for *'une sorte d' adoubement intellectuel'*.[30] Later in the same century the children of the Polish and Romanian elites went to France for similar reasons while those of prosperous American families studied in Europe as the culmination of a grand tour.[31]

The way in which students were pushed or pulled in a particular direction was influenced by information and by language. Information about possibilities flowed along channels created by the students: by the 1860s it was well known in Russia that Swiss universities were open to all.[32] Language could encourage or discourage. By the seventeenth century North American universities used textbooks in English which then displaced Latin first for conversation and teaching and then for formal occasions. Latin American universities increasingly taught in Spanish, rather than Latin. Europe followed suit and by the second half of the eighteenth century 70 to 80 per cent of even learned publications were in national languages.[33] The advantage this gave to universities working in French and German was in turn lost as English became the new lingua franca after the Second World War. Britain, North America and Australia, to be followed by India and Singapore, now gained the linguistic edge. Universities, not only in small-language states like Norway or the Netherlands, but even in Germany, began to accept dissertations and offer some courses in English.

Limitations at home, expectations and opportunities abroad, and finance, especially for the elite, encouraged students to travel to other rich and industrialised countries as they did to Britain.

Ideology played its part in shaping the movement of international students and brought with it tensions between conflicting institutional values. The American educator Clark Kerr identified one source of conflict:

> Universities are, by nature of their commitment to advancing universal knowledge, essentially international institutions, but they have been living in a world of nation states that have designs upon them. My basic question is: where does this dual identification position these institutions between a mythical academic Heaven and a

sometimes actual earthly Hell, and in what ways does it affect how they may act?...

It might...be expected that the academic profession would line up totally on the side of internationalisation, that it would be dedicated to the free advancement of learning everywhere and all the time – not bound by the parochial interest of nations, that it would be on the side of the universal God of learning and not the local Mammon of self-interest – those demons of cupidity. But reality, once again, is more complicated than this. Knowledge, as Socrates would have it, is the 'only one good' and is universal in value; but knowledge, as Bacon would have it, is also power, and power is particularised and those with the power may not want to share it. Which to serve: the universal truth or the particularised power?[34]

During the twentieth century there have always been individual academics, universities and institutions firmly on the side of the inter-nationalist angels. After 1918, academic cooperation was seen as one of the routes towards peace and mutual understanding. The International Committee on Intellectual Cooperation, a precursor of UNESCO, was set up as one step along that route. It published handbooks on university exchanges and, with the backing of Marie Curie, argued for travelling studentships and scholarships in the interest of 'achieving international rapprochement and intellectual cooperation'.[35] In America, the Institute of International Education was established in 1919 'to promote the inter-change of people and ideas for the development of a peaceful world'.[36] The optimism of the 1920s put internationalism ahead of national interest, at least in public rhetoric. Within Europe, internationalism again attracted support after 1945 when 'policies were especially focused on humanitarian aims of improving understanding between people for peaceful coexistence'.[37] The revival of academic exchanges and mobility across frontiers formed part of the post-war recovery, driven by a revived internationalism. In North America, the Canadian foreign minister and former university president Sidney Smith proposed establishing what became the Commonwealth Scholarship and Fellowship Plan arguing specifically for cooperation that went beyond economics and would reflect 'the free flow and exchange of ideas [that] has been and will continue to be one of the strongest bonds among the Commonwealth's members'.[38]

Throughout the century, however, governments often came down on the side of the particularised national power that Clark Kerr identified rather than that of internationalist values. One consequence is that the factors that encouraged students to move, or hindered them, were heavily influenced by national and international politics, and the ideologies that shaped them. These changed over time and can be illustrated by American scholarship policy, by the cold war, and by the new politics of Europe and of the market that followed it.

Early in the twentieth century the American government followed Cecil Rhodes' example of using scholarships for political ends. Western countries, including the United States, Britain and France, enjoyed extra-territorial rights in China that gave them an almost colonial status. Sir George Goldie, who had successfully brought Nigeria into the British empire, was all set to go to China with much the same idea when the Boxer Rising (1899–1902) broke out against the extra-territorial powers. The movement failed and the victorious allies imposed indemnities on China to compensate for their estimated losses. These indemnities were set so indefensibly high – estimated at $11 million too much – that by 1908 the United States decided they should return the money to China. But the Chinese were not trusted to use the money in their own or America's best interests so, rather than handing it back, the United States arranged to use the bulk of it to fund scholarships at American universities for Chinese students. This would encourage modernisation within China, make it a more solid trading partner, and create a cadre of well-educated young Chinese who should remain friends of America. Most of the money would be spent in America. Congratulations followed. The wife of the American minister in China explained in 1910 that the cancellation of the indemnity revealed 'an attitude too deep, too broad, too high for word expression. Does not this attitude reveal a strong current of sisterly good will, when it is able to sweep away the heavy weights of financial gain?' More prosaically the state department administrator who had taken part in the negotiations thought that the funds 'should be used to make China do some of the things we want' and expected of the beneficiaries:

> They will be studying American institutions, making American friends, and coming back here to favor America for China in its foreign relations. Talk about a Chinese alliance! The return of that indemnity was the most profitable work Uncle Sam ever did…They

will form a force in our favor so strong that no other government or trade element of Europe can compete with it. [39]

There were other views. One Chinese historian, T'ao Chii-yin, saw it as opening up a 'cultural leasehold' seeking to endanger Chinese culture and argued that 'Americans have called cultural investments "fertilizer for America's trade with China," and in substance it is completely like economic investment'.[40]

Boxer scholarships were duly established and took 1,300 Chinese students to America by the time the programme was re-formed in 1929. Britain, France and Japan followed the American example and created more modest programmes of their own. Theodore Roosevelt and his administrators had found a way of using education abroad for their own political ends and arranging that someone else would pay for it.

Scholarship programmes illuminate government policy. After the Second World War the United States demonstrated a mixed set of motives in establishing its Fulbright programme. William Fulbright was an academic lawyer, who had travelled to Oxford on a Rhodes scholarship, became president of the University of Arkansas at the age of 34, and served in Congress from 1943 to 1974. He gained national attention by persuading Congress in 1943 that America should abandon isolationism and engage with post-war peace-keeping machinery. He then got the support of his colleagues for a programme of international scholarships, whose name is his memorial, and which commemorates his internationalist and educational convictions. Calling on his own Rhodes experience, his knowledge of the Boxer precedent and his political acumen, he found an ingenious and uncontroversial way of funding them. At this time, many foreign countries were indebted to the United States while it held assets abroad whose movement was restricted by exchange controls. Overseas assets could be used to fund at least the offshore costs of a programme that would take Americans abroad and carry scholars to the United States. The purpose of the legislation was formally set out as 'authorizing the use of credits established through the sale of surplus properties abroad for the promotion of international goodwill through the exchange of students in the fields of education, culture and science'. Congress was persuaded and passed the legislation.[41]

The first exchanges were in 1948 when 35 students and one academic went to the United States and 85 Americans travelled overseas. Fulbright was successful in going on to get regular government funding for the programme so that it became an established and acclaimed part of American cultural diplomacy. By the twenty-first century it had 300,000 alumni including 28 heads of state or government and 43 Nobel Prize winners.[42] Fulbright took a clear internationalist view which went into the words of the basic legislation:

> to increase mutual understanding between the peoples of the United States and the people of other countries; to strengthen the ties which unite us with other nations by demonstrating the educational and cultural interests, developments, and achievements of the people of the United States and other nations, and the contributions being made toward a peaceful and more fruitful life for people throughout the world; to promote international cooperation for educational and cultural advancement; and thus to assist in the development of friendly, sympathetic, and peaceful relations between the United States and the other countries of the world.[43]

Fulbright later emphasised that 'the purpose of the program is not the advancement of science nor the promotion of scholarship. These are by-products of a program whose primary aim is international understanding'.[44] Fulbright's statements were interesting in their emphasis and in their omissions, with international understanding to the fore, friendship towards America only hinted at, and America's other political and economic interests barely visible. The awards were not initially about aid or development and made no reference to the Soviet Union or the cold war. Its chill winds were soon to blow. The French communist paper *L'Humanité* argued in May 1949 that many of those supported by the Fulbright programme would be 'simply agents, present or future, of the American intelligence service'.[45] Fulbright beneficiaries of the period deny this exaggerated claim but its existence demonstrates how the mutual understanding sought by Fulbright was rapidly displaced by mutual suspicion. This was to dominate intellectual exchanges for more than four decades.

During those years international politics, and with them the lives of international students, were dominated by the east-west conflict and by the southern pursuit of economic development. Each bloc tried to demonstrate the relevance and superiority of its ideology to the new countries of Africa and Asia.

East Africa was one of their playing fields. In 1959 the Kenyan politician Tom Mboya raised funds to charter a plane for 89 students offered university and college places in the United States. Thousands accompanied him to Nairobi airport to see them off at four in the morning, and succeeding years brought more flights. Mboya saw them as 'a challenge to the British Government, which only financed fourteen students to go to Britain in the year we organised eighty-one to go to America', although his arrangements were hurried and haphazard with many students ill-prepared for college study.[46] Not to be outdone, his political rival Oginga Odinga set up a programme that took cohorts to Moscow and east Europe. They had to manage with less fanfare as students travelled to Cairo or London to pick up air tickets, worried that the colonial authorities would take away their passports. Between 1960 and 1963 nearly 1,000 students travelled east for their higher education. East and west locked themselves into a competition for students and influence as a response to the new demand for higher education in the south, and to the new conviction that satisfying the demand was a necessary condition for development.[47]

The American response was to set up a raft of scholarship and support programmes that rapidly grew to carry more students to America than Fulbright. Students from Africa and Asia in the United States rose to 158,000 by 1963 and 351,000 by 1973.[48] The vice-president of the Institute of International Education summarised the aims of American policy. Peace came first but this was now 'deeply involved with another aim: that is, to withstand the extension of communism'. Then, those educated in America could be expected 'to have attitudes favourable to the United States and will be more competent in their jobs than if they had not been here'.[49] Language had moved on from Fulbright's internationalism. By 1959 the state department required American scholarship programmes

> to demonstrate to other people, by every possible means, the evidence of our own moral, spiritual and material strength, our determination to support the free nations of the world so that we may gain and hold the confidence of all free peoples in our efforts to halt Soviet aggression and Communist infiltration.[50]

Meanwhile the eastern bloc developed its own scholarship programmes which the west watched with alarm. By the mid-1980s the United States Congress was warned that the Soviet Union was making a long-term investment in students who upon returning home would 'form a leadership corps for Marxist revolutionary movements'. Jack Kemp, a New York

Congressman, urged Congress to support 'a program that could tell the world that the U.S. was also interested in educating Third World children of the poor, and that this activity was not a monopoly of the Soviet bloc countries'.[51] Congress wrote into law a claim that there were 12 times as many Soviet bloc government scholarships a year as there were from the United States. It came with a warning that 'this disparity entails the serious long-run cost of having so many of the potential future leaders of the developing world educated in Soviet bloc countries'.[52]

In Britain, where Members of Parliament echoed these warnings (see Chapter 6), its spies and diplomats were already on the job. As early as 1949 British diplomats kept an eye on foreign students in Prague and produced a 'Collation of materials on the use made by the communists of Prague as centre to stir up trouble in Colonial world'.[53] A brief drafted in 1964 suggests that the Soviet and east European programmes to recruit students were being monitored in Ghana, India, Kenya, Nigeria and Tanganyika.[54] Two years later the shadowy information research department of the Foreign Office was able to provide the prime minister's office with a confidential brief on 'Soviet and Chinese activities in Africa' including their scholarship programmes.[55] The east was always of concern to the west.

It is now possible to assess the scale and the nature of the Soviet scholarship and training programmes and to gauge how far western suspicions of it were justified. The Soviet Union always had some students from abroad. In 1921 it founded the University of Toilers of the East in the name of Stalin (*Kommunisticheskii Universitet Trudyashchikhsya Vostoka imeni Stalina* or *KUTV*) to train cadres who would work in the eastern Soviet Union and students from Africa, America and Asia intending to return home to promote communism. It was a tightly regulated organisation, with a 52-point secrecy code in the student rule book. The university had students in their hundreds, with the largest number from China, and, like Sandhurst and the London School of Economics, succeeded in attracting future political leaders so that its alumni included Ho Chi Min, Liu Shaoqi and Jomo Kenyatta. The latter was there in the early 1930s but, according to his tutors' report, had an attitude to the Soviet Union bordering on cynicism, and it was an LSE tie that he later wore as president of Kenya.[56] Alongside KUTV there was a smaller, and more short-lived, Lenin school, founded in 1926, with only 60 to 70 students who followed a three-year course and were generally at a 'higher level of political development' than those at KUTV.[57] While both KUTV and the Lenin school were clearly of potential interest to the west, they did not survive long and were closed down by the late 1930s.

By 1945 there were said to be only 20 foreign students in Soviet institutions of higher education.[58]

Foreign students began to travel to Russia again after the Second World War. During Stalin's lifetime most were from eastern Europe, Mongolia and above all China. One estimate suggests that 25,000 Chinese students were trained between 1948 and the early 1960s while another refers to 20,000 workers and 18,000 professionals.[59] Policy changed after his death when Khrushchev introduced a new third-world policy which was to bring increased numbers of students from Africa, Asia and Latin America alongside those from the second world of the Soviet bloc. The west was particularly taken aback when, within the framework of that policy, Khrushchev announced on 22 February 1960 the creation of a university dedicated to the needs of foreign students, the International Friendship University, later renamed the Patrice Lumumba University. Although it took only a minority of Russia's foreign students, many of whom continued to attend conventional institutions of higher education, it attracted particular interest, publicity and concern in the west. The university had faculties of engineering, medicine, science, agriculture, arts, and economics and law, with the largest group of students in the engineering faculty. Its degree programmes did not have the courses in Marxism-Leninism required in other universities. By 1965 it had produced 288 graduates, by 1975 5,000 and continued to expand, with 55,000 of its students gaining doctorates.[60] A recent Russian writer describes its aims in tones that have an almost Soviet lilt:

> The main purpose of the university was to provide assistance in training highly qualified national cadres, educated in the spirit of friendship among peoples, for the countries of Asia, Africa, and Latin America; the aim was to give young people there, first and foremost those from low-income families, the opportunity to acquire an education.[61]

The result of Khrushchev's policy was that foreign student numbers in higher education rose from 5,900 in 1950 to 126,500 in 1990, recorded in UNESCO's statistics. Beyond these numbers, there were also students in party, *komsomol*, and trade union schools amounting to a further 180,000 in 1990. By that year the Soviet Union had 11 per cent of the world's foreign students and was the third most popular destination after the United States and France.

Unlike the politically oriented, even Trotskyist, KUTV, most post-war students went to universities and technical institutes and most studied technical subjects – above all engineering, agriculture and medicine. The Soviet Union did not charge fees, and claimed that anyone within the country qualified to enter higher education could do so. Foreign students were paid a stipend which was more generous than that paid to nationals, and could be increased for those who got higher marks. A friendly American observer saw the long-term aim of Soviet policy in Africa as

> to deprive the West of its internationally sanctioned controls: economic, political, diplomatic, military, and cultural. In the long haul, the study pin-pointed the Soviet desire for an Africa predisposed to a Marxist-Leninist ideology and to a socialist mode of development.[62]

But, perhaps remembering Lenin's definition of communism as power plus electrification, in the short run the aim was to produce scientists, doctors and technologists rather than revolutionaries.

The Soviet programme always had to struggle against a series of difficulties. Before decolonisation, Soviet institutions could not recruit students through their own diplomatic missions or government channels; instead they were initially recruited through party organisations, trade unions, or clandestinely, and many lacked the necessary educational background to start on higher education. Only from the mid-1960s was it possible to set up more formal, and more efficient, mechanisms for recruitment. Courses were necessarily long, as students spent a year learning Russian, or Czech or German in the parallel programmes in those countries, before starting their professional studies. Some students were inevitably disappointed. One African student at Moscow State University complained:

> No cars, no cafés, no good clothes or good food, nothing to buy or inspect in the stores, no splash of color to relieve Moscow's damp gray. *Nothing but shortages and restrictions*. No opportunity to let go normally, breathe easily, and enjoy some harmless student fun.[63]

(The complaints echo those reported from streetwise young men from Soweto who found themselves in northern Nigeria in 1976 when Africa offered school places to those affected by the riots in South African schools.) More serious than shortages, African students, and no doubt others, encountered race prejudice in just the same way as their peers in Britain or North America. Confrontations between students and authorities escalated and the death of one student in 1960 attracted international publicity. Khrushchev was unsympathetic and was reported as saying at a Kremlin New Year's Eve reception:

> If they do not like it here we will give them their passports and a good send off. At home they can do anything they like, even stand on their head and shake their legs around. But here we do not do such things. They come here as our guests and we cannot allow them to demonstrate.[64]

Demonstrating students make the headlines but most worked, graduated and returned home. While there was colour prejudice it cannot have been universal if the reports are accurate that the 50,000 African students who studied in Russia from the 1950s left behind them between 15,000 and 17,000 Afro-Russian children.[65] The Soviet Union was proud of the fact that their students returned home and pointed out that, unlike western programmes, theirs did not contribute to brain drain.[66] Anecdotal evidence reports that the Soviet-trained agriculturalists and technologists were professionally well-qualified and played valuable roles back in their home countries. But Soviet qualifications were not always recognised, especially where recognition involved professional bodies tied to their metropolitan and western peers. Russian-trained doctors were often required to undergo further training if they were to practise in Commonwealth countries. There is some evidence that, given the choice, students valued American or western European programmes over those in the east. One rare study, which looked at the increased income that came with advanced qualifications, found that in east Africa in the 1970s, students with higher degrees from western European, American and local universities earned more than those who had studied in the east.[67] The numbers of foreign students in the Soviet Union never approached those travelling to the United States, despite the claim to Congress about the imbalance in government scholarships. In practice scholarships went to nearly all foreign students in the Soviet bloc but only to a minority of those in the United States.[68]

During the cold war the Soviet and western programmes for foreign students both resembled and suspected each other. Viacheslav Eliutin, Soviet minister of higher education, argued in 1985 that 'One of the factors obstructing the resolution of the urgent, vital problems facing the nations of the developing countries is backwardness in education and culture and a shortage of trained cadres'. This was the rationale for the Soviet programme.[69] It could equally have been an echo of a consensus reached by the mid-1950s 'among foundation officials, business leaders and Washington policymakers regarding the importance of the developing world... [that led] the Carnegie, Ford, and Rockefeller foundations to support educational projects' in the south. They expected to 'nurture through training in elite American universities, a cadre of political leaders whose outlook and values would insure their support of the dominant American social, economic and political institutions'.[70] The eastern programmes laid greater emphasis on the physical sciences and the western on social sciences. Suspicion was shared. Eliutin claimed that the American 'criterion for selecting students... is usually not their educational level or desire to acquire knowledge but a "loyal" attitude to American ways, the social status of the candidate (meaning membership of the ruling classes) etc'.[71] The British suspected Soviet trained students. In the 1960s it was claimed that their return to Northern Rhodesia would 'create a definite threat to the security of the territory' while, even after independence in Guyana, the Commonwealth Relations Office passed on good practice from Nigeria to the British high commission there in explaining how 'the Nigerian Special Branch and immigration authorities were often quite active in tracking down "unofficial" students' and deterring them by confiscating air tickets and passports.[72]

The eastern and western programmes of the Cold War were not mirror images – the western was always bigger than the eastern – but had much in common. Each accused the other of concealing long-term geopolitical aims behind a veil of technical assistance. Each was right to do so. Each assumed that students would benefit from the values they represented, with students in the United States learning to understand and admire the American way of life and those in the east grasping the strength of Marxism-Leninism as an intellectual tool. Each brought benefits to the south through programmes of training that had practical value as well as ideological trappings.

The contest between the two rival circles of international student mobility ended with the collapse of the Berlin Wall and the implosion of the Soviet Union. It soon became clear that in the new world of the 1990s and 2000s policy towards international students would be shaped by different interests from those that had predominated between 1945 and 1990. A study by OECD in 2004 identified four as all-important: the demand for skilled migration, the search for education in the interest of capacity building, the pursuit of mutual understanding and the generation of revenue.[73]

The first two of these had long been staples of foreign-student policy. In the search for skilled migrants, OECD explained that across Europe international students had been recruited and

> expected to contribute to the knowledge economy of the receiving country, especially in the context of an aging society.... [Twelve member countries] have developed domestic policies to recruit more international students. Countries like the United Kingdom or the Netherlands target talented students and graduates in fields like science and technology where interest among national students has declined. Countries such as France have endeavoured to attract foreign students from areas where historical or geographical links have been weak. Germany's policy is ambitious in both scale and funding... [with] initiatives to double the number of international students in German universities.[74]

There were now at least potential conflicts of interest between the industrialised countries of the OECD and the developing countries of the south. Both wanted the industrialised countries to recruit and train international students but in the one case to maintain their advanced economies and high-tech industries and in the other to produce graduates who would develop their own competitive economies. Economic competition now came ahead of the advancement of internationalist understanding and cooperation.

Mutual understanding was not, however, dead and drove activity within Europe with the establishment of the Erasmus programme. European cooperation in education had taken a long and winding road. Proposals for a European community university in the 1950s and for the harmonisation of education in the 1970s had come to nothing.[75] A decade of hesitation and negotiation followed before the council of ministers eventually approved the European Action Scheme for the Mobility of University Students or Erasmus on 14 May 1987, although with a budget less than half that proposed. The initial programme was expected to move an estimated 29,000 students, down from an original hope that 10 per cent of all European university students would spend some time in another European country.[76] Erasmus was followed by the Sorbonne agreement in 1998 to pursue harmonisation in higher education and the adoption by European universities of the Bologna process a year later intended to ease movement between them through a common approach to degree structures.[77]

The Erasmus programme had among its aims the strengthening of European higher education in the interest of economic development. But it was always more than this. One French study of the programme quotes Monnet, the architect of the European Community, as arguing 'if one were doing it again, I would begin with education'.[78] One of Erasmus's objectives was 'to contribute to the development of a pool of well-qualified, open-minded and internationally experienced young people as future professionals'. Study abroad was a way of developing the new European citizen.[79]

Erasmus never approached its original 10 per cent target and more students travelled outside the Erasmus framework than it supported. In 2005 it was argued that Europe suffered 'the chagrin of seeing many of the best students going to the US'.[80] It is difficult to establish how far it succeeded in creating European citizens as Erasmus students, understandably, showed more interest in job prospects and enjoying their travel than in concepts of citizenship. The evidence is mixed. On the one hand, it shows that while former Erasmus students showed valued their periods of study abroad, participation in the programme did not strengthen their support for the European Union.[81] On the other, Erasmus succeeded in creating not just mobile students but a more mobile workforce so that former Erasmus students were more likely than their peers to go on to work abroad.[82] For its part, the European Commission claimed the programme as 'the perfect example of a European success story: close to 3 million students have participated since it started in 1987, as well as over 300,000 higher education teachers and other staff since 1997' with more than 4,000 participating institutions in 33 countries. In 2010 it supported 231,000 students in Europe while the countries involved in Erasmus sent only 60,000 to the United States, albeit for longer periods of time as the average Erasmus student spent six months abroad.[83]

Whether a triumph or a disappointment Erasmus reaffirmed an internationalist view of higher education that often seemed more important to universities than to governments. At the same time, the late twentieth and early twenty-first centuries saw the pursuit of revenue – the fourth of the drivers identified by OECD – as profoundly influencing policy and pushing it in a quite different direction. While Erasmus was mainly concerned with movement within Europe, and inspired by political ideals as well as economics, international demand for education across borders was driven by economics. Both sending and host countries looked for economic benefits in what OECD identified as 'a global market for higher education … with certain countries exporting higher education and others importing it. This market was estimated to have an annual value of several billion US dollars'.[84] Britain, the United States and Australia, all benefiting from their use of English, led the world's governments and universities into this global market place (see also Chapter 6). The United States illustrated the change in the language and rationale of its policy in a presidential memorandum on 'International education policy' in 2000. It set out conventional arguments about economic development and attracting future leaders but also did the calculations to explain that international students contributed $9 billion a year to the American economy.[85]

Australia offers a case study, having moved from a position outside the 50 most popular destinations for foreign students in 1950 to second place in 2008. Its policies changed dramatically over this period. Under its 'White Australia Policy' it restricted immigration until 1973 and required most overseas students to return home after graduating. It accepted some students, particularly from south Asia, under the Colombo plan of technical assistance set up in 1950, which was seen as a useful way of checking Chinese influence in the region. In the 1980s, as it watched Britain grappling with overseas student fees and the funding of universities, the Australian government adopted a new foreign-student policy. Following the British lead it established the general principle that overseas students would pay full-cost fees, although these were waived for some students on scholarships and awards. This provided an incentive for universities to recruit internationally which was underpinned by government policy:

> The demand for education services throughout the Asian region is likely to be quite large for the next 20 or so years. The expansion of Australian education to meet this demand would encourage cultural exchanges and tourism. It would provide jobs for Australians directly, and there would be multiplier effects ... The development of an education 'export industry', particularly in the graduate field, would benefit the economy directly, and through research it would be linked to the 'high tech' and 'new tech' industries which Australia so strongly wishes to develop.[86]

International students were now a matter of trade not aid. A non-profit agency, IDP Australia, set up in 1960 in the context of the Colombo plan, had its remit changed in 1994 to focus on selling the Australian brand and recruiting students. Legislation was put in place in 2000 to build confidence in Australian higher education with codes of practice and measures of quality assurance. All this was remarkably successful with overseas university numbers rising to 74,000 in 1995, 138,000 in 2000 and 255,000 in 2005. Australian universities attracted students from their Asian hinterland and gained an international reputation, regarded askance by their British competitors, for their aggressive marketing.[87]

A desire to increase revenue also played a part in the expansion of overseas campuses, franchising and cross-border distance-learning programmes. Here, too, Australia played an active part, as did Britain and the United States. Again, growth was rapid so that, by 2010, there were more offshore students following programmes of this kind from British universities than there were students travelling conventionally to Britain. It was stimulated more by universities than by governments and driven by the search for revenue backed by interest in experimenting with new communication technologies. The programmes are significant, both for their students and for the universities offering them and have demonstrated a new form of international study and student mobility. But the students' experience is qualitatively different from that of students travelling to another country, as is their impact on the institutions themselves. They can therefore with some legitimacy be excluded from the definition of 'foreign student'.

Despite the growth of these programmes, conventional movement across borders grew more rapidly after the end of the cold war than before. While no longer driven and shaped by east-west conflict, it continued to respond to an international demand for student places, and continued to respond to national policies. European politics brought the expansion of the Erasmus programme in a new demonstration of internationalism. Worldwide economics and a new economic consensus brought a new language and new attitudes with higher education treated as a competitive market in a new way.

The similarities and contrasts between British policy towards foreign students and that of its neighbours, allies or competitors reflect Britain's position as an offshore European island, or archipelago. Language was at times a barrier, at times a bridge. National politics, in Britain as elsewhere in Europe, shaped student movement as did the British imperial and maritime legacy.

Religion, geography and empire all played their part in the international movement of students. It was influenced by the politics of religion from the twelfth to the nineteenth centuries which first encouraged international movement then tried to confine it within religious boundaries. Movement within Europe was easier than across the Channel so that many continental universities had more foreign or distant students than those in the British Isles. The establishment of the first and second British empires then reversed that trend, bringing new groups of students to Britain but also to other countries in Europe. In the early twentieth century the academic status of German universities often made them more attractive to foreign students than those in Britain. There was then a contrast between French and British imperial policy where, despite the French policy of *assimilation*, only tiny numbers of students from its empire went to study in France. The French legacy took a higher proportion of students from the Maghreb to France after the end of empire than before. While the United States did not have an imperial legacy, its overwhelming economic strength in the second half of the twentieth century drew international students as powerfully as Britain had done in the days of its empire.

The twentieth century also saw national and international political interests and competing ideologies pushing and pulling students. America demonstrated the potency of scholarship policy for political ends with its use of the Boxer indemnity and then a renewed commitment to internationalism inspired by Fulbright and the awards he established. The Soviet Union toyed with the use of foreign study for revolutionary ends but abandoned that attempt and moved into the use of education in the technologies as a better route to long-term influence. Europe saw cooperation in education as bringing political as well as economic benefits.

At least three ideological competitions were played out internationally, all of them paralleled by British experience. One was between the pursuit of cooperation in the interest of mutual understanding and the use of education for national interests, political, strategic or economic. Another, during the cold war, was between east and west in which both blocs wanted not only to teach and influence international students but also to demonstrate the superiority of their ideology as a route to development. The new respect for market forces marks a third competition where there is a conflict between what Kerr called 'the free advancement of learning everywhere and all the time' and the economic interests of institutions looking for revenue in the market place. The challenge for students has always been to reconcile their individual plans and aspirations with the forces that served to encourage or hinder them as they looked for their own chances to study abroad.

10
Conclusion: Policies, Purposes and Effects

Britain always drew some of its students from abroad, even when it was at the periphery of educated Europe. By the twenty-first century it had more foreign students than any of its continental neighbours. They had shaped and influenced its universities. To assess the significance of studying in Britain, we can look at numbers and policies, at students' backgrounds and experience, and at the outcomes or consequences of their period of study.

Numbers are sparse until the twentieth century but it seems that, in Britain as elsewhere in Europe, the number of foreign students rose during the later Middle Ages, though with setbacks, particularly from war, schism and plague. While the Reformation cut student numbers, British universities expanded in the seventeenth century and continued to attract students internationally. Oxbridge spent the eighteenth and early nineteenth centuries in a state of placid calm but Enlightenment Edinburgh and its medical school became an international magnet. Across Europe foreign student numbers rose as economies expanded in the early years of the twentieth century. By 1910 there were some 2,700 foreign students in British universities, about 10 per cent of the total, with others in schools and technical colleges. Many were from the empire but links with continental universities looked important in the apparent dawn of European amity that was shot down by Gavrilo Princip's revolver and the guns of the western front.

During the twentieth century, while foreign university numbers remained at a steady 10 per cent, with the European proportion rising in the 1930s and early 1940s, foreign students outside university also increased. By the early 1970s, alongside the 20,000 university students there were nearly as many in technical colleges and polytechnics, a similar number of trainee nurses and perhaps 5,000 to 10,000 in English language schools with 1,700 children at private secondary schools.

228

Numbers continued to grow, with the one exception of the nurses where recruitment fell in response to changes in immigration policy. By 2010, one in five university full-time students was from abroad and they made up more than half of all postgraduates. Alongside these 365,000 university students there were over 380,000 attending shorter courses at language schools and 23,000 in private-sector schools. Increasing numbers of students came from continental Europe while demand from Asia expanded dramatically in the late twentieth and early twenty-first centuries. Growing numbers of foreign students, and especially students from Asia, went in the same way to continental Europe, Russia, the United States and Australia. Travel from the developing to the industrial world had become a more powerful driver of international student numbers than movement between industrialised countries.

Changes in student numbers, and in practices affecting them, were often a response to foreign students and their circumstances rather than a consequence of deliberate policy. Medieval students were drawn to Oxford by the quality of its teaching, or kept away by suspicions of heresy, not by deliberate university policy. Edinburgh attracted medical students from Europe and North America, and the Inns of Court potential lawyers from India, Africa and the Caribbean, without developing overt policies of international recruitment. For its part government seldom spoke with one voice or from any clear policy. Tensions between restrictive attitudes to immigration and a welcome for foreign students go back to the bans imposed on Scots in 1306, and the exemptions then allowed to students. Early in the twentieth century government might have liked fewer Indian students, but saw no way of discouraging them.

Government policy and attitudes towards foreign students responded to changes in national and international politics and in economics. In turn, the politics of religion, of the empire, of the cold war, of Europe and of the market took students to Britain and affected policies towards them. Policies on trade and economics repeatedly shifted in the twentieth century, from the 1930s when the Board of Trade wanted foreign students and industry suspected them, to the 1990s when universities, ahead of government, began promoting foreign study as an article of trade.

Policy was always contested, often inconsistent and usually responsive rather than purposive. There were repeated conflicts between internationalist university values and national, economic and political interests. For much of the twentieth century there was a gulf between national expectations that university education, open to the empire, deserved gratitude and respect from colonial students, and their conviction that the downfall of the empire merited a lifetime commitment and justified their study in Britain. Later, as Britain was easing its way into the European Community, government accepted European students at the same fees as British in the confident and incorrect expectation that there would not be many of them. In the early twenty-first century a welcome for foreign students at the highest levels of government did not match immigration policy or make it cheap or easy to obtain and renew visas. The doubling of the proportion of overseas university students between the early 1990s and the late 2000s reflected individual university practice far more than deliberate or national policy.

Early university policy was shaped by the needs of the church and of an educated elite within what was seen as universal Christendom. The state was involved where secular needs had to be met by universities or where, for religious or political reasons, student activities needed to be watched or restrained. For their part, even after the Reformation, universities retained internationalist commitments which were symbolised by the journeys of Erasmus, and remembered as important by academics even when universities were at their most insular. From the sixteenth to the nineteenth century religion was a cause for exclusion, and a mark of identity, rather than a force for unity or universality. As its influence declined, the needs of the empire steadily grew in importance for British universities, and to a smaller extent for its schools and military academies.

Students from the West Indian plantocracy, from the colonies of settlement, and above all from India ushered in a period in which imperial hegemony powerfully shaped Britain's international educational policy. British universities were important for the empire, imperial policy affected the way students were treated, and students from the empire and then the Commonwealth dominated overseas numbers. Until decolonisation, and the changes in migration law that accompanied and followed it, imperial students had a right of access to Britain and so, in principle, to its educational system. Commonwealth numbers remained high until the 1980s. British imperial experience here is markedly different from French which attracted large numbers of students from its former colonies in the Maghreb only after their independence.

Major changes came in the 1980s when shifting ideologies, and changing geopolitics, moved education in a quite new direction. The 1979 government was unwilling to regard Commonwealth students more favourably than others. More significantly it respected market forces and expected others, including the educational establishment, to do so. Universities then moved ahead of government, seeing the vigorous and competitive recruitment of overseas students as a way of securing and increasing their income. By the early twenty-first century the government, its agency the British Council and the universities were using the language of the market to describe and explain their policies. Although academic values still influenced policy and internationalist convictions played their part in the decisions of universities and of university staff, students were increasingly recruited not to support an imperial ideal, or in the interest of international development or of disinterested scholarship, but to help balance the university books. In an unforeseen change, while Commonwealth student numbers made up a declining proportion of the whole, students travelling from continental Europe to Britain regained an importance they had lost some centuries before –with the first 14 years of the twentieth as a possible exception.

The forces that pushed or pulled students, identified in Chapter 1, mattered more than deliberate policy. At different times religion, politics and individual aspiration drew scholars to Britain. During the years when it was uniting western Europe, religion carried both monastic and lay scholars to England. Protestantism then drew scholars, predominantly from northern Europe. New forces then came into play. The Indian students of the late nineteenth century, moved by the opportunities that they saw were open to the 'England returned', were followed by the ambitious from the whole of the empire, including its future politicians, as demand for higher education outstripped the capacity of local institutions.

Many of the students came from prosperous families who could not find the education they wanted nearer to home in a pattern matched in the other major hosting countries. This was as true of the students from the black middle class of west Africa in the eighteenth century as of the increasing number of Indians and Egyptians a century later and of their twentieth-century successors. It remained true, for example, for Greek students in the 1980s when, as Greece was entering the European Community and their fees had to be determined, the English Department for Education explained that this was not 'a case of helping Greece where she is poor. We are concerned with a benefit not for poor Macedonian peasants, but for the children of the well-heeled Greek commercial and professional classes'.[1] Most students paid for themselves, or relied on their families, but a significant minority relied on scholarships, provided for institutional, political and economic reasons.

Gender kept out many students. Although small numbers of girls were sent to Britain for their education from the late eighteenth century onwards, universities were long closed to women. By the 1860s university doors were creaking ajar but it took more than another century before women came near to making up half of all foreign university students.

Until the twenty-first century it was only among exceptional groups of students that women were in a majority – among the trainee nurses recruited in the 1960s and 1970s and again among Erasmus students. Tracing the history of women students has, however, been hampered where, as was often the case, data were not disaggregated by gender.

Class, race and gender influenced student travel to Britain and went on to affect the lives of students after they arrived. While race was important in conditioning student experience, class often carried more weight: in the 1890s Ranjitsinhji was respected both for his skills as a university cricketer and because he was understood to be a prince. (Britain has always been good at recognising class distinctions that can be treated as matching its own.) Students had to grapple with issues of class and race, too, as they confronted shortage of accommodation and the challenge of prejudice. Over many years the coldness of the British weather and the coolness of the British character influenced their experience while rarely, it seems, deterring their successors.

Student experience is inadequately described if it is analysed solely in terms of the sober categories of class, race and gender, leave alone religion, politics and economics. This would be a distortion in leaving out fun for, as Lawrence Stone pointed out, an

> enduring latent function of the university has been to provide the undergraduate with access to a luxuriant and exciting adolescent subculture. Success in sport, sex, social climbing, or love has always counted more than academic success for the bulk of liberal arts students.[2]

That was as true for the medieval wandering scholars – or at least those who left us cheerful songs – as for the Erasmus students of the twenty-first century – or at least the 75 per cent who told researchers that 'to have fun' was very important in their decision to go abroad or the 95 per cent who found their time abroad personally rewarding even though far fewer of them thought it would help them get a job or an increased income. It influenced both their decision to travel and the quality of their life once they had done so.[3]

To fill out an analysis of foreign-student experience in Britain we can also to ask about its outcomes. Inevitably we know most about the famous and successful.

During his passage to England in 1968, when the Rhodes Trust still brought its American scholars by ocean liner, Bill Clinton had his first alcoholic drink ever and found that 'by far the best part of the voyage was just what it was supposed to be: being with the other Rhodes scholars'. Within 30 years he had appointed one as counsel to the Labor Department, one a federal judge in Boston, one as special advisor on Russia, one chief of the legal services corporation, one US attorney in San Diego, one to the ninth circuit court of appeals and one as secretary of labor. Yet another, who was already an admiral when Clinton became president, became commander of US forces in the Pacific though, Clinton explained, 'he got there without any help from me'. Rhodes is proud of its alumni and Clinton's list looks like a vote of confidence in Oxford, and in the Rhodes selectors, rather than a cheer for presidential patronage.[4]

Illuminated by the dying embers of empire, the London School of Economics could make as strong a claim to influence as the Rhodes Trust. According to one unidentified but 'well-known political leader' there was in the 1970s 'a vacant chair at every cabinet meeting in India. It is reserved for the ghost of Professor Harold Laski.' Within and beyond India – where its alumnus B. R. Ambedkar drafted its constitution – LSE could identify:

> Krishna Menon of India, Jomo Kenyatta of Kenya, Kwame Nkrumah and Hilla Liman of Ghana, Veeraswamy Ringadoo of Mauritius, Goh Keng Swee of Singapore, Kamisese Mara of Fiji, Errol Barrow of Barbados, Eugenia Charles of Dominica, Michael Manley of Jamaica, Shridath ('Sonny') Ramphal of Guyana and the Secretary-General of the Commonwealth – the list of leaders of new nations with an LSE past is long, all the way to the unfortunate Maurice Bishop who, as Prime Minister of Grenada, was killed during the 1983 coup on his island.[5]

Institutional pride in their foreign alumni is one indicator of their impor- tance and if political advance is the criterion of success, and selective illustration the source of evidence, then positive assessment is straight- forward. Similarly, if the younger researchers assisted by the Academic Assistance Council (now the Council for Assisting Refugee Academics) are regarded as postgraduate students, then we can use its record of 16 Nobel Prize winners and over a hundred fellows of the Royal Society and British Academy as an indicator of the benefits of welcoming foreign refugee students. Success stories are legion.

Moving beyond them becomes more difficult. Institutions, students and those funding them have rarely had simple or single aims that would help evaluation. Nor are there always records. Even in the case of the modest number of African Rhodes scholars – 638 of them up to 1990 – their historian concludes that we lack the prosopographical analysis to assess their impact.[6] At least as important, students' interests and hopes are seldom likely to coincide precisely with the philosophy and intentions of those funding them, whether these were their parents or a funding agency. We can therefore only ask, without expecting definitive answers, questions like: Where did students go next? How did their experience change them and what use did they make of their qualifications? Did they get rich? Did those funding them get what they hoped for? how did they influence their institutions within Britain?

Long before the term 'brain drain' was coined sponsors deplored the way in which students who came to learn stayed to settle. The Russian tsar wanted his students back in the seventeenth century while in the early twentieth nearly a quarter of colonial Rhodes scholars had not gone home despite their sponsors' expectations.[7] By the 1960s, health professionals were dismayed that of every seven qualified midwives from the British West Indies, four were in Britain along with one in four trained midwives from Commonwealth West Africa.[8] In the 2000s eastern European academics had begun to watch the development of a brain drain to Britain and Germany.[9] This has not always been seen negatively. The United States has recruited skilled labour for its workforce from former foreign students while studies of Erasmus have shown that its beneficiaries are more likely to go on and work abroad than their peers, with this seen as a contribution to the European labour market.[10] A proportion of foreign students always stayed in their host country and, although hard figures are scarce, it is possible to make some generalisations about those who stayed and those who returned home.

The drivers of student mobility had a bearing on decisions to stay or return. Many refugees – from the Huguenots to those fleeing Nazism and to the Hungarian students of 1956 – stayed and settled in Britain: some had no other choice. Similarly, many of the West Indian nurses who were recruited to train and work in Britain became permanent members of the workforce and the Caribbean diaspora. Some students stayed as their families established two-country or two-continent domiciles: intellectual middle-class Indian families like the Dutts offered a home for new generations of students in Britain. For more than a century academically gifted students followed Rutherford's path, remaining in Britain, or using it as a base for a mobile academic career. Returning home was never a realistic option for many of these who enriched their own lives and that of the universities that hosted them.

Individual preferences, geography and money influenced some decisions to stay. Among academics, students from industrialised countries were more likely to remain in Britain than those from developing countries. Academics from Australia were more likely to stay in Britain and those from Canada to return, possibly because of the scale of the opportunities open to them south of the forty-ninth parallel.[11] The Commonwealth Scholarship and Fellowship Plan was criticised in its early days because 'for Australia the net result has been loss rather than gain: good men had not returned to Australia and Britain had done a very good thing in buying their brains'.[12] Generally – and in contrast to this exception for academic careers – it has been suggested that the wider the difference between wages or salaries in students' home countries and those of their hosts, the more likely they are to stay, changing from students to migrants.[13]

While some students stayed, many returned home to pursue their domestic and vocational aims. There was limited choice for those who came on short-term vocational courses: they were under pressure to return and did not stay long enough to make the contacts that helped others to stay. Similarly Erasmus students, coming to follow one component of a course, had strong reasons to return home. Many longer-term students looked towards potential rewards at home. The Indian law students who troubled the British authorities in the early twentieth century expected to go home and make their fortune at a time when law was the best-paid profession. The potential politicians, from Nehru to Nyerere, returned home like the potential lawyers and professionals but to seek power (at least in the best cases) more than fortune. And some students returned home because they felt they belonged there. Recent students made the point in such terms as 'I never once entertained the idea of staying in the UK or anywhere outside Sierra Leone' and 'I always knew that I would come back [to post-apartheid South Africa]...our society is such an exciting place, and, to be able to inform that process and be part of it...I just wanted to be part of that'.[14]

Jobs for the educated were not always available and careers not always successful. In the early twentieth century many Indian students returned from Britain only to face unemployment while in the 1960s it was estimated that at least 55 per cent of those who had studied abroad were not working in the jobs for which they had been trained.[15] The less successful leave fewer records but the continuing and increasing flow of students from India suggest that they were a minority. More often, British qualifications became a universal currency, comparable to the medieval *ius ubique docendi*.

Along with their qualifications, and sometimes prestige, many former students also took home attitudes and contacts that were to influence their lives for better or worse. These, too, are difficult to weigh up. On the one hand, the Ugandan poet Okot p'Bitek warned that western education left the former student 'a lost victim of the school system, he cannot dance the dance or play the music of his own people'.[16] In India successful returning students were at risk of being 'derided as mimic-men and Brown Englishmen'.[17] But comments about their intellectual gains are, on the other hand, a recurring theme in student memoirs. For the Indian civil servant J. D. Shukla residence in Oxford exposed him 'to a great and long tradition of freedom and independence of spirit' just as, some decades later, Mboya found that Oxford enabled him to explore the 'line of politics that would be effective in our struggle' and helped him 'to think more analytically about problems and work out on paper how best to meet them'.[18]

Without seeking a balance between the two extremes of deracination and assured intellectual power we can identify one further consequence of study abroad: access to an international elite. International study could provide that access, partly through the activities of former students once they had returned home, partly through the work of the agencies that supported them. In India, among former Fulbright scholars, 'Those who show "good response" after their return…are repeatedly sent abroad. They become permanent, safe, contacts in various ministries, institutions, Universities, colleges, etc'.[19] Some students today become 'transnational' in the sense that they maintain contacts and social links – sometimes even passports – in both their home country and their country of study.[20] Rapid, cheap, transport has made this simpler than ever before.

It is easier to ask about money than about psychology but surprisingly difficult to find how far students who returned home benefited financially from studying abroad. Even without struggling with the counterfactual question of how students would have developed without travelling, we do not have good data. In his account of Rhodes scholars, Ziegler quotes without rebutting the charge that with all its prestige the scholars ended up as 'decent mediocrities – honourable men who served society in a humdrum way', which suggests they did not gain a passport to wealth.[21] Erasmus has not reported on financial benefits from the programme (which were not its aim) and an evaluation of three cohorts of its students found that only 16 per cent of its students thought they were better paid as a result of studying abroad, the same proportion as thought they were worse off. One possible conclusion is that 'the more participation in temporary study abroad grows, the less it seems to make a difference for employment and work'.[22]

There is, however, evidence of financial benefits. Students who migrate, remaining in their host country, are likely to earn more than they would at home. Among those who returned, the east African research on the outcomes of study abroad in the 1970s described in Chapter 9 showed a differential of almost 25 per cent between the salaries of those educated at home and abroad, with monthly mean salaries of $461 for local graduates and $574 for those with degrees from western Europe.[23] Similarly a recent study showed that New Zealand graduates with one or more years education abroad benefited financially as compared with those educated entirely at home.[24] It is reasonable to assume that those who were educated abroad gained financially, and to suggest that gains are likely to be greater for those who returned home to developing rather than to industrialised countries, but to go beyond that is to move from assumption to speculation.

Those who funded students have gone to varying lengths to see whether they were getting value for money. Each family that sent a second child abroad to study, or supported a grandchild or nephew or niece, demonstrated confidence in the first decision. Muhammad Ali's decision to continue funding missions to study abroad in the nineteenth century, or the US government's continuing support for Fulbright awards, showed a similar measure of confidence. Despite the difficulty of tracing alumni, funding agencies often found reason to be pleased with what they discovered, with repeated evidence of successful academic careers. The Great Exhibition trustees were repeatedly assured that their scholars were pursuing successful academic careers though they were also proud that three accompanied Captain Scott in the Antarctic.[25] The Commonwealth Scholarship Commission tracked its alumni and heard with pleasure in 1984 of the 104 Malaysian award holders working in universities, out of a national total of 220 alumni; in his pursuit of them the commission's secretary could almost go from one vice-chancellor's lodge to another when touring the Commonwealth. Scholarship schemes that sought good scholars were usually able to find evidence of their success in doing so.[26]

Other measures of success are more difficult and were not always seen as important. Once funds were identified, it was taken for granted that training doctors or foresters for the colonies was a worthwhile activity. Nor was it seen as necessary in 1939 to evaluate the impact of scholarship programmes designed to counteract those of Nazi Germany. Increasing pressure for evaluation brought studies of the technical cooperation and training programme in the 1980s and of Commonwealth scholars in the 2000s and of their contribution to meeting the international millennial development goals.[27] Hard evidence was gradually added to anecdotal reports from well-disposed alumni.

More often sponsors had to be satisfied with fuzzy evidence in relation to their grander aims, and to adjust these as time went on, with flexible expectations a necessity. Rhodes' trustees continued to make awards although his ambition of creating a cadre of imperial guardians was never achieved. Expenditure on Commonwealth scholarships was by 2001 justified in terms of international development rather than of Commonwealth cohesion. Programmes like Chevening and Marshall, designed to create friends for Britain, managed to sustain their budgets without much more than anecdotal evidence of their effects. They benefited from a conviction that funding higher education brings unarguable benefits, and from the institutional inertia that keeps programmes running almost in defiance of their initial purpose.

Finally, any assessment of the record of foreign students needs to ask how far they influenced institutions in this country. At one extreme the influence was probably negligible: Sandhurst would have been much the same even without its minority of overseas cadets. At the other extreme some institutions and some courses were created principally for overseas students. Language schools could not exist without them. In the heyday of colonial and post-colonial technical cooperation, specialist courses, from textbook production to agricultural development existed principally for overseas students. Since the 1980s many master's courses have been planned and set up mainly to attract them. Between those two extremes, there is consistent evidence across centuries that universities benefited from their international links and from the presence of overseas students. The reputation of the first British universities depended in part on a flow and exchange of students with continental Europe. New subjects came into the curriculum partly in response to imperial demand and partly for overseas students. Most strikingly the PhD degree came into existence at the end of the First World War to meet the interests of international students while, within two decades, a flow of international refugee students brought their dazzling intellectual verve to enrich their host universities.

The last word can therefore go to a vice-chancellor and former minister of education who reconciled university values with national interests in identifying the benefits that flowed from welcoming foreign students. In a House of Lords debate on student fees in 1979 Edward Boyle summarised his case:

> First, there is the wide recognition that without the contribution of overseas students British universities would be quite different institutions, of much less value.... We are a part of ... the international

confraternity of universities. By that I do not mean only, or perhaps even mainly, arcane contributions to learning. I mean the part that universities like Leeds and Manchester and Liverpool and Birmingham play in validating international standards of professional perform-ance that are held right across continental boundaries, and indeed right across ideological boundaries.

Secondly, I would make the point that fully one-quarter of overseas students are here to do research, and they play a vital part in the intellectual and scientific life of the nation and therefore in helping to keep academic disciplines alive. Thirdly...all over the world there are men and women, often in positions of influence, who have a real understanding of the United Kingdom because they spent some of their formative years of their lives being educated in this country.[28]

Notes

1 Introduction: Travelling Abroad to Study

1. R. Kanigel 1991 *The man who knew infinity*, London, 159.
2. Ibid., 168.
3. Ibid., 191–5.
4. Ibid., 313.
5. Ibid., 340–3.
6. 'Ambiguity and ambivalence' is used as a heading by C. Holmes (1991 *A tolerant country?*, London, 91) to characterise immigration policy.
7. Committee on higher education 1961 *Higher education* (Cmnd. 2154) (*Robbins Report*), London, 66.
8. C. W. Chitty 1966 'Aliens in England in the sixteenth century', *Race* 8: 2, 131.
9. See p. 70; J. Goatly to controller, 18.11.1959, NA, BW 1/552.
10. S. Lahiri 2000 *Indians in Britain*, London, 145.
11. G. de Freitas, *Hansard HC*, 3.7.1953, col. 743.
12. As explained in E. S. Lee 1966 'A theory of migration', *Demography*, 3: 1, E. G. Ravenstein presented a paper on 'The laws of migration' to the Royal Statistical Society in 1885. Push and pull factors in relation to students are discussed in H. de Wit 2008 'Changing dynamics in international student circulation', and P. Agarwal 2008 'The dynamics of international student circulation in a global context', in H. de Wit et al. (ed.) *The dynamics of international student circulation in a global context*, Rotterdam. Economic modelling of student flows is reported in, for example, V. Naidoo 2007 'Research on the flow of international students to UK universities', *Journal of Research in International Education* 6, 287 and M. R. Rosenzweig 2006 'Global wage differences and international student flows', in S. M. Collins and C. Graham (eds) *Brookings trade forum: Global labor markets?*, Washington, DC.
13. Interview, A. Niven, 5.5.2007.
14. W. D. Robson-Scott 1953 *German travellers in England 1400–1800*, Oxford, 105.
15. F. Youssoupoff 1953 *Lost splendour*, London, 137–44.
16. *Oxford Dictionary of National Biography*.
17. Personal communication, Lewis Elton. Cf. J. Seabrook 2013 *The refuge and the fortress*, Basingstoke, 30, 36–7.
18. E.g. L. Stone 1974 'The size and composition of the Oxford student body 1580–1909', in L. Stone (ed.) *The university in society vol. 1*, Princeton, NJ.
19. Including for Oxford J. Foster 1888–92 *Alumni Oxonienses*, Oxford, and for Cambridge the Venn data at http://venn.lib.cam.ac.uk/acad/search.html.
20. This typology follows that proposed by Runciman though I have preferred 'narrative' to his term 'reportage' (W. G. Runciman 1983 *A treatise on social theory: vol. 1*, Cambridge, 15–20).

2 Internationalism Reshaped, 1185–1800

1. C. Kerr 2002 *The uses of the university*, Cambridge, Mass., 115.
2. W. Rüegg 1992 'Foreword', in H. de Ridder-Symeons (ed.) *Universities in the middle ages*, Cambridge, xvii.
3. P. Nardi 1992 'Relations with authority', 102 in de Ridder-Symeons (ed.) *Universities*.
4. R. C. Schwinges 1992 'Admission', in de Ridder-Symeons (ed.) *Universities*, 171.
5. A. B. Cobban 1988 *The medieval English universities to c. 1500*, Aldershot, 44.
6. J. Verger 1992 'Patterns', in de Ridder-Symeons (ed.) *Universities*, 48–50.
7. H. de Ridder-Symoens 1992 'Mobility', in de Ridder-Symeons (ed.) *Universities*, 294–7.
8. T. H. Aston, G. D. Duncan and T. A. R. Evans 1980 'The medieval alumni of the University of Cambridge', *Past and Present*, 86: 1, 18–19.
9. P. Moraw 1992 'Careers of graduates', in de Ridder-Symeons (ed.) *Universities*, 268.
10. T. A. R. Evans 1984 'The number, origin and careers of scholars', in J. I. Catto and T. A. R. Evans (eds) *Late medieval Oxford*, Oxford, 496.
11. J. R. H. Moorman 1947 'The foreign element among the English Franciscans', *English Historical Review*, 62: 244, 301–2.
12. T. H. Aston 1977 'Oxford's medieval alumni', *Past and Present* 74: 1, 23.
13. V. H. H. Green 1974 *A history of Oxford University*, London, 25.
14. D. R. Leader 1988 *The university to 1546*, Cambridge, 198–9.
15. Aston 'Oxford's medieval alumni', 25.
16. Ibid., 21; Leader *University*, 120–1.
17. E. J. Ashworth and P. V. Spade 1992 'Logic in late medieval Oxford', in Catto and Evans (eds) *Late medieval Oxford*, 48–9.
18. Cobban *Medieval universities*, 144.
19. W. A. Hinnebusch 1964 'Foreign Dominican students and professors at the Oxford Blackfriars' in *Oxford studies presented to Daniel Callus*, Oxford, 112.
20. M. Asztalos 1992 'The faculty of theology', in de Ridder-Symeons (ed.) *Universities*.
21. Moorman 'Foreign element', 297.
22. H. Mackenzie 1929 'The anti-foreign elements in England 1231–1232', in C. H. Taylor (ed.) *Anniversary essays in mediaeval history by students of Charles Homer Haskins*, Boston, 183.
23. Hinnebusch 'Foreign Dominican students', 115.
24. Ibid., 123.
25. D. E. R. Watt 1986 'Scottish university men of the 13th and 14th centuries', in T. C. Smout (ed.) *Scotland and Europe, 1200–1850*, Edinburgh, 4–6.
26. A. B. Cobban 1999 *English university life in the middle ages*, London, 32.
27. Moorman 'Foreign element', 295–6.
28. R. F. Young 1923 'Bohemian scholars and students at the English universities from 1347 to 1750', *English Historical Review*, 38: 149, 73.
29. de Ridder-Symoens 1992 'Mobility', 287, 303.
30. L. W. B. Brockliss 1989 'The University of Paris and the maintenance of Catholicism in the British Isles, 1426–1789', in D. Julia and J. Revel (eds) *Les universités européennes du xvie au xviiie siècles, tome 2*, Paris, 578–9.

31. W. H. G. Armytage 1955 *Civic universities*, London, 54.
32. de Ridder-Symoens 1992 'Mobility', 284.
33. H. de Ridder-Symoens 1996 'Mobility', in H. de Ridder-Symoens (ed.) *Universities in early modern Europe*, Cambridge, 421.
34. Ibid., 419.
35. G. R. Elton 1955 *England under the Tudors*, London, 141.
36. M. H. Curtis 1959 *Oxford and Cambridge in transition*, Oxford, 49–50.
37. J. V. Luce 1992 *Trinity College Dublin*, Dublin, 60.
38. It was a complicated life in which he served in Parliament and survived supporting the American and French Revolutions and a trial for treason in 1794; Venn database.
39. L. Stone 1974 'The size and composition of the Oxford student body 1580–1909', in L. Stone (ed.) *The university in society*, Princeton, 16–17.
40. Curtis *Transition*, 58.
41. Stone 'Size and composition', 18–20; L. Stone 1964 'The educational revolution in England, 1560–1640', *Past and Present*, 28.
42. S. L. Greenslade 1986 'The faculty of theology', in J. McConica (ed.) *The collegiate university*, Oxford, 304.
43. S. Porter 1997 'University and society', in N. Tyacke (ed.) *Seventeenth century Oxford*, Oxford, 59.
44. Stone 'Size and composition', 68.
45. de-Ridder-Symoens 1996 'Mobility', 428–9.
46. H. Kellenbenz 1978 'German immigrants in England', in C. Holmes (ed.) *Immigrants and minorities in British society*, London, 74.
47. V. G. Kiernan 1978 'Britons old and new', in Holmes (ed.) *Immigrants and minorities*, 36.
48. Ibid., 40.
49. G. Gömöri 2005 *Hungarian students in England and Scotland 1526–1789*, Budapest, 114–15.
50. Leader *University*, 265, 319.
51. Curtis *Transition*, 160.
52. C. Cross 1979 'Continental students and the protestant reformation in England in the sixteenth century', in D. Baker (ed.) *Reform and reformation: England and the continent c. 1500–c. 1700*, Oxford, 55.
53. Curtis *Transition*, 213.
54. de Ridder-Symoens 1996 'Mobility', 437–9.
55. Brockliss 'University of Paris', 589–90.
56. de Ridder-Symoens 1996 'Mobility', 428.
57. E. Ashby 1966 *Universities: British, Indian, African*, London, 8–11.
58. Venn database 1501–1800 for West Indies, Antigua, Barbados, Dominica, Jamaica, Leewards, Montserrat, Nevis, St Kitts, St Lucia, Windwards, identifying those born in WI or whose mother or father were shown as from there. This calculation needs to be treated with caution because of the definitional complexities of admission and matriculation, but the orders of magnitude are probably sound.
59. J. Wright 1986 'Early African musicians in Britain', in R. Lotz and I. Pegg (eds) *Under the imperial carpet*, Crawley, 16, and E. Long 2002 [1774] *History of Jamaica*, Kingston Jamaica, vol. 2, 475–85.
60. W. R. Prest 1972 *The inns of court under Elizabeth I and the early Stuarts 1590–1640*, London, 23.

61. W. D. Robson-Scott quoted in P. Panayi (ed.) 1996 *Germans in Britain since 1500*, London, 32.
62. de Ridder-Symoens 1992 'Mobility', 292.
63. H. Kellenebenz 'German immigrants', 69.
64. A. G. Cross 1980 *'By the banks of the Thames': Russians in eighteenth century Britain*, Newtonville, 2.
65. V. Shestakov 2009 *Russkiye v britanskikh universitetakh*, St Petersburg, 151–3.
66. Ibid., 158–62.
67. J. Kerr 1913 *Scottish education school and university*, Cambridge, 109, 131.
68. de Ridder-Symoens 1996 'Mobility', 439.
69. Kerr *Scottish education*, 57.
70. C. A. McLaren 2005 *Aberdeen students 1600–1800*, Aberdeen, 59.
71. J. Roberts, Á. M. Rodriguez Cruz and J. Herbst 1996 'Exporting models', in de Ridder-Symoens (ed.) *Universities*, 279.
72. de Ridder-Symoens 1996 'Mobility', 438.
73. Shestakhov, *Russkiye*, 163–5.
74. de Ridder-Symoens 1996 'Mobility', 438.
75. R. B. McDowell and D. A. Webb 1982 *Trinity College Dublin 1592–1952*, Cambridge, 246–8, 324; Brockliss 'Catholic students', 589–90; D. Julia and J. Revel 1989 'Les pérégrinations académiques, xvie–xviiie siècles', in Julia and Revel *Les universités*, 71.

3 Revival and Reform, 1800–1900

1. F. K. Ringer 1979 *Education and society in modern Europe*, Bloomington, 226.
2. M. Sanderson 1972 *The universities and British industry, 1850–1979*, London, 3.
3. V. H. H. Green 1974 *A history of Oxford University*, London, 133–4.
4. C. Harvie 1997 'Reform and expansion, 1854–1871', in M. G. Brock and M. C. Curthoys (eds) *Nineteenth-century Oxford part 1*, Oxford, 714.
5. L. Stone 1983 'Social control and intellectual excellence', in N. Phillipson (ed.) *Universities, society, and the future*, Edinburgh, 21.
6. A. L. Turner 1919 *Sir William Turner*, Edinburgh, 340.
7. Sanderson *Universities and industry*, 19.
8. A. M. Birke 1987 *Britain and Germany*, London, 19.
9. A. Bullock 2000 '"A Scotch university added to the others?"', in M. G. Brock and M. C. Curthoys (eds) *Nineteenth century Oxford part 2*, Oxford, 203.
10. T. Pietsch 2013 *Empire of scholars*, Manchester, 93–4.
11. L. Stone 1974 'The size and composition of the Oxford student body 1580–1909', in L. Stone (ed.) *The university in society*, Princeton, 101.
12. T. Pietsch 2011 'Many Rhodes', *History of Education*, 40: 6, 738.
13. Stone 'Size and composition', 68.
14. R. D. Anderson 1983 *Education and opportunity in Victorian Scotland*, Oxford, 294–8.
15. Quoted in J. Walvin 1973 *Black and white*, London, 195.
16. J. Austen 1974 *Lady Susan; The Watsons; Sanditon*, London, 205–6.
17. C. Fyfe 1993 *A history of Sierra Leone*, Aldershot, 189, 205.
18. D. Killingray 1993 'An introduction', *Immigrants and Minorities*, 12: 2, 7–8.
19. Ibid.

20. Fyfe *Sierra Leone*, 261, 294–5, 406–7. Christopher Fyfe once told me of a PhD student who had considered writing a thesis, for which enough material was available, on 'The Negro in nineteenth century Edinburgh', though unfortunately rejected the idea.
21. Venn database. This analysis included all those born or educated in Australia or whose father was shown as 'of' there.
22. E. Ashby 1966 *Universities: British, Indian, African*, London, 37.
23. Ibid., 38.
24. R. Symonds 2000 'Oxford and the empire', 712, in Brock and Curthoys (eds) *Nineteenth century Oxford Part 2*.
25. Venn database. In this analysis all individuals are included who are shown as having been born or educated in Australia, or whose father is shown as 'of Australia'.
26. J. P. C. Roach 1967 *The City and University of Cambridge*, London, 267–8.
27. Pietsch *Empire*, 90–1.
28. D. M. Reid 1990 *Cairo University and the making of modern Egypt*, Cambridge, 17–18.
29. Egyptians recorded in Venn database.
30. C. Charle 2004 'Patterns', in W. Rüegg (ed.) *Universities in the 19th and early 20th centuries*, Cambridge, 67.
31. V. Shestakov 2009 *Russkiye v britanskikh universitetakh*, St Petersburg, 189.
32. J. Heyworthe-Dunne 1938 *An introduction to the history of education in modern Egypt*, London, 104–5, 261.
33. D. Arnold 2000 *Science, technology and medicine in colonial India*, Cambridge, 57–64.
34. J. D. Hargreaves 1994 *Academe and empire*, Aberdeen, 67–72.
35. P. J. Cain and A. G. Hopkins 2002 *British imperialism, 1688–2000 (2nd edition)*, Harlow, 286.
36. Ashby, *Universities*, 52.
37. quoted in S. Banerjee 2010 *Becoming imperial citizens*, Durham North Carolina, 22.
38. J. S. Gandhi and A. P. Bali 1998 *The prime movers of Indian society*, New Delhi, 24–8.
39. Banerjee *Becoming*, 160–1.
40. S. Lahiri 2000 *Indians in Britain*, London, 22.
41. H. Pratt 1860 *University education*, London, 21–2.
42. Ibid., 26.
43. R. Symonds 1986 *Oxford and empire: The last lost cause?* Basingstoke, 257–8.
44. A. M. Wainwright 2008 *'The better class of Indian'*, Manchester, 171–3.
45. J. Jones 1997 *Balliol College*, Oxford, 218.
46. Symonds *Oxford and empire*, 257.
47. S. Satthianadhan 1880 'Indian students and English universities', *Journal of the National Indian Association*, 603–6.
48. Lahiri *Indians in Britain*, 38.
49. M. H. Fisher, S. Lahiri and S. S. Thandi 2007 *A South-Asian history of Britain*, Oxford, 99–100.
50. C. Sorabji 1934 *India calling*, London, 20–31.
51. Fisher et al. *South-Asian history*, 100.
52. Venn database; Nolini Bannerjee married Col. Blair in 1899 and like her sister Sunila qualified in medicine. Sarojini Chattopadhyay became the first woman president.

4   Universities for the Empire, 1900–45

1. J. Nehru 1991 *An autobiography*, Delhi, 16.
2. R. Dahrendorf 1995 *LSE*, Oxford, 13. LSE was, and still is, part of the University of London.
3. W. H. G. Armytage 1955 *Civic universities*, London, 248–53.
4. E. Ashby 1966 *Universities: British, Indian, African*, London, 226.
5. *University Congress Proceedings* 1912. The existence of the ACU means that there are good statistics for overseas students from the early 1920s where there were only patchy totals before.
6. L. Stone 1975 'The size and composition of the Oxford student body 1580–1910', in L. Stone (ed.) *The university in society: Vol. 1*, London, 101.
7. P. Ziegler 2008 *Legacy*, New Haven, 48–9.
8. R. D. Anderson 1983 *Education and opportunity in Victorian Scotland*, Oxford 296–8.
9. Board of education 1912 *Reports for 1910–11 for universities and university colleges* (Cd. 6245–6).
10. Ziegler *Legacy*, 87.
11. *India Students' Department annual report 1913/14* (Cd.7719), 14ff.
12. J. Wilkie to Cabinet Office, 21.9.1926, NA, ED 24/1994.
13. T. Weber 2008 *Our friend 'The enemy'*, Stanford, 67–8.
14. J. M. Winter 1994 'Oxford and the First World War', in B. Harrison (ed.) *The twentieth century*, Oxford, 3.
15. S.W.R.D. Bandaranaike 1963 *Speeches and writings*, Colombo, 74–5.
16. *Report of the committee appointed to consider questions relating to the position of students holding scholarships in the United Kingdom granted by colonial governments*, 15.12.1899, NA, CO 885/7/16.
17. *Report of committee on state technical scholarships established by the government of India* (Cd. 6867), 1913, 9.
18. Nehru *Autobiography*, 13.
19. H. Miller 1959 *Prince and premier*, London, 37–43.
20. V. Shestakov 2009 *Russkiye v britanskikh universitetakh*, St Petersburg, 156, 183, 200–1.
21. J. W. Boag et al. 1990 *Kapitza in Cambridge and Moscow*, Amsterdam, 10.
22. Ibid., 50–1.
23. Sir Richard Temple 1914, quoted in R. Symonds 1986 *Oxford and empire*, Basingstoke, 146.
24. S. Mukherjee 2010 *Nationalism, education and migrant identities*, London, 110.
25. Symonds *Oxford and empire*, 261.
26. S. Lahiri 2000 *Indians in Britain*, London, 179.
27. R. Dahrendorf 1995 *LSE*, Oxford, 273–5.
28. Bandaranaike *Speeches and writings*, 81–4.
29. *Oxford Dictionary of National Biography*.
30. E. Williams *Inward hunger*, London, 46–7.
31. M. G. Brock 2000 'The Oxford of Asquith and Elmhirst', in M. G. Brock and M. C. Curthoys (eds) *Nineteenth-century Oxford, Part 2 (The history of the University of Oxford, vol. 7)*, Oxford, 802.
32. J. Seabrook 2013 *The refuge and the fortress*, 20–4. The figures are uncertain. Another estimate puts the total from central Europe in the 1930s at 56,000 (C. Holmes 1991 *A tolerant country?*, London, 31).

33. E. Hobsbawm 2002 *Interesting times*, London, 78.
34. Seabrook *Refuge*, 38–9.
35. Lahiri, *Indians*, 38.
36. J. Green 1986 'Dr J. J. Brown of Hackney', in R. Lotz and I. Pegg (eds) *Imperial carpet*, Crawley, 271.
37. *Times*, 22.12.1926, quoted in M. C. Morgan 1978 *Bryanston 1928–78*, Blandford.
38. C. Tyerman 2001 *A history of Harrow school 1324–1991*, Oxford, 463–5, an honourable exception to the generally hagiographic genre of school histories.
39. India Office 1927 *Report of the India Sandhurst committee*, London, 35, 43–4.
40. P. Daniel 1986 *Frensham Heights, 1925–49*, n.p., 121–2.
41. A. Shepperd 1980 *Sandhurst*, Feltham, 141–2; H. Thomas 1961 *The story of Sandhurst*, London, 199.
42. *India Sandhurst committee*, 10.
43. T. Pietsch 2013 *Empire of scholars*, Manchester, 142–5.
44. Evidence by E. M. Rich to Committee on overseas students, 20.7.1933, NA, BT 64/5.
45. H. E. S. Fremantle to Vice-Chancellor, 8.4.1902, NA, CO 885/8/5.
46. 'Official report of the allied colonial universities conference', 1904, *The Empire Review*, 6, 77.
47. R. Anderson 2006 *British universities past and present*, London, 57.
48. Dahrendorf *LSE*, 43.
49. *University Congress Proceedings* 1912, 58.
50. Ibid., 67.
51. R. Simpson 1983 *How the PhD came to Britain*, Guildford, 56, 93, 97.
52. *Hansard HL*, 7.3.1905, col. 532.
53. Ziegler, *Legacy*, 50–1, 110.
54. Leader, *The Times*, 1.9.1908.
55. The Lee-Warner report was not published at the time but appears as an appendix in the 1922 *Lytton report* (*Report of the committee on Indian students*), London.
56. *Lee–Warner report*, 8–9.
57. Ibid., 3–4.
58. Ibid., 49–50.
59. Ibid., 52.
60. Ibid., 17.
61. Lahiri, *Indians*, 5.
62. Symonds *Oxford and empire*, 259.
63. *Lytton report*, 47–8.
64. *Indian students' department annual report 1913/14*, 8.
65. *Indian students' department annual report 1915–16*, 13.
66. A. Basu 1974 *The growth of education and political development in India, 1898–1920*, Delhi, 28.
67. *Report of the committee on the system of state technical scholarships established by the government of India* (Cd. 6867) 1913 (*Morison report*), 21ff.; The problems were confirmed in annual reports of the Indian students' department, e.g. for 1920/21, 25.
68. *Lytton report*, 58–63.
69. Simpson *How the PhD came to Britain*, 145.

70. Ibid., 145–62.
71. R. Simpson 2009 *The development of the PhD degree in Britain, 1917–1959 and since*, Lewiston, 482
72. *Lytton report*, 12–13.
73. Ibid., 41.
74. Ibid., 27.
75. *Royal Commission on Oxford and Cambridge Universities* (Cmd. 1588) 1922, 33.
76. *University Congress Proceedings 1936*, 39.
77. *Report of Indian students department 1921/22*, 5.
78. C. Whitehead 1988 *Not wanted on the voyage*, London, 2–3.
79. Memorandum from faculty board of English, March 1929, quoted in Simpson, *Development of the PhD*, 281.
80. Dahrendorf *LSE*, 345.
81. UGC report 1930 quoted in Armytage, *Civic universities*, 250.
82. J. Jones 1997 *Balliol College*, Oxford, 253–4.
83. *Lytton report*, 34.
84. W. Ormsby Gore to Vice-chancellor, 22.10.1926; G. A. Weekes to Ormsby Gore, 18.12.1926, NA, CO 323/962/2.
85. *Indian students department annual report 1914–15*, 9.
86. Mukherjee, *Nationalism*, 64.
87. B. Wasserstein 1998 *Secret war in Shanghai*, London, 186.
88. *India Sandhurst committee*, 31; H. Stanley to H. R. Cowell, 29.6.1928, NA, CO 54/891/1/11; R. Nunn May to Lord Halifax, 10.7.1935, NA, WO 32/2738.
89. Internal brief, October 1935, NA, WO 32/2738.
90. S. D. Stewart to H. J. Creedy, 6.8.1936, NA, WO 32/2738.
91. A. J. Widdows to under secretary colonial office, 14.12.1935, NA, CO 323/1348/5.
92. J. E. W. Flood, minute, 2.3.1936, NA, CO 323/1348/5.
93. C. Parkinson to J. Shuckburgh, 13.3.1936, NA, CO 323/1348/5.
94. J. E. W. Flood, minute, 2.3.1936, NA, CO 323/1348/5.
95. W. Runciman to E. C. Grenfell, 26.5.1933, NA, BT 59/16.
96. Chairman's report, 5.10.1933, NA, BT 59/16 .
97. W. B. Brander, 13.7.1933; Committee paper 54 'Summary of replies from universities, February 1934, NA, BT 64/5.
98. R. Nunn May, 19.7.1933, NA, BT 64/5.
99. A. H. Ball to C. M. Pickthall, 2.12.1933, NA, ED 121/21.
100. Letter from federation, 11.1.1934, NA, BT 64/5.
101. W.R. Richardson to S. H. Wood 13.3.1935, NA, ED 121/121.
102. Note to Mr Holmes 13.3.1935, NA, ED 121/21.
103. A. J. S. White 1965 *The British Council*, London, 3.
104. *Hansard HC* 22.3.1935, col. 1483–4
105. British Council paper 'British cultural propaganda in Egypt', 5.3.1935, NA, ED 121/22.

5   Recovery and Expansion, 1945–79

1. G. Neave 2011 'Patterns', in W. Rüegg (ed.) *A history of the university in Europe Vol. IV*, Cambridge, 31.

2. R. Layard, J. King and C. Moser 1969 *The impact of Robbins*, Harmondsworth, 13.
3. W. Rüegg and J. Sadlak 2011 'Relations with authority', in Rüegg *History*, 73.
4. P. Hennessy 1992 *Never again*, London, 162.
5. Committee on higher education 1963 *Higher education* (Cmnd. 2154) (*Robbins report*), 15.
6. *University development 1948–52* (Cmd. 8875), 19–21.
7. *University development 1952–57* (Cmnd. 534), 82.
8. M. Young 1962 'Is your child in the unlucky generation?', *Where* 10, 3–5.
9. *Education: A framework for expansion* (Cmnd. 5174) 1972, 35.
10. Central Advisory Council for Education 1959, *15 to 18* (*Crowther report*), London, 8.
11. *Robbins report*, 73.
12. Lord Hailey 1938 *An African survey*, London, 1, 250.
13. E. Ashby 1966 *Universities: British, Indian, African*, London, 214.
14. Personal recollection.
15. R. Symonds 1966 *The British and their successors*, London, 90.
16. J. Useem and R. H. Useem 1955 *The western-educated man in India*, New York, 118.
17. Interview, Gajaraj Dhanarajan, 19.12.2008.
18. *Robbins report*, Appendix 2A, 257.
19. P. Ziegler 2008, *Legacy*, New Haven, 179.
20. A. T. Carey 1956 *Colonial students*, London, 109–10.
21. *Report of the committee on legal education for students from Africa* (Cmnd. 1255) 1961, 5.
22. *Robbins report*, Evidence, vol. F, 1790.
23. Ibid., 1804–5.
24. Evidence from G. Thompson, 7.2.1962, *Robbins report,* Evidence vol. E, 1539.
25. Personal recollection.
26. *Report of the Imperial education conference 1911* (Cd. 5666), 38–41.
27. *Robbins report*, 66.
28. Enoch Powell, later a scourge of immigration, was reported (R. Winder 2004 *Bloody foreigners*, London, 264) to have led one of these recruitment drives, before he became minister of health, though his biographers seem to have missed the story.
29. V. Chapman to director of Nigerian students, 18.9.1956, NA, CO 1028/39.
30. S. Walsh 1979 *Overseas nurses*, London, para. 4, 27–9.
31. G. Kalton 1966 *The public schools*, London, 33.
32. J. Rae 1981 *The public school revolution*, London, 166.
33. Figures from the 1970s from the Independent Schools Information Service *Annual census.*
34. C. Tyerman 2000 *A history of Harrow School*, Oxford, 465–6.
35. B. Scragg 1993 *Sevenoaks School*, Bath, 180–2.
36. F. Bell 1987 'The Bell schools and Cambridge', *Cambridge*, 21, 100–3.
37. D. W. Urwin 1982 *Specialist schools and colleges in Cambridge*, Cambridge, 5–6.
38. G. Williams and M. Woodhall 1979 *Independent further education*, London, 31–4.

39. 'Allotment of overseas vacancies to the RMA Sandhurst', 31.5.1955, NA, WO 32/17829.
40. J. B. Churcher, 9.9.1958, NA, WO 32/17829.
41. DMI to Director of Military Training, 22.8.1958, NA, WO 32/17829.
42. G. W. Lathbury to Gen. Stafford, 30.9.1958, NA, WO 32/17829.
43. P. R. Fraser to J. Mark, 26.12.1946, NA, FO 945/152.
44. A. Creech Jones circular to colonial administrations 'The welfare of colonial students overseas', 10.6.1948, NA, CO 537/5138.
45. P.R. Fraser to J. Mark, 26.12.1946, NA, FO 945/152.
46. *Hansard HC*, 2.7.1953 col. 728–30.
47. *Hansard HC*, 10.7.1953, col. 1584.
48. P. Lancaster 1962 *Education for Commonwealth students in Britain*, London, 23–4.
49. P. Williams 1981 'Overseas students in Britain: The background', in P. Williams (ed.) *The overseas student question*, London, 36–7.
50. Savingram to colonial governors 'Communism in the colonies', in D. Rees Williams to E. Bevin, 23.5.1949, NA, FO 1110/230.
51. D. Rees Williams to T. Lloyd, 16.2.1948, NA, CO 537/5138.
52. P. Sillitoe to O. Sargant, 23.12.1948, NA, CO 537/4312.
53. R.A.A. Badham to M. Logan, 26.5.1949, on the Coordinating Council; Box 500 to Colonial Office 16.7.1949, on Burnham, NA, CO 537/4312; R. R. Todd to J. B. Sidebotham, 1.9.1953, on Malayan students, NA, CO 968/263; see also Chapter 7.
54. G.H. Hall, Circular to the colonies, 15.11.1945, NA, CO 1045/207.
55. Colonial Office note (CO 194/49), 11.3.1949, NA, CO 537/5138.
56. P. R. C. Williams 1985 *They came to train*, London, 9.
57. Colonial Office note, 11.3.1949 (CO 194.49), NA, CO 537/5138.
58. Draft, SofS to officer administering government of Tanganyika, 24.8.1950, NA, CO 876/162.
59. *Robbins report* Appendix V, 1801–2.
60. *Technical Assistance from the UK for overseas development* (Cmnd. 1308), 1961, para. 6, para. 66.
61. ODM 1970 *Education in developing countries*, London 26.
62. *More help for the poorest* (Cmnd. 6270) 1975, 22.
63. D. Veale in *University Congress Proceedings* 1948, 229–33.
64. *University Congress Proceedings* 1963, 196.
65. H. Perraton 2009 *Learning abroad*, Newcastle upon Tyne, 5–11.
66. Ibid., 36.
67. Ibid., 31, 37.
68. Ibid., passim. With only three women at the founding conference, two of them arriving late because women had been so conspicuously absent, 'fathers' seems legitimate.
69. J. D. Hargreaves 1954 *Academe and empire*, Aberdeen, 43.
70. Irving memorial lecture, 8.11.1961, NA, OD 17/156.
71. *University Congress Proceedings* 1953, 83, 94.
72. R. Simpson 2009 *The development of the PhD degree in Britain, 1917–59 and since*, Lewiston, 209.
73. University of Oxford 1966 *Report of commission of inquiry*, para. 94–5.
74. S. Fisher 1961 'The overseas student in Oxford', *Isis*, 12 June.

75. ACU, CSC minutes, Paper 25/63, 26.9.1963.
76. ACU, CSC minutes, Paper 22/65, 24.11.1964.
77. Simpson, *Development of PhD*, 482. Her seven included the main providers: Cambridge, Edinburgh, Imperial, LSE, Manchester, Oxford, UCL.
78. PEP 1955 *Colonial students in Britain*, London; PEP 1965 *New Commonwealth students in Britain*, London; D. G. Burns 1965 *Travelling scholars*, Reading; A. Sen 1970 *Problems of overseas students and nurses*, Reading; Lancaster, *Education for Commonwealth students*; A. K. Singh 1963 *Indian students in Britain*, New York; L. Braithwaite 2001 *Colonial West Indian students in Britain*, Kingston, Jamaica; Carey *Colonial students*; B. R. Davison 1966 *Black British*, London.
79. J. Carswell 1985 *Government and the universities in Britain*, Cambridge, 10–11.
80. *Robbins report*, 213–14.
81. Ibid., 67.
82. G. E. Dudman to R. H. Stone, 7.1.1977, NA, ED 212/162.
83. Note, R. H. Stone, 17.1.1977, NA, ED 212/162.
84. Note, G. E. Dudman, 13.1.1977, NA, ED 212/162.
85. *Robbins report*, para. 178.
86. J. Wolfenden to vice-chancellors quoted in R. W. B. Clarke to J. Nicholls, 4.12.1963, NA, OD 17/111.
87. DES letter to G. R. Bell, 24.8.1966, NA, FO 924/1560.
88. R. Cecil to PS, 7.11.1966, NA, FO 924/1560.
89. E.G. Edwards, *University Congress Proceedings* 1968, 74.
90. *Hansard HC*, 23.2.1967, col. 2000.
91. *Hansard HL* 14.2.1967, col. 275.
92. *Hansard HL*, 14.2.1967, col. 247–8.
93. *Hansard HL*, 14.2.1967, col. 202–12.
94. R. Cecil to PS, FO, 7.9.1966, NA, FO 924/1560.
95. Carswell, *Government and universities*, 115–16.
96. *Hansard HL*, 14.2.1967, col. 234.
97. Position paper on RRA, 10.2.1977, NA, ED 212/162.
98. *Hansard HC*, 25.11.1976, col. 188.
99. S. Williams to J. Hart, 5.12/1977, NA, ED 212/163.
100. Williams 'Overseas students', 36–7.
101. *Hansard HC*, 13.3.1978, col. 182.
102. R. Bristow 1979 *Overseas students and government policy*, 1962–79, London, 8.
103. P. Hennessy 2001 *The Prime Minister*, London, 94.

6   Into the Market Place, 1979–2010

1. V Shestakov 2009 *Russkiye v britanskikh universitetakh*, St Petersburg, 285; CSCAR 1997.
2. *The development of higher education into the 1990s* (Cmnd. 9524) 1985, para. 3.5.
3. Figures are quoted in J. Pratt 1997 *The polytechnic experiment 1965–1992*, Buckingham, 27.

4. D. Watson and R. Bowden 2007 'The fate of the Dearing recommendations', in D. Watson and M. Amoah (eds) *The Dearing report ten years on*, London, 7.
5. *Higher education* (Cm. 114) 1987, para. 4.6.
6. Ibid., para. 3.3.
7. *The future of higher education* (Cm. 5735) 2003, 8
8. National Committee of Enquiry into Higher Education 1997 *Higher education in the learning society* (*Dearing report*), Recommendation 71.
9. *The future of higher education*, 2–8.
10. Ibid., 57.
11. Prime minister, Cabinet meeting, 17.5.1959, NA, CAB 128/66/2.
12. 'Public expenditure 1980–81 to 1983–84: The scope for reductions' (C (79) 25), 6.7.1979, NA, CAB 129 206/25.
13. Public expenditure: Memorandum by secretary of state for education and science, 10.7.1979, NA, CAB 129/206/29.
14. Conclusions of cabinet meeting, 25.10.1979, NA, CAB 128/66/18.
15. E. Parkes to A. Thompson, 10.8.1979; E. E. H. Jenkins to Mr King, 9.10.1979, NA, ED 212/167.
16. Note by E. Sharland, 14.2.1980, NA, FCO 13/950.
17. The exchange is in 3rd Report of House of Commons Foreign Affairs Committee, 1979/80, (HC553) pp. 4–9. Minutes of 18 and 20.2.1980 in NA, OD 52/2 confirm there was no paper. Bill Dodd, the chief educational adviser, returned to his office in uncharacteristic anger and embarrassment (private information).
18. Note by Lord N. G. Lennox, 12.3.1980, NA, FCO 13/947.
19. *Hansard HC*, 5.6.1980, col. 1691–2.
20. *Hansard HL*, 12.12.1979, col. 1296.
21. The Lords got in first on 5.7.1979 and 12.12.1979, and the Commons on 5.6.1980, with an adjournment debate on 10.7.1980.
22. *Hansard HC*, 10.7.1980, col. 909.
23. *Hansard HL*, 5.7.1979, col. 629–39.
24. *Hansard HL*, 5.7.1979, col. 587.
25. *Hansard HL*, 5.12.1979, col. 1285.
26. *Hansard HC*, 5.6.1980, col. 1695.
27. Ibid., col. 1722.
28. *Hansard HL*, 5.7.1979, col. 604.
29. *Times*, 12.12.1979.
30. Referred to by Lord Boyle; *Hansard HL*, 12.12.1979, col. 1332.
31. Lord Flowers and Albert Sloman both made this point at a seminar at All Souls, 15–16.1.1982, NA, ED 212/195/1.
32. E.g. Overseas Students Trust 1981 'Overseas students and British commercial interests' in P. Williams (ed.) *The overseas student question*, London.
33. 'The scope for reductions', 6.7.1979, NA, CAB 129/206/25.
34. N. Marten, 5.6.1980, *Hansard HC*, col. 1750.
35. M. Carlisle to P. Carrington, 17.3.1980, NA, ED 261/168.
36. G. Lennox to D. E. Lloyd Jones, 18.2.1980, NA, FCO 13/950.
37. M. Carlisle, *Hansard HC*, 5.6.1980, col. 1708–9.
38. *Hansard HC*, 10.7.1980, 905–12.
39. *Guardian*, 17.2.1983.
40. *Guardian*, 19.2.1981.

41. *Times*, 12.2.1981.
42. *Guardian*, 14.2.1980.
43. W. T. Hull (FCO) to M. J. Rabarts, 3.7.1980, NA, ED 261/169.
44. M. Brown to J. A. L. Morgan, 27.2.1980, NA, FCO 13/950.
45. P. A. Shaw note of call by Mr A. Michaelides, 2.12.1980, NA, ED 261/169.
46. Appendix to FCO paper for meeting of 6.10.1982, NA, ED 261/204.
47. *Hansard HC*, 8.2.1983, col. 879–88.
48. *Guardian*, 17.2.1983.
49. The policy was summarised by Pym in the House of Commons (8.2.1983) but then amplified in a lecture by Renton 'Government policy on overseas students' (First annual lecture of the London conference on overseas students), *Foreign policy document 143*, London, 1985.
50. 'Government policy'.
51. D. Elliott 1998 'Internationalizing British higher education: Policy perspectives', in P. Scott (ed.) *The globalization of higher education*, Buckingham, 36.
52. *Realising our potential* (Cm. 2250) 1993, 3.41.
53. Elliott 'Internationalizing', 33
54. National committee of enquiry into higher education 1997 *Higher education in the learning society* (*Dearing report*), London, para. 5.35.
55. J. Gordon and J.-P. Jallade 1996 '"Spontaneous" student mobility in the European Union: A statistical survey', *European Journal of Education*, 31: 2, 13, 139.
56. UGC and HESA statistics.
57. C. Humfrey 1999 *Managing international students*, Buckingham, 11–12, 145.
58. OECD 2004 *Internationalisation and trade in higher education*, Paris, 94, 114.
59. Interview, J. Stoddart, 15.5.2013.
60. These findings are consistent across various studies of Erasmus students including, for example, S. Opper et al. 1990 *Impact of study abroad programmes on students and graduates*, London, 38–9.
61. M. Paunescu 2008 'Students' perspectives upon their mobility', in M. Byram and F. Dervin (eds) *Students, staff and academic mobility in higher education*, Newcastle, 189.
62. K. Maxey 2006 *International student mobility in the Commonwealth: 2006 update*, London, 27.
63. From the mid-1990s some figures for overseas students were no longer disaggregated between full and part time which makes comparison difficult with earlier periods, where figures quoted are full time.
64. HESA statistics.
65. *Economist*, 2.2.2013.
66. Independent Schools Council *Annual census* (www.isc.co.uk, downloaded 14.5.2013).
67. *Economist*, 5.11.2009.
68. 'English UK' statistics, for which I am indebted to Tony Millns and Laura Underwood.
69. G. Conlon, A. Litchfield and G. Sadlier 2011 *Estimating the value to the UK of education exports*, London, 52–3; the figure for individual expenditure looks high in relation to those reported for university students.
70. Elliott, 'Internationalizing', 36.
71. 'Overseas students: Memorandum by the FCO', February 1989; HC Foreign Affairs Committee, 1.3.1989.

72. J Hanley, *Hansard HC*, 12.2.1997, col. 323.
73. River Path Associates 2003 *The FCO scholarship review*, n.p., 47.
74. 'Overseas students: Memorandum'.
75. H. Perraton 2009 *Learning abroad*, Newcastle, 56, 72.
76. Personal communication, Col. R. M. Crombie, RMA Sandhurst, 17.7.2013.
77. *International defence engagement strategy* www.gov.uk/government/uploads/attachment_data/file/73171/defence_engagement_strategy.pdf (downloaded 5.7.2013).
78. Crombie; FoI enquiry, Ministry of defence, 2.7.2013.
79. Personal information.
80. J. Battle, *Hansard HC*, 1.12.1999, col. 262W.
81. British Council, *PMI Overview*, http://www.britishcouncil.org/eumd-pmi2-overview.htm, (downloaded 29.5.2011).
82. K. Booth 2010 'Review of the Dorothy Hodgkin postgraduate award scheme', http://www.rcuk.ac.uk/documents/researchcareers/dhpa/DHPAReview2010.pdf (downloaded 7.6.2012).
83. British Council 2010 *Making it happen*, London, 1.
84. British Council 2008 *PMI*, London, http://www.ukcosa.org.uk/files/ppt/pmi/campaigns_and_marketing.ppt.
85. Theresa May, Home Secretary, *Hansard HC*, 23.11.2010, col. 169.

7 Student Experience

1. C. H. Cooper 1843 *Annals of Cambridge vol. 1*, Cambridge, 37.
2. M. H. Somers 1979 'Irish scholars in the Universities of Paris and Oxford before 1500', PhD thesis, City University of New York, 24–5.
3. A. B. Cobban 1999 *English university life in the middle ages*, London, 50.
4. R. W. Hays 1968 'Welsh students at Oxford and Cambridge in the Middle Ages', *Welsh History Review* iv, 334.
5. W. P. Griffith 1981 'Welsh students at Oxford, Cambridge and Inns of Court during the sixteenth and early seventeenth centuries', PhD thesis, University of Wales, 8–9.
6. D. R. Leader 1988 *The university to 1546*, Cambridge, 38.
7. L. Fowler and H. Fowler 1984 *Cambridge commemorated*, Cambridge, 4.
8. J. P. C. Roach 1967 *The City and University of Cambridge*, London, 77.
9. R. C. Schwinges 1992 'Student education, student life', in H. de Ridder-Symoens (ed.) *Universities in the middle ages*, Cambridge 225–6.
10. Cobban *University life*, 190, 45.
11. Ibid., 53.
12. Griffith 'Welsh students', 8.
13. W. H. G. Armytage 1955 *Civic universities*, London, 41.
14. T. H. Aston 1977 'Oxford's medieval alumni', *Past and Present*, 74: 1, 23.
15. V. H. H. Green 1974 *A history of Oxford University*, London, 15; J. R. H. Moorman 1947 'The foreign element among the English Franciscans', *English Historical Review*, 62: 244, 293.
16. A. B. Cobban 1988 *The medieval English universities to c1500*, Aldershot, 246.
17. Cobban *University life*, 137–9.
18. E. Waugh 1964 *A little learning*, London, 168.
19. Cobban *University life*, 138–9.

20. Ibid., 201.
21. Roach *Cambridge*, 192.
22. F. A. Taylor (ed.) 1946 *Voltaire – Lettres philosophiques*, Oxford, xxxv–xxxvi.
23. L. R. Farnell 1934 *An Oxonian looks back*, London, 33.
24. P. R. Deslandes 2005 *Oxbridge men*, Bloomington, 210–13.
25. C. A. Bristed 2008 *An American in Victorian Cambridge*, Exeter, 31–3.
26. Quoted in G. A. Shepperson 1983 'An early African graduate', in G. Donaldson (ed.) *Four centuries*, Edinburgh, 92.
27. Quoted from A. C. Benson 1901 'A life of E. W. Benson', in Fowler and Fowler (eds) *Cambridge commemorated*, 209–10.
28. R Symonds 2000 'Oxford and the empire', in M. G. Brock and M. C. Curthoys (eds) *Nineteenth-century Oxford, part 2*, 714–15.
29. S. Satthianadhan 1893 *Four years in an English university*, Madras, 23–4.
30. N. Koyama 2004 *Japanese students at Cambridge University in the Meiji era, 1868–1912*, Fukuoka, 182.
31. C. Sorabji 1934 *London calling*, London, 22, 30–1, and passim.
32. L. Stone 1964 'The educational revolution in England, 1560–1640', *Past and Present*, 28, 73.
33. Green *History of Oxford*, 71–2.
34. C. Cross 1979 'Continental students and the Protestant Reformation in England', in D. Baker (ed.) *Reform and Reformation*, Oxford, 41–2.
35. Roach *Cambridge*, 225.
36. Ibid.
37. Green *History of Oxford*, 116.
38. W. Everett 1867 *On the Cam*, Cambridge: 130 ff.
39. Satthianadhan *Four years*, 36–45.
40. G. Midgley 1996 *University life in eighteenth century Oxford*, New Haven, 66–7.
41. Bristed 2008 *An American*, 32–3, 50–8.
42. E. Ashby 1966 *Universities: British, Indian, African*, London, 6.
43. V. Morgan 2004 *A history of the University of Cambridge: Vol. 2 1546-1750*, Cambridge, 298.
44. Cooper *Annals vol. 2*, 169.
45. R. B. McDowell and D. A. Webb 1982 *Trinity College Dublin 1592–1952*, Cambridge, 106.
46. Midgley, *University life*, 87.
47. Bristed *An American*, 78.
48. W. D. Robson-Scott 1953 *German travellers in England 1400–1800*, Oxford, 14, 48, 53–4.
49. N. Amhurst quoted in Midgley *University life*, 77.
50. Bristed *An American* 308–11.
51. Sorabji *London calling*, 33–4.
52. J. J. Thomson 1936 *Recollections and reflections*, London, 138.
53. K. P. S. Menon 1965 *Many worlds: An autobiography*, London, 49.
54. B. Gould 1995 *Goodbye to all that*, London, 31; Scholars' reports, 8.10.968, CSC Minutes.
55. J. Green 1990 *Them*, London, 99–100.
56. *Report of the committee on Indian students* 1922 (*Lytton report*), Appendix IV (*Lee-Warner report*), 50.

57. *India students' department report 1913–1914* (Cd. 7719), 4.
58. PEP 1955 *Colonial students in Britain*, London, 38.
59. M. Thomas and J. M. Williams *Overseas nurses in Britain*, London, 4.
60. E. Reid 1989 *Radical mandarin*, Toronto, 49.
61. S. Fisher 1961 'The overseas student in Oxford', *Isis*, 12 June, 6–11.
62. Green *Them*, 130.
63. K. Akinsemoyin 1949 'An undergraduate at Glasgow', *West African Review*, 20: 264.
64. F. Youssoupoff 1953 *Lost splendour*, London, 142.
65. V. Nabokov 1965 *Speak memory*, London, 198; V. Nabokov 2012 *Collected poems*, 29ff.
66. D. Obolensky 1999 *Bread of exile*, London, 223.
67. Menon *Many worlds*, 57; M. C. Chagla 2000 *Roses in December*, Mumbai, 37.
68. S. W. R. D. Bandaranaike 1963 *Speeches and writings*, Colombo, 41.
69. *Oxford dictionary of national bibliography*.
70. D. Lewis 1981 *The good fight*, Toronto, 51.
71. Gould *Goodbye to all that*, 37, 45.
72. *Report of Indian students' department 1920–21*, 4.
73. *Lytton report*, 34; R. Symonds 1986 *Oxford and empire,* Basingstoke, 262–5.
74. *Report of the colonial students committee*, 1938, NA, CO 885/52.
75. Lewis *The good fight*, 77.
76. E. Atiyah 1946 *An Arab tells his story*, London, 103.
77. H. T. Tizard, 19.7.1933, NA, BT 64/5.
78. S. Lahiri 2000 *Indians in Britain*, London, 120.
79. Note, H. Vischer, 9.1.1929, NA, CO 323/1025/9.
80. M. Sadler to A. Mayhew, 20.11.1930, NA, CO 323/1113/2.
81. *Report of the colonial students committee*, 1938, 24, NA, CO 885/92.
82. Note F. H. Ruxton, 5.1. 1929, NA, CO 323/1025/9.
83. Waugh *A little learning*, 184.
84. H. Vischer, Note, 9.1.1929, NA, CO 323/1025/9; L. Braithwaite 2001 *Colonial West Indian students in Britain*, Kingston, Jamaica, 23.
85. PEP 1955 *Colonial students*, 84–5.
86. PEP 1965 *New Commonwealth students in Britain*, London, 149.
87. Thomas and Williams *Overseas nurses*, 38.
88. Scholars' reports, 22.9.1965, CSC Minutes.
89. Carey *Colonial students*, 105–7.
90. PEP *New Commonwealth students*, 151.
91. Perraton *Learning abroad*, 147.
92. Scholars reports, 5.10.1982, CSC Minutes.
93. Scholars reports, 5.10.1993, CSCS Minutes.
94. W. M. Macmillan 1975 *My South African years*, Cape Town, 66..
95. Youssoupoff *Lost splendour*, 137; Bandaranaike *Speeches and writings*, 34.
96. *Lee-Warner report*, 15; *Lytton report*, 32.
97. A. Kenny 2001 'The Rhodes Trust and its administration', in A. Kenny (ed.) *The history of the Rhodes Trust*, Oxford, 88.
98. J. W. Boag et al. 1990 *Kapitza in Cambridge and Moscow*, Amsterdam, 114.
99. Extract from *East Africa and Rhodesia*, 12.2.1948, NA, CO 537/2574.

100. J. M. Lee 2006 'Commonwealth students in the United Kingdom, 1940–1960', *Minerva* 44, 4–10.
101. Braithwaite *West Indian students*, 167.
102. B. G. Stone to D. L. Skidmore, 29.12.1950, NA, CO 876/119.
103. Carey *Colonial students*, 51–7.
104. PEP *Colonial students*, 75.
105. PEP *New Commonwealth students*, 159.
106. F. Maiworm, W. Steube and U. Teichler 1991 *Learning in Europe*, London, 80–98.
107. B. Bamford 1959 *The substance*, Cape Town, 38–41.
108. H. Perraton 2009 *Learning abroad*, Newcastle upon Tyne, 140–1.
109. R. Simpson 2009 *The development of the PhD degree in Britain, 1917–1959 and since*, Lewiston, 18–19.
110. T. Holland 1931 'Facilities for overseas students in British universities', *University Congress Proceedings*, 180–9.
111. Perraton *Learning abroad*, 151–2.
112. Holland 'Facilities', 184–9.
113. PEP *Colonial students*, 116–18.
114. E. N. Goody and C. M. Croothues 1977 'The West Africans: Cultural and social change among migrants in Britain', in J. L. Watson (ed.) *Between two cultures*, Oxford, 164.
115. Kenny, *Rhodes Trust*, 88.
116. Personal communication.
117. P.R.C. Williams 1985 *They came to train*, London, 6.
118. S. Rothblatt 2011 'Curriculum, students, education', in W. Rüegg (ed.) *Universities since 1945*, Cambridge, 272.
119. A. K. Smith and C. Weiner 1980 *Robert Oppenheimer*, Cambridge Mass., 86–7.
120. E. Forsey 1990 *A life on the fringe*, Toronto, 37.
121. E. N. Mangait Rai 1973 *Commitment my style*, Delhi, 41.
122. S. Fisher 1961 'The overseas student in Oxford' *Isis*, 12 June.
123. Kenny *Rhodes Trust*, 87–8, 98.
124. *Report of Indian students' department 1922–23*, 6.
125. Waugh *A little learning*, 184; Lewis *The good fight*, 53, 76–7.
126. *Lee-Warner report*, 18, 50; *The Times*, 1.9.1908.
127. *Manchester Guardian*, 27.12.1910.
128. *Lytton report*, 65.
129. R. Dahrendorf 1995 *LSE*, Oxford, 273–5.
130. M. Sherwood 1993 'Kwame Nkrumah: The London years 1945–47', *Immigrants and Minorities* 12: 3, 167–84.
131. C. Walton 2013 *Empire of secrets*, London, 220–1.
132. T. Mboya 1963 *Freedom and after*, London, 57–8.
133. Braithwaite *West Indian students*, viii.
134. CSC Minutes 24.5.1966.
135. CSC Minutes 23.9.1964.
136. Lewis *The good fight*, 48, 74.
137. T. E. B. Howarth 1978 *Cambridge between two wars*, London, 170.
138. Ziegler *Legacy*, 217–23.
139. Menon *Many worlds*, 14.

140. Lahiri, *Indians in Britain*, 121–2.
141. Carey *Colonial students*, 60–3.
142. Menon *Many worlds*, 52–61; Waugh *A little learning*, 169.
143. Lahiri *Indians in Britain*, 122.
144. J. A. P. Majumdar 2003 *Family history*, New Delhi, 85, 102.
145. Cf. Carey *Colonial students*; Braithwaite *West Indian students*; R. D. Lambert 1956 *Indian students on an American campus*, Minneapolis, 41.
146. Carey *Colonial students*, 122.
147. Braithwaite *West Indian students*, 216ff.
148. Carey *Colonial students*, 193–4.
149. Ibid.
150. A. K. Singh, 1963 *Indian students in Britain*, New York, 68.
151. Carey *Colonial students*, 124.
152. Braithwaite, *West Indian students*, 221.
153. Ibid., 87, 90.
154. PEP *Colonial students*, 99.
155. Carey *Colonial students*, 220.
156. Ibid., 189.
157. E. Murphy-Lejeune 2002 *Student mobility and narrative in Europe*, London, 158.

8   Poor Scholars and Endowed Scholars

1. A. B. Cobban 1999 *English university life in the middle ages*, London, 35.
2. F. Pegues 1956 'Royal support of students in the thirteenth century', *Speculum*, 31: 3, 462.
3. Cobban *University life*, 37–9.
4. T. A. R. Evans 1992 'The number, origins and careers of scholars', in J. I. Catto and T. A. R. Evans (eds) *Late medieval Oxford*, Oxford, 502–3.
5. L. Stone 1964 'The educational revolution in England, 1560–1640', *Past and Present*, 28, 71.
6. S. Porter 1997 'University and society', in N. Tyacke (ed.) *Seventeenth century Oxford*, Oxford, 87.
7. W. R. Prest 1972 *The Inns of Court under Elizabeth I and the early Stuarts 1590–1640*, London, 28.
8. Porter 'University and society', 87.
9. R. O'Day 1982 *Education and society 1500–1800*, London, 198.
10. P. Searby 1997 *A history of the University of Cambridge vol. III 1750–1870*, Cambridge, 78.
11. Ibid., 80.
12. A. M. Wainwright 2008 *'The better class' of Indian*, Manchester, 171–4.
13. Ibid., 202.
14. *Journal of the National Indian Association* 1880, 614.
15. A. Kenny 2001 'The Rhodes Trust and its administration', in A. Kenny (ed.) *The history of the Rhodes Trust 1902–99*, Oxford,18; H. Hobhouse 2002 *The Crystal Palace and the Great Exhibition*, London, 239.
16. J. A. P. Majumdar 2003 *Family history*, New Delhi, 19.
17. S. Mukherjee 2010 *Nationalism, education and migrant identities*, London, 113.

18. G. A. Shepperd 1980 *Sandhurst*, Feltham, 131.
19. H. Perraton 2009 *Learning abroad*, Newcastle, 144; ACU, CSC 20/64, 24.11.1964.
20. D. Dewar 1926 *A student of St Andrew's a hundred years ago*, Glasgow, 108–12.
21. A. McLaren 2005 *Aberdeen students 1600–1860*, Aberdeen, 127.
22. Figures from a survey in *Commonwealth Universities Yearbook 1936*; although Oxford and Cambridge provided detailed estimates the other figures are more difficult to interpret without knowing how amply hostels and halls fed their residents.
23. ACU, D. Crapper 2003 *Review of Stipends and Allowances Paid by DfID and the FCO*, 36, 3.
24. H. Phelps Brown and S. V. Hopkins 1981 *A perspective of wages and prices*, London, 11–12; details of RPI and its predecessors are in *Economic Trends*, 604, March 2004.
25. Costs shown in square brackets are in constant 2010 currency.
26. Figures from ACU, papers CSC41/71, CSC39/80, 51st *Annual report* figures for university staff scholar
27. http://www.constructionrates.co.uk/RICS_Prime_Cost_of_Daywork_UK_Construction_Industry_6th_April_2009.htm (accessed 11.09.12).
28. *Oxford University commission 1852*, 30–33.
29. ACU, CSC 13/60 of 9.3.1960; this figure is higher than that quoted below, probably because of the effect of extra fees such as bench fees.
30. R. C. Schwinges 1992 'Admission', in H. de Ridder-Symoens (ed.) *Universities in the middle ages*, Cambridge, 184.
31. *Cambridge University commission 1852*, 74–6; *Oxford University commission 1852*, 33.
32. A. L. Turner 1933 *History of the University of Edinburgh 1883–1933*, London, 44.
33. L. Stone 1974 'The size and composition of the Oxford student body 1580–1909', in L. Stone (ed.) *The university in society vol. 1*, Princeton, 36.
34. E. Sagarra 1991 'From the pistol to the petticoat', in C. H. Holland (ed.) *Trinity College Dublin and the idea of a university*, Dublin, 111.
35. E. S. Bates 1987 *Touring in 1600*, London, 328–35.
36. T. J. Hatton and J. G. Williamson 2004 *Global migration and the world economy*, Cambridge, Mass., 9, 40–1.
37. Majumdar 2003 *Family history*, *passim*.
38. Advertisements in *The Times* 1.1.1880; 13.4.1895.
39. ACU, CSC 13/60, 9.3.1960.
40. ACU, CSC 33/79, 25.9.1979.
41. F. Maiworm et al. 1991 *Learning in Europe*, London, 118.
42. CSC *51st annual report*, 46.
43. Ibid., 56.
44. M. Harper and S. Constantine 2010 *Migration and empire*, Oxford, 190.
45. Letter to editor, 'Indian students in England', *Manchester Guardian*, 27.12.1910.
46. *Report of the Indian Students' Department 1920/21*, London, 14, 32; *Report 1926/27*, i, 15.
47. *Report of the Indian Students' Department 1920/21*, 31.
48. H. Vischer, Note 9.1.1929, NA, CO 323/1025/9.
49. *Report of the colonial students committee*, 1938, NA, CO 885/52.

50. *Report of the Indian Students' Department 1923/24*, London, 6.
51. *Report of the Education Department 1925/26, Indian High Commission*, London, 23.
52. P. Z. Ezechiel 'The supervision of colonial government scholars and other students from the colonies', 2.4.1927, NA, ED 121/119.
53. E. Atiyah 1946 *An Arab tells his story*, London 83, 126.
54. *Report of the Indian Military College Committee*, 1931, London, 13, NA, WO 32/3789.
55. Circular from secretary of state to colonial administrations 'The welfare of colonial students overseas', 10.1.1948, CO 537/5138; PEP 1955 *Colonial students in Britain*, London, 55.
56. Committee on higher education 1961 *Higher education (Robbins report)* (Cmnd. 2154) *Appendix 2A*, London, 274.
57. E. N. Goody and C. M. Croothues 1977 'The West Africans: Cultural and social change among migrants in Britain', in J. L. Watson (ed.) *Between two cultures: Migrants and minorities in Britain*, Oxford, 164.
58. K. Maxey 2000 *Student mobility on the map*, London, 45.
59. K. Maxey 2006 *International student mobility in the Commonwealth: 2006 update*, London, 39–44.
60. F. Maiworm et al. 1991 *Learning in Europe*, London, 123.
61. The title of his book, *Nigger at Eton* (1972, London), is perhaps more surprising than his history. School fee from *Whitaker's almanack* 1968.
62. D. W. Urwin 1982 *Specialist schools and colleges in Cambridge*, Cambridge, A7; K. Brennan and N. Cheeseman 1996 *Bournemouth summer school industry report*, Bournemouth, 15.
63. G. Conlon, A. Litchfield and G. Sadlier 2011 *Estimating the value to the UK of education exports*, London, 52–3.
64. C. Fyfe 1993 *A history of Sierra Leone*, Aldershot, 122.
65. *Hansard HC*, 29.7.1903, col. 671–2.
66. Cabinet memorandum 'Employment of native born administrators in the higher grades of colonial civil services' (CP (50) 171), 17.7.1950, NA, CAB/129/41.
67. P. R. C. Williams 1985 *They came to train*, London, 5–12.
68. *Minutes of evidence*, 1.3.1989, House of Commons Foreign Affairs Committee (1988/89 HC 242-i), 2–3.
69. G. Williams and M. Woodhall 1979 *Independent further education*, London, 63, 34.
70. M. Thomas and J. M. Williams 1972 *Overseas nurses in Britain*, London, 42–3.
71. G. F. Lytle 1974 'Patronage patterns and Oxford colleges', in L. Stone et al. (ed.) *The university in society vol. 1*, Princeton, 123.
72. H. Hobhouse 2002 *The Crystal Palace and the Great Exhibition*, London, 93–4.
73. Ibid., 238–9.
74. Ibid., 322–4.
75. Ibid., 345.
76. Ibid., 379.
77. *Minutes of evidence*, 1.3.1989, House of Commons Foreign Affairs Committee (1988/89 HC 242-I), 6–7.
78. Pegues 'Royal support', 454–5.

79. *Encyclopaedia Britannica (11th edition)*, 1911, 23: 257; The entry was written by Lady Lugard, wife of the first British governor of Nigeria, an appropriate writer on imperialism.
80. Ibid.
81. Ibid.
82. Chinese Association for the promotion of education 1924 *Boxer indemnity and Chinese education*, London, 29–45.
83. F. Donaldson 1984 *The British Council*, London, 62.
84. Note of meeting, 11.10.1944; D. L. Keith 'Note on British Council awards to colonial students for study in the UK',11.4.1944, NA, CO 859/127/1.
85. *Oxford commission report*, 1852, 28.

9   International Comparisons

1. J. Verger 1992 'Patterns', in H. de Ridder-Symoens (ed.) *Universities in the middle ages*, Cambridge, 48.
2. P. Nardi 1992 'Relations with authority', in de Ridder-Symoens (ed.) *Universities*, 48.
3. C. H. Lawrence 1994 *The friars*, London, 84–6.
4. W. Rüegg 1992 'Themes', in de Ridder-Symoens (ed.) *Universities*, 19–20.
5. Nardi 'Relations', 102.
6. A. B. Cobban 1999 *English university life in the middle ages*, London, 29.
7. H. de Ridder-Symoens 1992 'Mobility', in de Ridder-Symoens (ed.) *Universities*, 286–7.
8. R. C. Schwinges 1992 'Admission', in de Ridder-Symoens (ed.) *Universities*, 188.
9. M. R. di Simone 1996 'Admission', in H. de Ridder-Symoens (ed.) *Universities in early modern Europe*, Cambridge, 293–5.
10. C. Roth 1951 *The Jews of medieval Oxford*, Oxford, 126.
11. H. de Ridder-Symoens 1996 'Mobility', in de Ridder-Symoens (ed.) *Universities*, 419–26, 442.
12. Ibid., 437.
13. N. Hammerstein 1996, 'Epilogue', in de Ridder-Symoens (ed.) *Universities*, 624.
14. K. H. Jarausch 1983 'Higher education and social change', in K. H. Jarausch (ed.) *The transformation of higher learning 1860–1930*, Chicago, 13.
15. O. Klineberg 1976 *International educational exchange*, The Hague, 76, 113.
16. N. Tikhonov 2003 'Migrations des étudiants et feminisation de quelques universités européennes', in H. R. Peter and N. Tikhonov (eds) *Universitäten als Brücken in Europa*, Frankfurt, 43–4.
17. K. H. Jarausch 1995 'American students in Germany, 1815–1914', in H. Geitz et al. (ed.) *German influence on education in the United States to 1917*, Cambridge, 195, 203.
18. 'Universities', *Encyclopaedia Britannica, 11th edition*, 27: 777.
19. A. Latreche 2003 'Les étudiants de nationalités étrangères en France', in Peter and Tikhonov (eds) *Universitäten*, 138–40.
20. V. Karady 2003 'Les logiques des échanges inégaux', in Peter and Tikhonov (eds) *Universitäten*, 23.

21. J. A. Harley 1931 *International understanding*, Stanford, 39.
22. *Students abroad*, 6, May 1934, 15, 20.
23. Figures in this and the following paragraphs are drawn generally from *UNESCO statistical yearbook* and from online data of the UNESCO Institute for statistics, together with W. K. Cummings 1993 'Global trends in overseas study', in C. D. Goodwin (ed.) *International investment in human capital*, New York; Latreche 'Les étudiants'; V. Lasanowski 2009 *International student mobility*, London.
24. *Open doors* 2010, 5.
25. Latreche 'Les étudiants', 141ff.
26. T. N. Bonner 1992 *To the ends of the earth:*, Cambridge, Mass., 27–9.
27. *Students abroad*, 6, May 1934, 26.
28. J. C. Albisetti 1995 'German influence on the higher education of American women, 1865–1914', in Geitz et al. *German influences*, 240.
29. R. Brooks and J. Waters 2011 *Student mobilities*, Basingstoke, 99.
30. Karady 'Les logiques', 20–1.
31. Ibid., 22; H. de Wit 2002 *Internationalization of higher education in the USA and Europe*, Westport, 9.
32. Bonner *To the ends of the earth*, 34.
33. N. Hammerstein 1996 'Epilogue', in de Ridder-Symoens (ed.) *Universities*, 624.
34. C. Kerr 1990 'The internationalisation of learning and the nationalisation of the purposes of higher education', *European Journal of Education* 25: 1, 5–6.
35. *Students abroad*, 1, October 1931, 6; 2, April 1932, 4.
36. W. Johnson and F. J. Colligan 1965 *The Fulbright program*, Chicago, 16.
37. M. Van der Wende 1997 'International comparative analysis and synthesis', in T. Kälvermark and M. Van der Wende (ed.) *National policies for the internationalisation of higher education in Europe*, Stockholm, 227.
38. 'Universities and the Commonwealth', address at ACU Congress, Montreal, 1.9.1958.
39. M. H. Hunt 1972 'The American Remission of the Boxer Indemnity', *Journal of Asian Studies*, 31: 3, 540, 557–8.
40. Ibid., 541.
41. H. Johnson and B. G. Gwertzman 1969 *Fulbright*, London, 108–9.
42. www.fulbright.org.uk/about/what-we-do (downloaded 14.3.2013).
43. Johnson and Colligan *Fulbright program*, vii–viii.
44. Ibid., 42.
45. Ibid., 37.
46. T. Mboya 1963 *Freedom and after*, London, 138–41.
47. O. Odinga 1967 *Not yet uhuru*, London, 187–8.
48. Cummings 'Global trends', 32.
49. J. M. Davis 1965 'Government policy and international education: USA', in S. Fraser (ed.) *Government policy and international education*, New York, 218.
50. Johnson and Colligan *Fulbright program*, 69.
51. Y. G.-M. Lulat et al. 1986 *Governmental and institutional policies on foreign students*, Buffalo, 21–2.
52. http://law.justia.com/codes/us/2010/title22/chap57/sec4702/ (downloaded 15 March 2013).
53. 'Collation', 1949, NA, FO 1110/230.

54. 'Foreign students in communist countries', December 1964, NA, FCO 95/417.
55. H. F. T. Smith to PM office, 17.2.1966, NA, PREM 13/1931.
56. I. Filatova 1999 'Indoctrination or scholarship?', *Paedagogica Historica* 35: 1, 47–8, 61; C. Walton 2013 *Empire of secrets*, London, 270.
57. H. Haywood 1978 *Black Bolshevik: Autobiography of an Afro-American communist*, Chicago, 198.
58. E. Pis'mennaia 2010 'The migration of foreign students to Russia', *Russian Education and Society* 52: 10, 71.
59. Ibid.; J. Sigurdson 1981 'The reverse brain drain and the lack of educated manpower', in A. B. Zahlan (ed.) *The Arab brain drain*, London, 268.
60. H. D. Weaver 1985 'Soviet training and research programs for Africa', EdD thesis University of Massachusetts, 121–37; http://www.rudn.ru/en/?pagec=49, downloaded 20.3.2013.
61. Pis'mennaia 'Migration', 72.
62. Weaver 'Soviet training', 196.
63. M. Matusevich 2007 'Visions of grandeur…interrupted', in M. Matusevich (ed.) *Africa in Russia, Russia in Africa*, Trenton, 363.
64. 'Foreign students in communist countries', December 1964, NA, FCO 95/417.
65. A. Blakeley 2007 'African imprints on Russia', in Matusevich *Africa in Russia*, 53.
66. V. P. Eliutin 1985 'The international activity of Soviet higher education', *Soviet Education*, 27: 9–10, 156.
67. T. M. Maliyamkono et al. 1982 *Training and productivity in eastern Africa*, London, 271.
68. Pis'menaia 'Migration', 71–3.
69. Eliutin 'International activity', 155.
70. E. H. Berman 1980 'The foundations' role in American foreign policy', in R. F. Arnove (ed.) *Philanthropy and cultural imperialism*, Boston, 207.
71. Eliutin 'International activity', 141.
72. 'Training of Northern Rhodesian students in communist bloc countries', 19.3.1963, NA, DO 183/183; M. K. Ewans to H. M. S. Reid, 22.7.1966, NA, FCO 13/296.
73. OECD 2004 *Internationalisation and trade in higher education*, Paris, 221–31.
74. Ibid., 223.
75. A. Corbett 2005 *Universities and the Europe of knowledge*, Basingstoke, 25ff.
76. Ibid. 145.
77. A. Barblan 2011 'From the university in Europe to the universities of Europe', in W. Rüegg (ed.) *Universities since 1945*, Cambridge, 567–9.
78. M. Anquetil 2006 *Mobilité Erasmus et communication interculturelle*, Bern, 26.
79. http://ec.europa.eu/education/programmes/llp/erasmus/action2_en.html (downloaded 27.2.2013).
80. Corbett *Universities*, 7.
81. E. Sigalas 2010 'The role of personal benefits in public support for the EU', *West European Politics*, 33: 6, 1355. These findings are consistent with those of T. Kuhn 2012 'Why educational exchange programmes miss their mark', *Journal of Common Market Studies*, 50: 6.
82. M. Parey and F. Waldinger, 2010 'Studying abroad and the effect on international labour market mobility', *Economic Journal*, 121, 220; H. Oosterbeek and

D. Webbink 2011 'Does studying abroad induce a brain drain?', *Economica* 78, 361–4.

83. http://ec.europa.eu/education/lifelong-learning-programme/erasmus_en.htm; figures from *Open doors* and EC data.
84. OECD *Internationalisation*, 94.
85. de Wit *Internationalization*, 29–30.
86. *Report of the committee to review the Australian aid programme (Jackson report)* 1984, Canberra, 93–4 quoted in A. Chandler 1989 *Obligation or opportunity*, New York, 61.
87. K. Gürüz 2011 *Higher education and international student mobility in the global knowledge economy* Albany, 170, 263.

10 Conclusion: Policies, Purposes and Effects

1. W. O. Ulrich to Mr Thompson, 8.4.1980, NA, ED 261/168.
2. L. Stone 1983 'Social control and intellectual excellence', in N. Phillipson (ed.) *University, society and the future*, Edinburgh, 5.
3. E. Krzaklewska 2008 'Why study abroad?', in M. Byram and F. Dervin (eds) *Students, staff and academic mobility in higher education*, Newcastle, 92; O. Bracht et al. 2006 *The professional value of ERASMUS mobility*, Kassel, 78.
4. B. Clinton 2004 *My life*, New York, 136–7.
5. R. Dahrendorf 1995 *LSE*, Oxford, 408, 403.
6. A. Kirk-Greene 1993 'Doubly elite', *Immigrants and Minorities*, 12: 3, 232.
7. P. Ziegler 2008 *Legacy*, New Haven, 80.
8. O. Gish 1971 *Doctor migration and world health*, London, 138.
9. J. Guth and B. Gill 2008 'Motivations in east-west doctoral mobility', *Journal of Ethnic and Migration Studies*, 34: 5.
10. M. Parey and F. Waldinger 2010 'Studying abroad and the effect on international labour market mobility', *Economic Journal*, 121, 221.
11. R. Symonds 1986 *Oxford and empire*, Basingstoke, 274.
12. H. Perraton 2009 *Learning abroad*, Newcastle, 32.
13. M. R. Rosenzweig 2006 'Global wage differences and international student flows', in S. M. Collins and C. Graham (eds) *Brookings trade forum: Global labor markets?*, Washington, DC, 85.
14. Ibid., 159.
15. S. Mukherjee 2010 *Nationalism, education and migrant identities*, London, 115; A. S. Livingstone 1964 *The international student*, Manchester, 52.
16. O. p'Bitek 1973 *Africa's cultural revolution*, Nairobi, 13.
17. Mukherjee *Nationalism*, 141.
18. Ibid., 131; T. Mboya 1963 *Freedom and after*, London, 58.
19. Granthagar quoted in S. Mohanty 1997 (ed.) *In search of wonder*, New Delhi, 56.
20. J. Waters and R. Brooks 2012 'Transnational spaces, international students', in R. Brooks et al. (eds) *Changing spaces of education*, London, 25–8.
21. Ziegler *Legacy*, 152.
22. Bracht *Mobility*, 75.
23. See p. 221 and T. L. Maliyamkono et al. 1982 *Training and productivity in eastern Africa*, London, 271.

24. J. Poot and M. Roskruge 2013 'Internationalisation of education and returns in the labour market', *IZA Discussion paper*, 7696.
25. H. Hobhouse 2002 *The Crystal Palace and the Great Exhibition*, London, 279, 311, 379.
26. Perraton *Learning abroad*, 106.
27. P. R. C. Williams 1985 *They came to train*, London; CSC 2009 *Evaluating Commonwealth scholarships in the United Kingdom*, London.
28. *Hansard HL*, 5.7.1979, col. 1333.

Bibliography

Primary

Oxford University Commission (1482) 1852.
Cambridge University Commission (1559) 1852.
'Official report of the allied colonial universities conference', 1904, *The empire review*
Report of the Imperial education conference 1911 (Cd. 5666).
Congress of universities of the empire: Report of proceedings, London, 1912 (later *Congress of universities of the Commonwealth*) cited as *University Congress Proceedings*.
Reports for 1910–11 for universities and university colleges (Cd. 6245–6) 1912.
India Students' Department annual report 1913/14 and later years.
Report of committee on state technical scholarships established by the government of India (*Morison report*) (Cd. 6867) 1913.
Report of the committee on Indian students (*Lytton report*) 1922, London: HMSO.
Royal Commission on Oxford and Cambridge University: Report (Cmd. 1588) 1922.
India Office 1927 *Report of the India Sandhurst committee*, London.
University development: Report on the years 1948–52 (Cmd. 8875) 1953.
University development: Report on the years 1952–57 (Cmnd. 534) 1958.
Central Advisory Council for Education 1959, *15 to 18* (*Crowther report*), London: HMSO.
Commonwealth Scholarship Commission Annual Report 1960 (cited as CSCAR).
Report of the committee on legal education for students from Africa (Cmnd. 1255) 1961.
Technical Assistance from the UK for overseas development (Cmnd. 1308) 1961.
Committee on higher education 1963 *Higher education* (Cmnd. 2154) (*Robbins report*).
University of Oxford *Report of the commission of inquiry* (*Franks report*), 1966.
Public schools commission: First report (vol. 1 report) 1968 London: HMSO.
ODM 1970 *Education in developing countries*, London.
Education: A framework for expansion (Cmnd. 5174) 1972.
More help for the poorest (Cmnd. 6270) 1975.
The development of higher education into the 1990s (Cmnd. 9524) 1985.
Renton, T. 1985 'Government policy on overseas students', *Foreign policy document 143*, London.
Higher education: Meeting the challenge (Cm. 114) 1987.
Realising our potential: A strategy for science, engineering and technology (Cm. 2250) 1993.
National Committee of Enquiry into higher education 1997 *Higher education in the learning society* (*Dearing report*), London: HMSO.
The future of higher education (Cm. 5735) 2003.
Ministry of defence n.d. *International defence engagement strategy* (www.gov.uk/government/uploads/attachment_data/file/73171/defence_engagement_strategy.pdf downloaded 5.7.2013).

ACAD – A Cambridge Alumni Database (venn.lib.cam.ac.uk/acad/search.html) (cited as Venn database).
Association of Commonwealth Universities archives on Commonwealth Scholarship (cited as CSC).
National Archives files (cited as NA).
Parliamentary debates house of commons and house of lords (cited as *Hansard HC* and *Hansard HL*).

Secondary

Agarwal, P. et al. 2008 'The dynamics of international student mobility in a global context: Summary, conclusions and recommendations', in de Wit et al. (ed.) *Dynamics of international student circulation*.
Akinsemoyin, K. 1949 'An undergraduate at Glasgow', *West African Review*, 20: 264.
Albisetti, J. C. 1995 'German influence on the higher education of American women, 1865–1914', in Geitz et al. (eds) *German influences on education in the United States to 1917*.
Anderson, R. 2006 *British universities past and present*, London: Hambledon Continuum.
Anderson, R. D. 1983 *Education and opportunity in Victorian Scotland*, Oxford: Clarendon.
Anquetil, M. 2006 *Mobilité Erasmus et communication interculturelle: Une recherche-action pour un parcours de formation*, Bern: Peter Lang.
Armytage, W. H. G. 1955 *Civic universities: Aspects of a British tradition*, London: Benn.
Arnold, D. 2000 *Science, technology and medicine in colonial India*, Cambridge University Press.
Ashby, E. 1966 *Universities: British, Indian, African*, London: Weidenfeld & Nicolson.
Ashworth, E. J. and Spade, P. V. 1992 'Logic in late medieval Oxford', in Catto and Evans (eds) *Late medieval Oxford*.
Aston, T. H. 1977 'Oxford's medieval alumni', *Past and Present*, 74: 1.
Aston, T. H., Duncan, G. D. and Evans, T. A. R. 1980 'The medieval alumni of the University of Cambridge', *Past and Present*, 86: 1.
Asztalos, M. 1992 'The faculty of theology', in de Ridder-Symeons (ed.) *Universities in the middle ages*.
Atiyah, E. 1946 *An Arab tells his story: A study in loyalties*, London: Murray.
Austen, J. 1974 *Lady Susan; The Watsons; Sanditon*, London: Penguin.
Bamford, B. 1959 *The substance: The story of a Rhodes scholar at Oxford*, Cape Town: Beerman.
Bandaranaike, S. W. R. D. 1963 *Speeches and writings*, Colombo: Department of Broadcasting and Information.
Banerjee, S. 2010 *Becoming imperial citizens: Indians in the late-Victorian empire*, Durham, NC: Duke University Press.
Barblan, A. 2011 'From the university in Europe to the universities of Europe', in Rüegg *Universities since 1945*, Cambridge University Press.
Basu, A. 1974 *The growth of education and political development in India, 1898–1920*, Delhi: Oxford University Press.

Bates, E. S. 1987 *Touring in 1600: A study in the development of travel as a means of education*, London: Century.

Bell, F. 1987 'The Bell schools and Cambridge', *Cambridge*, 21.

Berman, E. H. 1980 'The foundations' role in American foreign policy', in Arnove, R. F. (ed.) *Philanthropy and cultural imperialism: The foundations at home and abroad*, Boston: G. K. Hall.

Birke, A. M. 1987 *Britain and Germany: Historical patterns of a relationship*, London: German Historical Institute.

Blakeley, A. 2007 'African imprints on Russia', in Matusevich (ed.) *Africa in Russia, Russia in Africa*.

Boag, J. W., Rubinin, P. E. and Shoenberg, D. 1990 *Kapitza in Cambridge and Moscow: Life and letters of a Russian physicist*, Amsterdam: North Holland.

Bonner, T. H. 1992 *To the ends of the earth: Women's search for education in medicine*, Cambridge, Mass.: Harvard University Press.

Bracht, O. et al. 2006 *The professional value of ERASMUS mobility*, International Centre for Higher Education Research, University of Kassel.

Braithwaite, L. 2001 *Colonial West Indian students in Britain*, Kingston, Jamaica: University of the West Indies Press.

Brennan, K. and Cheeseman, N. 1996 *Bournemouth summer school industry report*, Bournemouth Borough Council.

Bristed, C. A. 2008 *An American in Victorian Cambridge*, University of Exeter Press.

Bristow, R. 1979 *Overseas students and government policy, 1962–1979*, London: Overseas Students Trust.

British Council 2010 *Making it happen*, London: British Council.

Brock, M. G. 2000 'The Oxford of Raymond Asquith and Willie Elmhirst', in Brock and Curthoys (eds) *Nineteenth-century Oxford*.

Brock, M. G. and Curthoys, M. C. (eds) 2000 *Nineteenth-century Oxford, Part 2 (The history of the University of Oxford, vol. 7)*, Oxford: Clarendon.

Brockliss, L. W. B. 1989 'The University of Paris and the maintenance of catholicism in the British Isles, 1426–1789: A study in clerical recruitment', in Julia and Revel (eds) *Les universités européennes du xvie au xviiie siècles*.

Brooks, R. and Waters, J. 2011 *Student mobilities, migration and the internationalization of higher education*, Basingstoke: Palgrave Macmillan.

Brown, F. H. 1913 'Indian students in Great Britain', *Edinburgh Review*, 217.

Bullock, A. 2000 '"A Scotch University added to the others"? The non-collegiate students', in Brock and Curthoys (eds) *Nineteenth-century Oxford*.

Burns, D. G. 1965 *Travelling scholars*, Reading: NFER.

Byram, M. and Dervin, F. (eds) 2008 *Students, staff and academic mobility in higher education*, Newcastle: Cambridge Scholars Publishing.

Cain, P. J. and Hopkins, A. G. 2002 *British imperialism, 1688–2000 (2nd edition)*, Harlow: Pearson Education.

Carey, A. T. 1956 *Colonial students: A study of the social adaptation of colonial students in London*, London: Secker & Warburg.

Carswell, J. 1985 *Government and the universities in Britain: Programme and performance 1960–1980*, Cambridge University Press.

Catto, J. I. and Evans, T. A. R. 1992 *Late medieval Oxford (The history of the University of Oxford, vol. 2)*, Oxford: Clarendon.

Chagla, M. C. 2000 *Roses in December: An autobiography*, Mumbai: Bharatiya Vidya Bhavan.

Chandler, A. 1989 *Obligation or opportunity: Foreign student policy in six major receiving countries*, New York: Institute of International Education.

Charle, C. 2004 'Patterns', in Rüegg (ed.) *Universities in the 19th and early 20th century*.

Chinese Association for the Promotion of Education 1924 *Boxer indemnity and Chinese education*, London.

Chitty, C. W. 1966 'Aliens in England in the sixteenth century', *Race*, 8: 2.

Clinton, B. 2004 *My life*, New York: Knopf.

Cobban, A. B. 1988 *The medieval English universities to c. 1500*, Aldershot: Scolar.

—— 1999 *English university life in the middle ages*, London: UCL Press.

Commonwealth Scholarship Commission 2009 *Evaluating Commonwealth scholarships in the United Kingdom: Assessing impact in key priority areas*, London.

Conlon, G., Litchfield, A. and Sadlier, G. 2011 *Estimating the value to the UK of education exports*, London: Department of Business Innovation and Skills.

Cooper, C. H. 1842–53 *Annals of Cambridge*, Cambridge: n.p.

Corbett, A. 2005 *Universities and the Europe of knowledge: Ideas, institutions and policy entrepreneurship in European Union higher education policy, 1955–2005*, Basingstoke: Palgrave Macmillan.

Cross, C. 1979 'Continental students and the protestant reformation in England in the sixteenth century', in Baker, D. (ed.) *Reform and reformation: England and the continent c. 1500–c. 1700*, Oxford: Blackwell.

Cross, A. G. 1980 *'By the banks of the Thames': Russians in eighteenth century Britain*, Newtonville, Mass.: Oriental Research Partners.

Cummings, W. K. 1993 'Global trends in overseas study', in Goodwin, C. D. (ed.) *International investment in human capital: Overseas education for development*, New York: Institute of International Education.

Curtis M. H. 1959 *Oxford and Cambridge in transition 1558–1642*, Oxford: Clarendon.

Dahrendorf, R. 1995 *LSE: A history of the London School of Economics and Political Science 1895–1995*, Oxford University Press.

Daniel, P. 1986 *Frensham Heights, 1925–49*, n.p.

Davis, J. M. 1965 'Government policy and international education: USA', in Fraser, S. (ed.) *Government policy and international education*, New York: Wiley.

Davison, B. R. 1966 *Black British: Immigrants to England*, London: Oxford University Press.

de Ridder-Symeons, H. 1992 'Mobility', in de Ridder-Symoens (ed.) *Universities in the middle ages*.

—— (ed.) 1992 *Universities in the middle ages (A history of the university in Europe, vol.1)*, Cambridge University Press.

—— 1996 'Mobility', in de Ridder-Symoens (ed.) *Universities in the middle ages*.

—— (ed.) 1996 *Universities in early modern Europe (A history of the university in Europe, vol. 2)*, Cambridge University Press.

de Wit, H. 2002 *Internationalization of higher education in the USA and Europe*, Westport, Conn.: Greenwood.

—— 2008 'Changing dynamics in international student circulation: Meanings, push and pull factors, trends, and data', in de Wit et al. (eds) *The dynamics of international student circulation in a global context*.

de Wit, H. et al. (eds) 2008 *The dynamics of international student circulation in a global context*, Rotterdam: Stone.

Deslandes, P. R. 2005 *Oxbridge men: British masculinity and the undergraduate experience 1850–1920*, Bloomington: Indiana University Press.

Dewar, D. 1926 *A student of St Andrew's a hundred years ago*, Glasgow: Jackson, Wylie & Co.

di Simone M. R. 1996 'Admission', in de Ridder-Symoens (ed.) *Universities in the middle ages*.

Donaldson, F. 1984 *The British Council: The first fifty years*, London: Jonathan Cape.

Eliutin, V. P. 'The international activity of Soviet higher education', *Soviet Education*, 27: 9–10.

Elliott, D. 1998 'Internationalizing British higher education: Policy perspectives' in Scott, P. (ed.) *The globalization of higher education*, Buckingham: SRHE.

Elton, G. R. 1955 *England under the Tudors*, London: Methuen.

Evans, T. A. R. 1992 'The number, origin and careers of scholars', in Catto and Evans (eds) *Late medieval Oxford*.

Everett, W. 1867 *On the Cam: Lectures on the University of Cambridge in England* (2nd edition), Cambridge: Sever & Francis.

Farnell, L. R. 1934 *An Oxonian looks back*, London: Martin Hopkinson.

Filatova, I. 1999 'Indoctrination or scholarship? Education of Africans at the Communist University of the Toilers of the East in the Soviet Union, 1923–1937', *Paedagogica Historica* 35: 1.

Fisher, M. H., Lahiri, S. and Thandi, S. 2007 *A South-Asian history of Britain: Four centuries of peoples from the Indian sub-continent*, Oxford: Greenwood.

Fisher, S. 1961 'The overseas student in Oxford', *Isis* 12 June.

Forsey, 1990 *A life on the fringe: The memoirs of Eugene Forsey*, Toronto: Oxford University Press.

Foster, J. 1888–92 *Alumni Oxonienses*, Oxford: Parker & Co.

Fowler, L. and Fowler, H. 1984 *Cambridge commemorated: An anthology of university life*, Cambridge University Press.

Fyfe, C. 1993 *A history of Sierra Leone*, Aldershot: Gregg Revivals.

Gandhi, J. S. and Bali, A. P. 1998 *The prime movers of Indian society*, New Delhi: National Book Organisation.

Geitz, H., Heideking, J. and Herbst, J. (ed.) 1995 *German influences on education in the United States to 1917*, Cambridge University Press.

Gish, O. 1971 *Doctor migration and world health*, London: Bell.

Gömöri, G. 2005 *Hungarian students in England and Scotland 1526–1789*, Budapest: Eötvös Loránd Tudományegyetem Levéltára.

Goody, E. N. and Croothues, C. M. 1977 'The West Africans: Cultural and social change among migrants in Britain' in Watson, J. L. (ed.) *Between two cultures: Migrants and minorities in Britain*, Oxford: Blackwell.

Gordon, J. and Jallade, J.-P. 1996 'Spontaneous student mobility in the European Union: A statistical survey', *European Journal of Education*, 31: 2.

Gould, B. 1986 'Dr J. J. Brown of Hackney (1882–1953)', in Lotz and Pegg (eds) *Under the imperial carpet*.

—— 1995 *Goodbye to all that*, London: Macmillan.

Green, J. 1986 'Dr J. J. Brown of Hackney (1882–1953)', in Lotz and Pegg (eds) *Under the imperial carpet*.

—— Green, J. 1990 *Them: Voices from the immigrant community in contemporary Britain*, London: Secker & Warburg.

Green, V. H. H. 1974 *A history of Oxford University*, London: Batsford.

Greenslade, S. J. 1986 'The faculty of theology', in McConica. J. (ed.) *The collegiate university* (*The history of the University of Oxford, vol. 3*), Oxford: Clarendon.

Griffith, W. P. 1981 'Welsh students at Oxford, Cambridge and Inns of Court during the sixteenth and early seventeenth centuries', PhD thesis, University of Wales.

Gürüz, G. 2011 *Higher education and international student mobility in the global knowledge economy*, Albany, NY: State University of New York Press.

Guth, J. and Gill, B. 2008 'Motivations in east-west doctoral mobility', *Journal of ethnic and migration studies*, 34: 5.

Hailey, Lord 1938 *An African survey: A study of problems arising in Africa south of the Sahara*, London: Oxford University Press.

Hammerstein, N. 1996 'Epilogue', in de Ridder-Symoens (ed.) *Universities in the middle ages.*

Hargreaves, J. D. 1994 *Academe and empire: Some overseas connections of Aberdeen University 1860–1970*, Aberdeen University Press.

Harley, J. A. 1931 *International understanding: Agencies educating for a new world*, Stanford, Calif.: Stanford University Press.

Harper, M. and Constantine, S. 2010 *Migration and empire*, Oxford University Press.

Harvie, C. 1997 'Reform and expansion, 1854–1871', in Brock, M. G. and Curthoys, M. C. (eds) *Nineteenth-century Oxford, Part 1* (*The history of the University of Oxford, vol. 6*), Oxford: Clarendon.

Hatton, T. J. and Williamson, J. G. 2004 *Global migration and the world economy: Two centuries of policy and performance*, Cambridge, Mass.: MIT Press.

Hays, R. W. 1969 'Welsh students at Oxford and Cambridge in the middle ages', *Welsh History Review* 4:4.

Haywood, H. 1978 *Black Bolshevik: Autobiography of an Afro-American communist*, Chicago: Liberator Press.

Hennessy, P. 1992 *Never again: Britain 1945–1951*, London: Jonathan Cape.

—— 2001 *The prime minister: The office and its holders since 1945*, London: Penguin.

Heyworthe-Dunne, J. 1938 *An introduction to the history of education in modern Egypt*, London: Luzac.

Hinnebusch, W. A. 1964 'Foreign Dominican students and professors at the Oxford Blackfriars', in *Oxford studies presented to Daniel Callus*, Oxford Historical Society.

Hobhouse, H. 2002 *The Crystal Palace and the Great Exhibition: A history of the Royal Commission for the exhibition of 1851*, London: Athlone.

Hobsbawm, E. 2002 *Interesting times: A twentieth-century life*, London: Abacus.

Holmes, C. (ed.) 1978 *Immigrants and minorities in British society*, London: Allen & Unwin.

—— 1991 *A tolerant country? Immigrants, refugees and minorities in Britain*, London: Faber.

Howarth, T. E. B. 1978 *Cambridge between two wars*, London: Collins.

Humfrey, C. 1999 *Managing international students: Recruitment to graduation*, Buckingham: Open University Press.

Hunt, M. H. 1972 'The American remission of the boxer indemnity: A reappraisal', *Journal of Asian Studies*: 31: 3.

Jarausch, K. H. 1983 'Higher education and social change; Some comparative perspectives', in Jarausch, K. H. (ed.) *The transformation of higher learning 1860–1930*, University of Chicago Press.
—— 1995 'American students in Germany, 1815–1914: The structure of German and US matriculants at Göttingen University', in Geitz et al. (eds) *German influences on education in the United States to 1917*.
Johnson, H. and Gwertzman, B. G. 1969 *Fulbright: The dissenter*, London: Hutchinson.
Johnson, W. and Colligan, F. J. 1965 *The Fulbright program: A history*, University of Chicago Press.
Jones, J. 1997 *Balliol College: A history*, Oxford University Press.
Julia, D. and Revel, J. 1989 'Les pérégrinations académiques, xvie-xviiie siècles', in Julia and Revel (eds) *Les universités européennes du xvie au xviiie siècles.*
—— (eds) 1989 *Les universités européennes du xvie au xviiie siècles, tome 2,* Paris: Editions de l'école des hautes études en sciences sociales.
Kalton, G. 1966 *The public schools: A factual survey of Headmasters' Conference schools in England and Wales*, London: Longmans.
Kanigel, R. 1991 *The man who knew infinity: A life of the genius Ramanujan*, London: Scribners.
Karady, V. 2003 'Les logiques des échanges inégaux', in Peter and Tikhonov (eds) *Universitäten als Brücken in Europa.*
Kellenbenz, H. 1978 'German immigrants in England', in Holmes (ed.) *Immigrants and minorities in British society.*
Kenny, A. 2001 'The Rhodes Trust and its administration', in Kenny, A. (ed.) *The history of the Rhodes Trust*, Oxford University Press.
Kerr, C. 1990 'The internationalisation of learning and the nationalisation of the purposes of higher education', *European Journal of Education* 25: 1.
—— 2001 *The uses of the university*, Cambridge, Mass.: Harvard University Press.
Kerr, J. 1913 *Scottish education school and university: From early times to 1908*, Cambridge University Press.
Kiernan, V. G. 1978 'Britons old and new', in Holmes (ed.) *Immigrants and minorities in British society.*
Killingray, D. 1993 'An introduction', *Immigrants and Minorities*, 12: 2.
Kirk-Greene, A. 1993 'Doubly elite', *Immigrants and Minorities*, 12: 3.
Klineberg, O. 1976 *International educational exchange: An assessment of its nature and its prospects*, The Hague: Mouton.
Koyama, N. 2004 *Japanese students at Cambridge University in the Meiji era, 1868–1912: Pioneers for the modernization of Japan*, Fukuoka: Lulu.
Krzaklewska, E. 2008 'Why study abroad?', in Byram and Dervin (eds) *Students, staff and academic mobility in higher education.*
Kuhn, T. 2012 'Why educational exchange programmes miss their mark: Cross-border mobility, education and European identity', *Journal of Common Market Studies*, 50: 6.
Lahiri, S. 2000 *Indians in Britain: Anglo-Indian encounters, race and identity 1880–1930*, London: Cass.
Lambert, R. D. 1956 *Indian students on an American campus*, Minneapolis: University of Minnesota Press.
Lancaster, P. 1962 *Education for Commonwealth students in Britain*, London: Fabian Commonwealth Bureau.

Lasanowski, V. 2009 *International student mobility: Status report 2009*, London: OBHE.

Latreche, A. 2003 'Les étudiants de nationalités étrangères en France. Le cas des étudiants maghrébins au XXe siècle', in Peter and Tikhonov (eds) *Universitäten als Brücken in Europa*.

Lawrence, C. H. 1994 *The friars: The impact of the early mendicant movement on western society*, London: Longman.

Layard. R., King, J. and Moser, C. 1969 *The impact of Robbins*, Harmondsworth: Penguin.

Leader, D. R. 1988 *A history of the University of Cambridge, vol. 1: The university to 1546*, Cambridge University Press.

Lee, E. S. 1966 'A theory of migration', *Demography* 3: 1.

Lee, J. M. 2006 'Commonwealth students in the United Kingdom, 1940–1960: Student welfare and world status', *Minerva* 44.

Lewis, D. 1981 *The good fight: Political memoirs 1909–1958*, Toronto: Macmillan.

Livingstone, A. S. 1964 *The international student*, University of Manchester.

Long, E. 2002 [1774] *The history of Jamaica*, Kingston, Jamaica: Randle.

Lotz, R. and Pegg, L. (eds) 1986 *Under the imperial carpet: Essays in black history 1780–1850*, Crawley: Rabbit.

Luce, J. V. 1992 *Trinity College Dublin: The first four hundred years*, Trinity College Dublin Press.

Lulat, Y. G-M., Altbach, P. G. and Kelly, F. H. 1986 *Governmental and institutional policies on foreign students: An overview and bibliography*, Buffalo, NY: Comparative Education Center, SUNY.

Lytle, G.F. 1974 'Patronage patterns and Oxford colleges c. 1300–c1530', in Stone (ed.) *The university in society*.

McDowell, R. B. and Webb, D. A. 1982 *Trinity College Dublin 1592–1952: An academic history*, Cambridge University Press.

MacKenzie, H. 1929 'The anti-foreign movement in England 1231–1232', in Taylor, C. H. *Anniversary essays in mediaeval history by students of Charles Homer Haskins*, Boston: Books for Libraries Press.

McLaren, C. A. 2005 *Aberdeen students 1600–1860*, Aberdeen: University of Aberdeen.

Macmillan, W. M. 1975 *My South African years: An autobiography*, Cape Town: David Philip.

Maiworm, F., Steube, W. and Teichler, U.1991 *Learning in Europe: The ERASMUS experience*, London: Jessica Kingsley.

Majumdar, J. A. P. 2003 *Family history* (ed. A. Burton), New Delhi: Oxford University Press.

Maliyamkono, T. L., Ishumi, A. G. M., Wells, S. J. and Migot-Adhola, S. E. (eds) 1982 *Training and productivity in eastern Africa*. London: Heinemann.

Mangait Rai, E. N. 1973 *Commitment my style: Career in the Indian Civil Service*, Delhi: Vikas.

Matusevich, M. (ed.) 2007 *Africa in Russia, Russia in Africa: Three centuries of encounters*, Trenton, NJ: Africa World Press.

—— 2007 'Visions of grandeur ... interrupted: The Soviet Union through Nigerian eyes', in Matusevich (ed.) *Africa in Russia, Russia in Africa*.

Maxey, K. 2000 *Student mobility on the map: Tertiary education in the Commonwealth on the threshold of the 21st century*, London: UKCOSA.

—— 2006 *International student mobility in the Commonwealth: 2006 update*, London: Council for Education in the Commonwealth.

Mboya, T. 1963 *Freedom and after*, London: Deutsch.

Menon, K. P. S. 1965 *Many worlds: An autobiography*, London: Oxford University Press.

Midgley, G. 1996 *University life in eighteenth-century Oxford*, New Haven, Conn.: Yale University Press.

Miller, H. 1959 *Prince and premier: A biography of Tunku Abdul Rahman Putra Al-Haj, first prime minister of the Federation of Malaya*, London: Harrap.

Mohanty, S. (ed.) 1997 *In search of wonder: Understanding cultural exchange – The Fulbright program in India*, New Delhi: Vision.

Moorman J. R. H. 1947 'The foreign elements among the English Franciscans', *English Historical Review*, 62: 244.

Moraw, P. 1992 'Careers of graduates', in de Ridder-Symeons (ed.) *Universities in the middle ages*.

Morgan, M. C. 1978 *Bryanston 1928–78*, Blandford: Bryanston School.

Morgan, V. 2004 *A history of the University of Cambridge: Vol. 2 1546–1750*, Cambridge University Press.

Mukherjee, S. 2010 *Nationalism, education and migrant identities: The England-returned*, London: Routledge.

Murphy-Lejeune, E. 2002 *Student mobility and narrative in Europe: The new strangers*, London: Routledge.

Nabokov V. 1965 *Speak memory*, London: Gollancz.

—— 2012 *Collected poems*, London: Penguin.

Naidoo, V. 2007 'Research on the flow of international students to UK universities: Determinants and implications', *Journal of Research in International Education* 6: 287.

Nardi, P. 1992 'Relations with authority', in de Ridder-Symeons (ed.) *Universities in the middle ages*.

Neave, G. 2011 'Patterns', in Rüegg (ed.) *Universities Universities since 1945*.

Nehru, J. 1991 *An autobiography*, Delhi: Oxford University Press.

Obolensky, D. 1999 *Bread of exile: A Russian family*, London: Harvill.

O'Day, R. 1982 *Education and society 1500–1800: The social foundations of education in early modern Britain*, London: Longman.

Odinga, O. 1967 *Not yet uhuru: The autobiography of Oginga Odinga*, London: Heinemann.

OECD 2004 *Internationalisation and trade in higher education*, Paris: OECD.

Onyeama, D. 1972 *Nigger at Eton*, London: Frewin.

Oosterbeek, H. and Webbink, D. 2011 'Does studying abroad induce a brain drain?' *Economica*, 78.

Opper, S., Teichler, U. and Carlton, J. 1990 *Impacts of study abroad programmes on students and graduates*, London: Jessica Kingsley.

Overseas Students Trust 1981 'Overseas students and British commercial interests' in Williams, P. (ed.) *The overseas student question: Studies for a policy*, London: Heinemann.

Panayi, P. (ed.) 1996 *Germans in Britain since 1500*, London: Hambledon.

Parey, M. and Waldinger, F. 2010 'Studying abroad and the effect on international labour market mobility: Evidence from the introduction of Erasmus', *Economic Journal*, 121.

Paunescu, M. 2008 'Students' perspectives upon their mobility', in Byram and Dervin (eds) *Students, staff and academic mobility in higher education.*

p'Bitek, O. 1973 *Africa's cultural revolution*, Nairobi: Macmillan.

Pegues, F. 1956 'Royal support of students in the thirteenth century', *Speculum*, 31: 3.

PEP 1955 *Colonial students in Britain*, London: PEP.

—— 1965 *New Commonwealth students in Britain*, London: Allen & Unwin.

Perraton, H. 2009 *Learning abroad: A history of the Commonwealth Scholarship and Fellowship Plan*, Newcastle upon Tyne: Cambridge Scholars Publishing.

Peter, H. R. and Tikhonov, N. (ed.) 2003 *Universitäten als Brücken in Europa*, Frankfurt: Peter Lang.

Phelps Brown, H. and Hopkins, S. V. 1981 *A perspective of wages and prices*, London: Methuen.

Pietsch, T. 2011 'Many Rhodes: Travelling scholarships and imperial citizenship in the British academic world, 1880–1940', *History of Education*, 40: 6.

—— 2013 *Empire of scholars: Universities, networks and the British academic world 1850–1939*, Manchester University Press.

Pis'mennaia, E. 2010 'The migration of foreign students to Russia', *Russian education and society*, 52: 10.

Poot, J. and Roskruge, M. 2013 'Internationalisation of education and returns in the labour market', *IZA Discussion paper*, 7696.

Porter, S. 1997 'University and society', in Tyacke, N. (ed.) *Seventeenth-century Oxford* (*The history of the University of Oxford, vol. 4*), Oxford: Clarendon.

Pratt, H. 1860 *University education*, London: Ridgway.

Pratt, J. 1997 *The polytechnic experiment 1965–1992*, Buckingham: SRHE.

Prest, W. R. 1972 *The inns of court under Elizabeth I and the early Stuarts 1590–1640*, London: Longman.

Rae, J. 1981 *The public school revolution: Britain's independent schools 1964–1979*, London: Faber.

Reid, D. M. 1990 *Cairo University and the making of modern Egypt*, Cambridge University Press.

Reid, E. 1989 *Radical mandarin: The memoirs of Escott Reid*, University of Toronto Press.

Ringer, F. K. 1979 *Education and society in modern Europe*, Bloomington: Indiana University Press.

River Path Associates 2003 *The FCO scholarships review*, n.p.

Roach, J. P. C. 1967 *The city and University of Cambridge* (*Victoria county history of Cambridge, vol. 3*), London: Dawson.

Roberts, J., Rodriguez Cruz, Á. M. and Herbst, J. 1996 'Exporting models', in de Ridder-Symeons (ed.) *Universities in the middle ages.*

Robson-Scott, W. D. 1953 *German travellers in England 1400–1800*, Oxford: Blackwell.

Rosenzweig, M. R. 2006 'Global wage differences and international student flows', in Collins, S. M. and Graham, C. (eds) *Brookings Trade Forum: Global labor markets?*, Washington, DC: Brookings Institution Press.

Roth, C. 1951 *The Jews of medieval Oxford*, Oxford: Clarendon.

Rothblatt, S. 2011 'Curriculum, students, education', in Rüegg (ed.) *Universities since 1945.*

Rüegg, W. 1992 'Foreword' in de Ridder-Symeons (ed.) *Universities in the middle ages.*

—— 1992 'Themes', in de Ridder-Symoens (ed.) *Universities in the middle ages*.

—— (ed.) 2004 *Universities in the 19th and early 20th centuries* (*A history of the university in Europe, vol. 3*), Cambridge University Press.

—— (ed.) 2011 *Universities since 1945* (*A history of the university in Europe, vol. 4*), Cambridge University Press.

Rüegg, W. and Sadlak, J. 2011 'Relations with authority', in Rüegg (ed.) *Universities since 1945*.

Runciman, W. G. 1983 *A treatise on social theory vol 1: The methodology of social theory*, Cambridge University Press.

Sagarra, S. 1991 ' From the pistol to the petticoat? The changing student body 1592–1992', in Holland, C. H. (ed.) *Trinity College Dublin and the idea of a university*, Trinity College Dublin Press.

Sanderson, M. 1972 *The universities and British industry, 1850–1970*, London: Routledge.

Satthianadhan, S. 1880 'Indian students and English universities', *Journal of the National Indian Association*, 119.

—— 1893 *Four years in an English university* (2nd edition), Madras: Srinivasa, Varadachari and Co.

Schwinges, R. C. 1992 'Admission', in de Ridder-Symeons (ed.) *Universities in the middle ages*.

—— 1992 'Student education, student life', in de Ridder-Symeons (ed.) *Universities in the middle ages*.

Scragg, B. 1993 *Sevenoaks school: A history*, Bath: Ashgrove

Seabrook, J. 2013 *The refuge and the fortress: Britain and the persecuted 1933–2013*, Basingstoke: Palgrave Macmillan.

Searby, P. 1997 *A history of the University of Cambridge: Vol. 3 1750–1870*, Cambridge University Press.

Sen, A. 1970 *Problems of overseas students and nurses*, Slough: NFER.

Shepperd, A. 1980 *Sandhurst: The Royal Military Academy Sandhurst and its predecessors*, Feltham: Country Life Books.

Shepperson, G. A. 1983 'An early African graduate' in Donaldson, G. (ed.) *Four centuries: Edinburgh university life 1583–1983*, University of Edinburgh.

Sherwood, M. 1993 'Kwame Nkrumah: The London years 1945–47', *Immigrants and Minorities*, 12: 3.

Shestakov, V. 2009 *Russkiye v britanskikh universitetakh: Opyt intellektualnoi istorii i kulturnogo obmena*, St Petersburg: Nestor-Istoria.

Sigalas, E. 2010 'The role of personal benefits in public support for the EU: Learning from the Erasmus Students', *West European Politics*, 33: 6.

Sigurdson, J. 1981 'The reverse brain drain and the lack of educated manpower', in Zahlan, A. B. (ed.) *The Arab brain drain*, London: Ithaca Press.

Simpson, R. 1983 *How the PhD came to Britain: A century of struggle for postgraduate education*, Guildford: SRHE.

—— 2009 *The development of the PhD degree in Britain, 1917–1959 and since: An evolutionary and statistical history in higher education*, Lewiston, NY: Edwin Mellen.

Singh, A. K. 1963 *Indian students in Britain: A survey of their adjustment and attitudes*, New York: Asia Publishing House.

Smith, A. K. and Weiner, C. 1980 *Robert Oppenheimer*, Cambridge, Mass.: Harvard University Press.

Somers, M. H. 1979 'Irish scholars in the Universities of Paris and Oxford before 1500', PhD thesis, City University of New York.

Sorabji, C. 1934 *India calling: The memories of Cornelia Sorabji*, London: Nisbet.

Stone, L. 1964 'The educational revolution in England, 1560–1640', *Past and Present*, 28.

—— 1974 'The size and composition of the Oxford student body 1580–1909', in Stone (ed.) *The university in society*.

—— (ed.) 1974 *The university in society, vol. 1: Oxford and Cambridge from the 14th to the early 19th century*, London: Princeton University Press.

—— 1983 'Social control and intellectual excellence: Oxbridge and Edinburgh 1560–1983', in Phillipson, N. (ed.) *Universities, society, and the future*, Edinburgh University Press.

Symonds, R. 1966 *The British and their successors: A study in the development of the government services in the new nations*, London: Faber.

—— 1986 *Oxford and empire: The last lost cause?* Basingstoke: Macmillan.

—— 2000 'Oxford and the empire', in Brock and Curthoys (eds) *Nineteenth-century Oxford*.

Taylor, F. A. (ed.) 1946 *Voltaire: Lettres philosophiques*, Oxford: Blackwell.

Thomas, H. 1961 *The story of Sandhurst*, London: Hutchinson.

Thomas, M. and Williams, J. M. 1972 *Overseas nurses in Britain: A PEP survey for UKCOSA*, London: PEP.

Thomson, J.J. 1936 *Recollections and reflections*, London: Bell.

Tikhonov, N. 2003 'Migrations des étudiants et feminisation de quelques univer-sités européennes', in Peter and Tikhonov (eds) *Universitäten als Brücken in Europa*.

Turner, A. L. 1919 *Sir William Turner: A chapter in medical history*, Edinburgh: Blackwood.

—— (ed.) 1933 *History of the University of Edinburgh 1883–1933*, London: Oliver & Boyd.

Tyerman, C. 2000 *A history of Harrow school 1324–1991*, Oxford University Press.

Urwin, D. W. 1982 *Specialist schools and colleges in Cambridge: Draft subject plan*, Cambridge City Council.

Useem, J. and Useem, R. H. 1955 *The western-educated man in India: A study of his social roles and influence*, New York: Dryden.

Van der Wende, M. 1997 'International comparative analysis and synthesis', in Kälvemark, T. and van der Wende, M. (eds) *National policies for the internation-alisation of higher education in Europe*, Stockholm: Högskolevrket.

Verger, J. 1992 'Patterns', in de Ridder-Symoens (eds) *Universitiesin the middle ages*.

Wainwright, A. M. 2008 *'The better class' of Indian: Social rank, imperial identity and south Asians in Britain 1858–1914*, Manchester University Press.

Walsh, S. ?1979 *Overseas nurses – Training for a caring profession*, London: Royal College of Nursing.

Walton, C. 2013 *Empire of secrets: British intelligence, the cold war and the twilight of empire*, London: Harper.

Walvin, J. 1973 *Black and white: The negro and English society 1555–1945*, London: Allen Lane.

Wasserstein, B. 1998 *Secret war in Shanghai*, London: Profile.

Waters, J. and Brooks, R. 2012 'Transnational spaces, international students: Emergent perspectives on educational mobilities', in Brooks, R., Fuller, A. and Waters, J. (eds) *Changing spaces of education: New perspectives on the nature of learning*, London: Routledge.

Watson, D. and Bowden, R. 2007 'The fate of the Dearing recommendations', in Watson, D. and Amoah, M. (eds) *The Dearing report ten years on*, London: Institute of Education.

Watt, D. E. R. 1986 Scottish university men of the 13th and 14th centuries', in Smout, T. C. (ed.) *Scotland and Europe, 1200–1850*, Edinburgh: John Donald.

Waugh, E. 1964 *A little learning: The first volume of an autobiography*, London: Chapman & Hall.

Weaver, H. D. 1985 'Soviet training and research programs for Africa', EdD thesis, University of Massachusetts.

Weber, T. 2008 *Our friend 'The enemy': Elite education in Britain and Germany before World War I*, Stanford University Press.

White, A. J. S. 1965 *The British Council: The first 25 years 1934–1959*, London: British Council.

Whitehead, C. 1988 *'Not wanted on the voyage': A study of the colonial department, ULIE 1927–56*, London: Institute of Education.

Williams, E. 1969 *Inward hunger: The education of a prime minister*, London: Deutsch.

Williams, G. and Woodhall, M. 1979 *Independent further education*, London: Policy Studies Institute.

Williams, P. 1981 'Overseas students in Britain: The background' in Williams, P. (ed.) *The overseas student question: Studies for a policy*, London: Heinemann.

Williams, P. R. C. 1985 *They came to train*, London: Overseas Development Administration.

Winder, R. 2004 *Bloody foreigners: The story of immigration to Britain*, London: Little, Brown.

Winter, J. M. 1994 'Oxford and the first world war' in Harrison, B. (ed.) *The twentieth century (The history of the University of Oxford, vol. 8)*, Oxford: Clarendon.

Wright, J. 1986 'Early African musicians in Britain', in Lotz and Pegg (eds) *Under the imperial carpet*.

Young, M. 1962 'Is your child in the unlucky generation?' *Where,* 10.

Young, R. F. 1923 'Bohemian scholars and students at the English universities from 1347 to1750', *English Historical Review,* 38: 149.

Youssoupoff, F. 1953 *Lost splendour*, London: Jonathan Cape.

Ziegler, P. 2008 *Legacy: Cecil Rhodes, the Rhodes Trust, and the Rhodes Scholarships*, New Haven, Conn.: Yale University Press.

Statistics

Except where otherwise shown statistics are generally drawn from:

Association of Commonwealth Universities Yearbook (previously *Yearbook of the Universities of the Empire*).

British Council *Overseas students in Britain.*

Department for Education and Science *Statistical bulletin.*

Department for Education and Science/University Grants Committee *University statistics.*

Higher Education Statistics Agency *Students in higher education institutions.*

International Institute of Education *Open doors.*

UNESCO Institute for Statistics database *(*www.uis.unesco.org) and *Global education digest.*

UNESCO *Statistical yearbook.*

Index

Printed and bound by CPI Group (UK) Ltd, Croydon, CR0 4YY